RAF LIBERATORS OVER BURMA

RAF LIBERATORS OVER BURMA

FLYING WITH 159 SQUADRON

BILL KIRKNESS DFM AND MATT POOLE

FONTHILL

Fonthill Media Language Policy

Fonthill Media publishes in the international English language market. One language edition is published worldwide. As there are minor differences in spelling and presentation, especially with regard to American English and British English, a policy is necessary to define which form of English to use. The Fonthill Policy is to use the form of English native to the author. Bill Kirkness was born and educated in the United Kingdom; therefore British English has been adopted in this publication.

Fonthill Media Limited
Fonthill Media LLC
www.fonthillmedia.com
office@fonthillmedia.com

First published in the United Kingdom and the United States of America 2017
Reprinted 2020

British Library Cataloguing in Publication Data:
A catalogue record for this book is available from the British Library

ISBN 978-1-78155-656-6

Typeset in 10pt on 13pt Sabon
Printed and bound in England

Foreword

A Publishing Dream Fulfilled

I am so happy to see my late father's goal come to fruition. I know that Dad—Bill Kirkness—would have been elated to hold this book in his hands. He died in 1994, having failed to find a publisher.

Bill's individual wartime exploits are worth bringing to the public's attention even now, more than seventy years after the events described. With the printing of his memoir, the B-24 Liberator bomber component of 'The Forgotten Air Force' (as the RAF in the Far East has been labelled) is also better remembered.

Place names use the historical spellings found in Dad's memoir and the 159 Squadron Operations Record Book.

This work could never have been completed without Matt Poole's dedication and painstaking attention to detail. I wholeheartedly thank Matt on Bill's behalf for all the effort he put into researching, typing, checking, and cross-checking the material in Bill's raw manuscript. Matt, you are a gem.

I extend my very best wishes to those reading this book, and I honour the courage of all, including Dad, who faced the trials, and sometimes horrors, of the 1939 to 1945 war.

In loving memory of my dad, William Arthur Kirkness DFM. Thanks, Dad!

Susan Olsson (née Kirkness)

CONTENTS

Introduction

July 1942

I was sitting on the garden wall when the postman delivered the telegram. 'This came last night, but it's not urgent,' said the postman as he handed it to me. 'Don't suppose we'll lose the war with you on leave for a while,' he quipped.

I was wearing the uniform of an RAF sergeant. On the left breast was the half-wing brevet signifying an air gunner, and on the right upper arm, the wireless operator's 'sparks' badge. Reluctantly, I accepted the telegram. 'Thanks, Archie,' I sighed.

'Did your employer extend your leave?' asked Archie with a chuckle.

'No such luck,' I replied, eyeing the telegram.

'You are posted to RAF Burn, near Selby', it read. My leave had been cancelled and my flying career would continue at RAF Burn.

The postman refused the small tip I offered. 'Nay, Bill,' said Archie, 'reckon we owe you young 'uns something.' Archie had lost part of his jaw in the First World War and appeared almost embarrassed as he spoke. 'Don't forget, Bill, fly low and slow,' he advised. This was his way of saying be careful. With mixed feelings, I thanked Archie again and went indoors.

It was July 1942, and I had been on leave after returning home from a journey into harm's way to help deliver a Wellington bomber to Egypt. From Egypt, I had sailed to Cape Town, South Africa, where I eventually boarded a second ship sailing back to the UK. It had been an exhausting journey, and at times a dangerous one, especially in Malta. The leave had done me the world of good, but I had been strangely restless. Everything was too quiet and I missed the companionship of like-minded airmen.

The telegram's details suggested that I was inching closer to a posting on an operational squadron, which would have pleased me two weeks earlier, but since learning of my girlfriend's death in a recent air raid on Hull, nothing seemed very important anymore. My main pastime on leave had been taking my mongrel bitch for long walks in the woods close to the house.

My parents were both employed on war work—Dad at the Avro aircraft factory at Yeadon and Mum at an armaments factory in a neighbouring town—so I had to wait until the evening to inform them of the telegram. I spent the day packing and visiting the rail transport officer in town to obtain my travel warrant.

During the evening meal, I told my parents and sister, Sheila, that I was leaving next morning. After some initial fuss from Mum, the news was digested along with the Spam and limp lettuce that, together with the National Loaf brown bread, constituted our evening meal.

I awoke after my parents had left for work and Sheila for school. After bidding a fond farewell to my dog, I caught the bus to Leeds railway station, then the train to Selby. As it was the usual suburban train, it had no corridor so there was no easy way of knowing who else was aboard. It was with some pleasure, then, that I spotted an old pal from our time together at No. 15 Operational Training Unit at Harwell when we both left the train at the same destination. He was also a wireless operator/air gunner.

'Hello Arnie. You posted to Burn?' I asked of Arnie Bridgman.

'Yes, I suppose it's a bomber unit,' he answered. 'Wonder what kind of kites we'll be flying.'

'No need to wonder much longer. Here comes the gharry,' I said, as a 15-cwt utility vehicle pulled up near us.

We would shortly commence the next phase of our wartime service aboard American-built B-24 Liberator bombers of 1653 Conversion Unit at nearby RAF Burn. Further adventures would take us far afield to India, where challenging Liberator flying awaited us.

Only I would return home.

1

Earlier in 1942: A Wellington Delivery Adventure to Egypt

The Escapade Begins: Flying from the UK to Gibraltar

In 1940, Arnie and I joined the RAF in Leeds at the same time, and we trained as wireless operators together. We were jointly posted to No. 7 Air Gunnery School at Stormy Down, Wales, where we had a whale of a time. The war still seemed relatively remote back then in the last months of 1941.

Flying in old twin-engine Whitleys and firing at drogues seemed an appealing way to pass the days while we spent evenings enjoying life in a different sort of way, with the local brew and lasses.

Postings to No. 15 Operational Training Unit at Harwell followed in January 1942. There, we were crewed up on Wellington aircraft, but in separate crews. We were led to believe that eventual assignment to a squadron in the Middle East would follow, but the evolving war situation altered these plans.

The crew on which I was second wireless operator/air gunner was skippered by Plt Off. Wilkinson; it was not a happy one, but I stuck with them. On 8 May 1942, the Wilkinson crew, with me in the front turret, flew Wellington ES994 from Harwell to Portreath on the first stage of a delivery flight to Cairo, Egypt. Two days later, on a grey and drizzly morning, ES994 departed Blighty bucking strong headwinds *en route* to Gibraltar.

Arrival in Gibraltar occurred nine hours and fifty-five minutes later in brilliant sunshine. After being shown our billets, we went into town and were astounded at the abundance of food, particularly oranges, which in wartime England were almost non-existent.

At the briefing next morning, for onward routing to Malta, we were told there were shortages at Malta of most things, and that the garrison there would especially appreciate a delivery of cigarettes. We spent that afternoon buying cigarettes to bring with us. Our actions were not entirely altruistic as we hoped to make a small profit when we sold them on arrival in Malta.

Gibraltar to Malta and a Brief Stay in Malta

On 12 May, we took off in the afternoon daylight on the next leg of our journey. Take-off was timed so that we would fly the most dangerous part of the route, the roughly 150 miles from Pantelleria to Malta, in darkness. Jerry (the Germans) controlled much of the eastern Mediterranean airspace, and Malta was taking a real pounding. We had no radio aids to assist us so navigation was purely by dead reckoning. Being an inexperienced crew, we were more than a little apprehensive.

As the ETA for Malta approached, all eyes were strained for a sight of the island. The skipper was very excitable and becoming more so by the minute when I reported from the front turret, 'Searchlights on the port beam.'

Turning towards the lights, we realised that, by the amount of flak being thrown up at Jerry, we had arrived during a raid. Prudently, the skipper flew large figure eights until things quieted down, by which time we were in contact with the tower. Shortly afterwards, we landed and were guided to a dispersal pen by a 15-cwt Bedford truck.

An officer waiting there told us to report to the Flight Office at 9 a.m. When we had removed our gear from the aircraft, the Bedford, he said, would take us to the 'poor house', as it was called, for overnight accommodation.

Upon the departure of the officer, the small crowd that had gathered suddenly converged on us to buy the cigarettes that were in the aircraft. We did a brisk business.

Suddenly, the air raid siren started its mournful moaning, and my crewmates and I found ourselves alone beside the aircraft. 'Get in the shelter, you dozy lot of buggers,' shouted a voice, whereupon we hurried at a shambling run towards its owner. As we were still in our flying kit, our speed was not impressive.

'Now it's our turn. Fourth raid today,' came a voice from the gloom of the shelter.

'Might be going for the docks again,' added another, but as if on cue, the shelter trembled as high explosives fell on the airfield.

The raid was short and sharp. As soon as the 'all clear' sounded, we emerged, stunned by what we saw. Aircraft were burning, including Wellington ES994—our aircraft. The unique geodetic framing of the fuselage and wings was recognisable, but the aircraft was clearly a write-off.

'Bastards,' remarked someone. Amid murmurs of acquiescence, it slowly sank into our heads that the war was not fought by knights of the air, as was the romanticised popular depiction. Warfare was something much grimmer and it was not at all romantic. The first rule was survival.

'What now?' someone on the crew asked of no one in particular.

Our doubts were answered by the arrival of the 15-cwt truck. 'Get in. You won't be going far in that,' grinned the driver, with a nod towards the wreckage. He took us off the airfield and pulled up outside a solidly built two-storey building. 'Poor house, here we are,' he said. 'Pick you up at 9 a.m.'

'When do we get something to eat?' enquired the rear gunner, who was always hungry.

'Tomorrow if you are lucky,' the driver replied. 'By the way, you sleep upstairs and the Mess is downstairs,' he remarked before disappearing up the road in a cloud of dust.

The room we entered upstairs was quite large, almost like a hospital ward, and several of the beds were already occupied. In order not to disturb the occupants, we selected a bed each, shed our flying gear and eventually fell asleep.

We awakened next morning to an intensity of daylight to which we were unaccustomed. Going over to the window (made glassless by the bombing), we looked out with some curiosity at a sandstone-coloured landscape without much greenery. There was a fair amount of bomb damage in the near vicinity, although the main targets were not in the area.

After washing downstairs, we went into the Mess for an unappealing breakfast of fried tomatoes and goat's meat, with goat's milk for the tea. Apart from one or two grumbles, however, we ate the meal and waited outside for the truck to take us to the Flight Office for orders.

'You still here?' queried the driver. 'No going off into the wild blue yonder for you for a while, I'm thinking.' With a nod to the back of the truck, he added, 'You don't half look a scruffy lot!'

This last remark caused us to have a good look at each other, and we were compelled to agree with him. We never flew in our best blues, and we gunners, in particular, had oil stains on our trousers from the slight leaks which had developed in the gun turrets. We had no collars or ties as we had flown in the standard issue white sweaters, which were ideal in the air but hardly suitable for wear on a Mediterranean island.

We were also unshaven as all our kit had been destroyed, so it was with some trepidation that the meeting with the Flight Commander occurred. To our surprise, he never remarked about the appearance of the six untidy airmen before him, but, with a wave of his hand towards some chairs, he told us to sit down.

'You lost your aircraft last night,' he said quite casually. 'Until such time as we can provide another, you will make yourselves generally useful.' He looked up, and for the first time, his youth became apparent as did the lines of fatigue in his face.

'Intelligence has informed us that the enemy is preparing to invade Malta. The bombing that we are undergoing is a prelude to the main invasion, and therefore you will carry your sidearms at all times. As the enemy is doing his best to prevent supplies from reaching us, we are on short rations, short of fuel, spares, and ammunition, so we must husband our resources. Pilots will go on the duty pilots roster, the navigator will assist in the Map Section, and air gunners will assist the armourers to make up ammunition belts. Now report to Stores and draw some more suitable clothing. You are free for the rest of the day, but the navigator will report to the operations room at 8 p.m. this evening. Dismiss.'

The cockiness with which we had been infected when at training units had now largely evaporated, and it was a quiet and pensive crew that presented itself to the Stores sergeant.

He looked us up and down thoughtfully and without a word placed a khaki drill shirt before each of us. 'Sign here,' he said, indicating some 664b forms. 'We have nothing else.'

As we had been ordered not to report to our various sections until the following morning, Taffy and I decided to walk from the airfield, named Luqa, down to the main town and port of Valletta to have a look at the place. Taffy was the rear gunner and a fairly withdrawn individual. The air raid warning had sounded some time before we set out, but in the short period the crew had been on the island, with the resilience of youth, most of us had already come to accept a raid as part of the general inconvenience of the place.

Walking down the dusty road provided us with a sweeping view of the raid as it developed on the dock installations below us in Valleta. The Spitfires and Hurricanes, having taken off some time before, headed south in order to gain altitude. It appeared that the enemy was going to encounter no fighter opposition. The Ju 87s came slanting down the clear blue sky at an incredible angle with Bofors shells exploding just behind their tailplanes, while the Bf 109s circled above.

Suddenly, Taffy pointed. I then witnessed what appeared to be a column of midges speeding towards the action over the harbour. British fighters dove through the middle of the Bf 109s as though the enemy fighters were inconsequential, and they attached themselves to the Stukas' tails. As the dive bombers released their ordnance and started to level out, we heard short bursts from the Spits and Hurricanes, and the doomed Ju 87s either exploded, broke up in flames, or continued their dives straight into the Mediterranean. The RAF fighters then zoomed up, usually with German fighters on their tails, whereupon real old-fashioned dogfights ensued.

Sadly, it was not always the Spitfires and Hurricanes that were victorious. One Spitfire destroyed a Stuka, then immediately destroyed a Bf 109 that flew across his nose. Whether the RAF pilot was a novice or wildly exhilarated will never be known as he was himself shot down after foolishly performing a victory roll.

Within a short time, it was all over. The only indication of the intensity of the action, just finished, were a few fires in the town and the beautiful blue sky stained by the obscene-looking mushrooms of smoke from the recent heavy Ack-Ack barrage.

Taffy and I were aware that an airman, gently descending by parachute, was going to land nearby. The wearer of the chute actually came to earth in the middle of a stony field alongside the road on which we were standing. I noticed some women running towards the recent arrival from the other side of the field. With a shout to Taffy, I vaulted over the low wall and ran towards the uninjured man, who had by now divested himself of his parachute harness and was standing uncertainly beside the collapsed chute.

As Taffy and I neared him, it became obvious he was not RAF, so we decided he must be the enemy. We were correct; he was a Luftwaffe pilot. With some embarrassment, we drew our revolvers and covered him. Since the women appeared none too friendly, and now two revolvers were pointed at his middle, the enemy airman was justifiably scared. When I calmed the women a little, I discovered that they were more interested in the parachute than in the airman, so, after telling them to help themselves, Taffy and I prepared to deliver our captive into more secure hands. Immediately, it became obvious what the women's knives were for. Within the space of less than two minutes, the parachute had been dissected into its many panels, and the women were on their way laughing and chattering about their silken prizes.

Taffy and I regained the road with our prisoner, not quite knowing what to do with him. Suddenly, Taffy pulled out his revolver once again and pointed it at the German. I was startled, but the German was terrified, thinking he was about to be shot.

'What the hell are you doing, Taff?' I demanded. 'He's harmless.'

'Like hell he's harmless! He's still got his gun. Take it off him!' snapped Taffy.

'Oh hell, so he has,' I said, shamefaced. Turning the young German around, I removed his automatic.

By this time, the enemy pilot was so frightened that he was trembling. Feeling pity, I patted him on the shoulder and offered him one of my few remaining cigarettes, which was accepted with obvious relief and a wan smile.

The descent of the enemy pilot had been observed by personnel more accustomed than Taffy or I to dealing with prisoners. It was with relief that we welcomed the arrival of a military police vehicle, out of which stepped two beefy MPs.

'Come on, Jerry, let's have you,' said one, jerking his head towards the vehicle. The German, understanding the gesture if not the words, climbed into the wagon. As it was about to set off, I gave the German's gun to the MP.

'Blimey, forgot that. Thanks. By the way, where's his parachute?' the MP asked questioningly.

'Some local women got it,' I answered.

'Pity. You can have a good bird for some parachute silk,' he added to our mild amusement. With a grin and a wink, he slammed the vehicle into gear and left us by the roadside.

'Taffy, what do you think of the enemy, now that we have met him face to face?' I asked.

'Not much,' said Taffy. 'That example of the master race didn't frighten me.'

I grinned, 'You certainly scared the pants off him when you drew your revolver the second time. Thought he was going to shit himself.'

Chuckling, Taffy replied, 'Maybe he did; he smelled a bit ripe when he climbed into the wagon.'

We had now arrived at a gated entrance similar to the ones found in York. Once through, we were stunned by the devastation. Piles of rubble lined each side of the narrow street. Most of the buildings were damaged to some degree, but being of solid stone construction, they had withstood the bombing remarkably well. What impressed us most was the spirit of the Maltese. The ones we spoke to had a calmness and self-assurance that, after all that they were going through, was most impressive and made us feel considerably less conceited.

Taffy and I found ourselves in 'the Gut', a street of bars much frequented by the Navy over many years. Ensconced in The John Bull with a beer apiece, we were in the process of chatting up two hostesses when the air raid warning sounded once again. Patrons calmly stopped what they were doing and walked to the shelter. This was at least thirty feet deep and cut out of solid rock. Perhaps it had been a wine cellar in happier times.

Although we were safe in the shelter, when a bomb thudded down a fine dust descended from the roof. It was with satisfaction that all concerned eventually climbed back up to street level.

By mutual consent, Taffy and I decided to return to our billets; to expedite our return, we hired a horse-drawn four-wheeled landau type of vehicle.

'Just like Blackpool,' I said.

'Not a bit,' replied Taff, 'Too many bloody flies and not enough popsies.'

Another air raid was developing over the harbour, but the driver of our gharry paid no attention to it, although the sky over Valletta was black with flak bursts.

On arrival at the poor house, we paid the driver and were just in time for tea, which was not exciting, with goat prominent on the menu in the form of rissoles and goat's milk again in the tea.

The next morning, the wireless operators and air gunners reported to the Armoury, but we were sent to the Flights to assist. We thought it would be a soft job, but a shock awaited us. The non-commissioned officer in charge shattered our complacency immediately. 'Latest orders,' he offered. 'When the air raid warning sounds, you will each go to an allotted aircraft, assist the fitter to start the port engine to activate the hydraulics, man the turrets, and await the attacks.'

'Balls to that,' muttered Taff. 'That's just plain bloody stupid. A Wimpy with an engine running will attract every Jerry fighter around.' Wimpy was RAF slang for the Vickers Wellington bomber.

The NCO, having overheard the remark, had the decency to temper his response. 'That's enough of that,' he said. 'I didn't hear it, and I only give the orders; I don't make them.'

Shortly after this exchange, the sirens did sound, and with some trepidation we went to the aircraft. To my surprise, Taffy climbed straight into the kite while I was assisting the fitter. Once the engine was running, I also climbed in to find Taffy already installed in the front turret.

'Crafty bastard,' I grumbled. I finally entered the rear turret, cocked the guns, and, with some apprehension, sat and waited.

The attack was not long in coming. Two Ju 88s came streaking in, and I could see the cannon shells running across the airfield towards me. Without thinking, I pushed the firing button, and, keeping the button depressed, I moved the grips as if gently stirring a pudding bowl.

The guns in the Frazer Nash turret immediately began to churn out 1,150 rounds per minute per gun, filling a lot of sky with lead. I had the satisfaction of seeing the two enemy attackers veer slightly in their approach. It was sufficient. The cannon shells swept past the turret, damaging the port elevator and wing and silencing the engine.

The prop had only just stopped turning when Taffy and I bolted from the aircraft and ran like hell for the shelter. When eventually everyone emerged once again, the sight that met our eyes shocked us. Another Wellington had also been hit, and an air gunner, obviously dead, was being lifted into an ambulance. The other AG was screaming, not in fear, but in sheer blind temper.

'The stupid, stupid bastard who issued that order wants putting in one of these turrets,' he bellowed, 'and we should be allowed to shoot at him with 20-mm cannon! Not only are we losing aircraft, now the stupid sods are wasting bloody good blokes for nothing!'

The turret order, as it was known, was rescinded that evening.

Malta to Egypt

Gradually, my crewmates and I were becoming accustomed to the strange way of life in besieged Malta, which was so different from the comparative safety of our England postings recently left behind. Apart from the occasional moments of fear, a feeling almost of boredom began to set in, so it was with pleasure when on 18 May, we were informed by the adjutant that an aircraft was ready for us.

'You will inspect the aircraft today,' spoke the adjutant. 'She will be fuelled up this evening, and you will air test her at 6 a.m. tomorrow morning. If the air test is satisfactory, you will set course tomorrow early evening for a landing ground near Cairo. You, navigator, will be given the position before you leave this building and can prepare your charts this afternoon. You, wireless op, will receive call signs and frequencies from the wireless officer on leaving this room. That's all. Cheerio and good luck.'

With these words, the adjutant dismissed us, and with the exception of the navigator and wireless operator, we climbed aboard a 15-cwt truck to have a look at our new baby. We pulled up beside a Wellington wearing the serial number DV670, but its peculiar paint scheme, upon first glimpse, rendered us open-mouthed and speechless. The fuselage and tailplane were painted in the dark earth and olive-green colours of the European theatre, while the wings were in desert colours of sand and brown.

'It's a bitzer—reassembled bits and pieces from more than one Wimpy wreck!' marvelled one. All recognised that this Wellington had been cobbled together utilising parts of the many damaged aircraft lying around.

'Its got measles,' remarked another with an attempt at humour. The cause of this quip was the red oxide-coloured patching, which seemed to cover the rear of the fuselage. The navigator and wireless operator had by this time joined the rest of the crew at the aircraft.

Clambering aboard, we proceeded to ground test various pieces of the Wimpy. The wireless operator seemed satisfied with the radio, although the intercom was not brilliant, being somewhat crackly. As 2nd W/op, I fulfilled the duties of front gunner and noticed that the twin Brownings were rusty, but being unable to test them on the ground, I could not do much about it. I smiled wryly to myself. Five days ago, we had been ordered to fire Wimpy guns at enemy aircraft while sitting helplessly on the ground. Now it was considered unsafe to try them.

Plt Off. Wilkinson had by this time started running up the engines, allowing Taffy and I to test the mechanics of the turrets to our satisfaction. We climbed out to compare notes after the engines were shut down. 'We'll get this kite to Egypt if we have to carry it on our backs,' said the skipper, 'unless, of course, you all like it here. One good point—the engines seem very good, so none of you horrible lot find anything wrong on the air test tomorrow.'

We agreed with Plt Off. Wilkinson, and after the usual miserable evening meal, we soon retired, ready for an early call next morning. We had not been asleep long, however, when the racket of another air raid woke us, so it was a bleary-eyed crew that climbed aboard the aircraft next day.

The early morning light cast a pearly glow over the airfield as *The Bitzer*, DV670's obvious nickname, taxied to the end of the runway ready for take-off. Running the two Pegasus engines caused the aircraft to vibrate in an alarming manner, which was probably no worse than usual, but it did not help that we, her crew, were in a nervous state to begin with.

A green Verey light shot up from the watch office and we felt the engines open up as the skipper ran to full throttle against the brakes. When he released them, the aircraft trundled forward, slowly at first, but with ever-increasing speed, until it was going fast enough for Taffy, in the rear turret, to become airborne. His standard joke was that he should do a shorter tour than the rest of the crew because he spent longer in the air, becoming airborne when the tail wheel left the ground and remaining so until the tailwheel finally sank to the ground once again when we landed.

Standing between the two pilots, I watched the end of the runway coming towards us but felt the cessation of bumps with some relief as the aircraft became airborne a good fifty feet before the runway's end. By this time, the sun had risen above the horizon. I took my place in the front turret, where I could feel the warmth of the day beginning to permeate the Perspex.

On the quick fifteen-minute air test, per the skipper's wishes, no abnormalities were reported. We wanted to get out of Malta that evening, and nothing was going to interfere.

We were aloft in DV670 at 5.40 p.m. on 19 May with just over two hours of daylight remaining. After a circuit of the field, Smithy, the navigator, gave a course to the skipper, and we set off for Egypt, thankful not to have been caught by enemy fighters.

Testing the twin Brownings soon thereafter, I discovered that one was defective. After reporting this to the skipper, I was told to forget it as I would never be able to hit anything anyway. Shortly afterwards, the intercom to the turret went out. With only my thoughts to occupy me, it was not long before I fell asleep.

A sudden bang of my head on the turret side awoke me with a start. The sea below, spinning, grew closer and closer as the Wellington fell from the sky. Unable to call the crew on my useless intercom and realising there was insufficient time to vacate the turret, I could only watch in horror and await the end.

The end did not come, though. The spinning decreased, then stopped. The aircraft levelled off roughly 100 feet above the sea, and slowly, agonisingly slowly, it began to climb to a safer altitude.

Grateful to have survived, yet curious as to the circumstances behind our near-death experience, I left the turret and went aft for enlightenment. I learned that as the skipper rose up from the left-hand seat to allow the second pilot to take over, his parachute harness or the straps of his Mae West caught on the control column. As he moved towards the rear of the aircraft, the control column was inadvertently yanked back, initiating the immediate Wellington stall. Swift, instinctive reaction in the cockpit averted disaster.

Satisfied that it was not some quirk of *The Bitzer*, I resumed my place in the front turret with a grand sigh of relief. After my brief sleep, and with the jolt of the aircraft's sudden stall, I felt fully alert and began to enjoy the flight. I was surprised at being able to see the bottom of the Mediterranean at times and did not give much for a submarine's chances against an air attack.

Following sunset, there was scarce illumination from the crescent moon. At length, we spotted a convoy and skirted gingerly around it, as Allied ships were as likely to shoot at us as was the enemy; such was the state of the war in the Med at that time.

Although the navigation on the flight had all been dead reckoning, the landfall in Mersa Matruh, Egypt, appeared 10 miles to starboard. This was not too bad considering the poor drifts given by Taffy in the rear turret to Smithy, the navigator.

After minor corrections, the old Wimpy headed for our final destination, 108 Maintenance Unit (MU), a desert airstrip outside of Cairo. Late in the first hour of 20 May, and after seven hours and fifteen minutes aloft, we landed in darkness, throwing up a cloud of dust in the parched night air.

2

Egypt, South Africa, and Back to the UK

On the Ground in Egypt, into Cairo

The speed with which things occurred in the next twenty-four hours was positively surprising as the usual RAF system seemed to be one decision followed by an interminable wait for the next one. Our first surprise was in being whisked into a tent and given a tasty, if somewhat sandy, meal of eggs and chips cooked in the tent on a Primus kerosene stove. There was also bully beef and bread. The bully beef was rather liquified due to the heat, but after the fare on Malta, it all tasted like ambrosia.

Next, my crew and I were relieved of the packets of foreign currency given to us when we left England to aid our escape should we be unfortunate enough to be shot down in enemy territory. A pay sergeant then gave each of us 250 piastres (about £2.50).

The order to board an old bus surprised us as it was assumed by all that our next flight would be to join a squadron in the desert. More mystifying still, the bus headed in an easterly direction until it finally hit the road to Cairo.

The first sight of this ancient city was quite different from what any of us imagined. The buildings were impressive ultra-modern blocks of flats and other well-designed structures flanking broad avenues, along which travelled large American cars, as well as the expected donkeys and camels. Finally, we were deposited at The Manhattan House, a modest but comfortable hotel where the first aircrew member I saw was Arnie Bridgman, my pal from 15 OTU.

Arnie grinned, 'Took your time. What kept you?'

I answered regretfully, 'Jerry blasted our kite, and we had to wait for another.'

After a certain amount of leg pulling, it was decided that I would join Arnie in his room, where there was a spare bed; so, bidding the rest of my late crew farewell, I moved my sparse kit into Arnie's room.

Perplexed, I asked my roommate why he was still in Cairo instead of on a squadron up in the 'blue', as the desert was known.

'Dunno really,' replied Arnie. 'All sorts of rumours are going around. That new bloke, Montgomery, is doing the new broom caper, and the griff is that there will be a big offensive shortly. How it will affect us is anybody's guess.'

At that moment, I jumped up apprehensively, thinking the air raid warning had sounded. Arnie roared with laughter. 'Sit down, you silly bugger,' he said, 'it's only a tram!' Sheepishly, I did so, but it took me some time to become accustomed to the sound sufficiently enough to hear it without feeling alarmed.

After luxuriating in a hot bath followed by a shave with Arnie's razor, I felt better than I had for a while. In short time, Arnie was showing me the sights of Cairo. We had tea in a place named Jolley's and then proceeded to tour the town. We found ourselves in a bar with a floor show where a large Egyptian lady was belly dancing, much to the amusement of some Aussie soldiers who kept urging her on by throwing coins towards her on the floor.

'Come on girl, let's see it all!' This and other remarks in a similar vein were being shouted at her, but she managed to keep everything covered until one soldier, drunker than the rest, managed to catch hold of her and tear off her bra. Two of the biggest breasts imaginable were displayed for all to see. A roar went up from the crowd, which was quieted by the appearance of half a dozen MPs.

As an MP went up to one inebriated Aussie, someone threw a bottle that smashed at the feet of the Redcap. It triggered off the most intense free-for-all Arnie and I had ever been involved in. Tables and chairs flew, mirrors crashed to the floor, and men were brawling in one great and glorious melee, fought without any malice and to the accompaniment of uproarious laughter. The MPs had retired to await reinforcements, and in a lull, Arnie separated me from an Aussie and pushed me outside.

'Now follow me and run like hell!' cried Arnie. The two of us set off like hares up one street and down the next until the sounds of pursuit died away and we had time to rest in order to regain our breaths.

'Does this sort of thing happen often?' I questioned.

'Only now and again,' answered Arnie. 'It's mostly high-spirited fun from blokes who have been up in the blue and are here on leave.'

'Who pays for the damage to the property?' I asked, slightly confused.

'Don't know, didn't wait to find out!' grinned Arnie.

Cairo was an experience for both of us. It had a strange and not unpleasant dry, musty smell: a mixture of Egyptian tobacco, camels, spices, all manner of cooking odours, and bodies—brown bodies, white bodies, black bodies, every shade and level of humanity from beggars in their rags to disdainful wealthy women in Buicks and Cadillacs who did little to hide their contempt for British troops. With Rommel then being at El Alamein, less than 150 miles away, it was obvious that many would welcome him in Cairo should he manage to break through.

The following evening, a small booze-up was underway as it was the twenty-first birthday of another W/op named Wilkinson. When the vocal chords had been suitably lubricated, various RAF songs were sung with gusto by all concerned, such as:

Oh, we're leaving Khartoum,
By the light of the moon,
We're sailing by night and by day.
We've passed Kasfareet,
We've had eff all to eat,
'cos we've thrown all our rations away!

So—sail on, Somersetshire,
The skipper looks on her with pride.
He'd have a blue fit,
If he saw any shit,
On the side of the Somersetshire!

This is my story, this is my song,
I've been in this air force too bloody long.
So roll out the Rodney, Revenge and Renown,
But we can't say the Hood 'cos the blighter's gone down!

At the end of each song, a cheer went up and someone would start the next. One that confused me at first started as follows:

There's a street in Cairo,
full of sin and shame,
Sharia El Berka is its sodding name.
Russian, French and Greek bints all 'round I see,
Come all you air force lads,
Abide with me.

The song went on for verse after verse and told the story of an airman who squandered his pay each pay day in the brothels, until one sad day, he was told he had VD by the medical officer (MO). After weeks of treatment, he is pronounced cured and immediately resumes his old habits, and so the song starts all over again.

'Arnie, what's this place we've been singing about?' I queried.

'Not a place to be recommended to a lad like you,' laughed Arnie. 'Remember all those slides we were shown when training at Blackpool? It's the military brothel area, and you might end up a few ounces lighter if you go there.'

Noting my puzzlement, Arnie sighed in exasperation, 'Your cock might drop off, you gormless bugger.' With a shake of his head, he took a long drink of his beer.

It should be noted here that I was nearly twenty years of age while Arnie was twenty-two, and the difference in our ages caused Arnie to assume the role of elder brother in all decision making then, and in our subsequent time together in the RAF.

Almaza Transit Camp Outside of Cairo

Appearing next morning with varying degrees of hangovers, we found that the noticeboard displayed a piece of paper telling us to be ready to move that afternoon to a transit camp at Almaza, outside of Cairo, at which place we duly arrived at 4 p.m.

Almaza turned out to be a huge tented camp. The tents were like small marquees set down in the sand until only the roofs were above ground level, and the coolness inside was in marked contrast to the heat outside.

'Wonder who does all the digging?' I mused, almost to myself.

'Eyetie prisoners,' answered a darkly tanned figure from the corner of the tent in which we found ourselves. He continued, 'Make the sods sweat a bit, and let us have a rest now we are down from the blue.'

Arnie and I, feeling somewhat embarrassed, informed the speaker that we were not veterans like himself, but replacements awaiting posting to a squadron. During the ensuing conversation, the veteran, whose name was Dick, became quite interested on hearing of my short stay in Malta.

'Got a younger brother stationed there as an armourer,' spoke Dick. 'He's a lazy sod, and I haven't heard from him for some time. Is it as rough as they say?'

I hesitated before replying and then said, 'It's not too bad once you've learned to keep your head down when the shit starts flying.' Hearing this, Dick seemed much relieved. In order not to worry Dick any more than necessary, I omitted to tell him of the news we had been given of Jerry's impending invasion of the island.

'There's a rumour going around that some blokes are being posted back to Blighty, but I don't suppose I'll be one of them,' said Dick. He added with a grin, 'That particular rumour will not be of interest to you two either, seeing as you've just arrived.'

'Trying to understand the workings of the RAF mind is a pointless occupation,' offered Arnie. 'Wouldn't surprise me that having brought us all the way out here with difficulty and at great expense, the powers that be will decide to keep blokes like you here and send us back home to start the whole pointless exercise again.'

Seeing Dick's look of apprehension, he added, 'Don't worry, I'm only joking,' but his remark was to become startlingly true.

Reporting in for further instructions, I noticed that the various departments were housed in what appeared to be wooden huts. On closer inspection, however, they were revealed as the discarded packing crates of Hurricane fighters that had been shipped out to the Middle East in knocked-down form and assembled in Egypt. When all necessary details had been provided to the satisfaction of the Orderly Room, Arnie and I were directed to the Sergeants' Mess and told to keep our eyes on the noticeboard for an announcement of our posting to a squadron.

The Sergeants' Mess turned out to be several packing crates knocked together to form a reasonably large hut. As Almaza was a transit camp with personnel passing through all the time, little had been done to make the place comfortable. The main essential was there, however, in the shape of a bar that stretched across the entire width of one wall and at which stood men of many nationalities. British airmen were the most numerous, but there were also many Australians, New Zealanders, Canadians, a sprinkling of Americans, South Africans, Rhodesians, and two lonely Frenchmen sitting in a corner regarding the rest of us with utter boredom.

Above the general hubbub, raised voices were heard in one corner until a gunshot, which shattered a bottle at the back of the bar, created instant silence. We then saw an Aussie waving a revolver before two very apprehensive South Africans. Calmly, a rather small Australian pilot strolled over to the group, belted his fellow countryman on the chin, and took his gun from him before he had even hit the floor.

'Piss off, you two, before he comes round,' he snapped at the South Africans.

They did not need telling twice and left immediately. Much bad feeling had been generated between the Australians and South Africans over Tobruk with regards to the epic siege when the Aussies held out against Rommel for so long. Tobruk had been denuded of many of its defences and would fall to the Germans in June. Blaming the South Africans was hardly fair, but fairness is a scarce commodity in wartime; hence the bad feeling.

Events in the Mess had now returned to normal and the incident forgotten, but it served to show the tensions running under the surface. Arnie and I returned to our tent in a quiet and thoughtful mood.

Sailing from Egypt to South Africa

Three days after arriving in the camp, Arnie's words to Dick in the tent came true with uncanny accuracy. A long list appeared on the noticeboard, and, sure enough, there were the names of Arnie and myself listed for posting back to the UK. The name of our tent mate, Dick, was not on the list, but he took it philosophically and wished us luck before we left.

The way home took a completely different route from the one everyone expected. Where it was assumed by all concerned that groups of us would be flown to the UK as aircraft were available, orders directed us to Port Tewfik on the Suez Canal. There, the *Nieuw Amsterdam*, a large modern Dutch liner, awaited us and, as the Mediterranean was almost closed to Allied shipping, our route home would be via South Africa.

The aircrew members were ferried out to the ship aboard large flat-bottomed lighters. As there were only sixty aircrew allocated to each ship, the task was soon accomplished. Arnie and I were accommodated in a cabin on 'C' Deck, and on entering, we were greeted by Wilky, the chap who had celebrated his twenty-first birthday in Cairo, and an air gunner neither of us knew. As the cabin only held two bunk beds, we two new arrivals stowed our kit on the top two beds; the lower ones had already been claimed by Wilky and the air gunner whose name we discovered was Joe.

Joe turned out to be a natural born comic with a Liverpudlian accent, of which he was not ashamed, and which he used to good effect on some of the more snobbish officers, particularly Navy types. He said the reason for the accent was the draught from the Mersey Tunnel affecting his adenoids.

Stowing of kit completed, we four decided on an inspection tour of the ship, and we were amazed at the evidence of magnificent peacetime luxury. Great marble staircases, beautifully panelled walls, and remnant pieces of the main carpets remaining in odd corners gave us some idea of the opulence that had existed, but which was probably gone forever.

Having been brought up in the less salubrious part of Horsforth, and with a father who in peacetime struggled to make a living as a signwriter, this other side of life was slightly disturbing to me.

The four of us were, by this time, leaning on the ship's rail watching the bum boats clustered round the ship selling everything from fruit to leather goods. Haggling took place between vendor and customer with shouted offers and mock-horrified refusals from the traders in the small boats until agreement was reached on both sides, whereupon the necessary money was lowered in a container attached to a thin rope. Upon receipt of the money, the purchased article was placed in the container and hauled aboard.

With something like twenty transactions taking place simultaneously at the side of the vessel, the noise was intense, but it sounded like a whisper when the ship's siren sounded. All concerned were startled by the sheer intensity of the noise but were pleased to note that it presaged our imminent departure. Within a surprisingly short space of time, the ship was under way.

There was an audible click on a public address system, and a tinny voice started issuing times of meal sittings. As food was a favourite subject, my pals and I gave the announcement our whole attention. Joe spoke, 'We're first sitting for tea. We'd better hurry.'

Without another word, he was on his way with the rest of us close behind, and after some wrong turns we eventually found the Mess Deck. Here, another pleasant surprise awaited us as the food was better than the usual RAF food, with fresh bread rolls and butter, decent soup, a main course, and a sweet. The men who served us food were Italian Prisoners of War *en route* to captivity in South Africa. We were later detailed to guard the entrance to the deck way down in the lower depths of the ship, where the main body of prisoners were housed.

In the days that followed, life assumed a routine that was quite pleasant: boat drill in the morning, some free time until lunch, and games in the afternoon. Arnie and I enjoyed the deck hockey and became good enough to be selected to join the team that would represent the RAF in the upcoming competition against the Navy and the Army.

The games were fairly straightforward, played on hands and knees with Indian clubs used as hockey sticks and a rubber puck instead of a ball. In the final, between the RAF and the Navy, I was goalkeeper. The action was intense as there was great rivalry between the two services. The Navy personnel, in particular, were not happy to admit that a battleship was vulnerable without air cover.

Nearing the game's end, the RAF was leading by three goals to two when the Navy attacked. As I went forward to retrieve the puck, I was aware of someone holding me back. Keeping my eye on the puck, I swung the club behind me and heard a yelp and a crack. Clearing the puck, I was able to look behind to see a Navy captain nursing a shin, and obviously in some pain.

The final whistle sounded, resulting in victory for the RAF, whereupon I stood up and confronted the captain. 'Sorry, sir, is it broken?' I asked, nodding towards the injured leg and feeling like Fletcher Christian on the HMS *Bounty*. The officer regarded me coolly and then slowly grinned, shook his head, and limped away. Some sailors who had witnessed the incident looked at me with awe.

'Blimey,' breathed a cockney able seaman. 'You belted a captain and got away with it. How does it feel?'

'Bloody marvellous,' I answered, letting out a great sigh of relief. 'Thought he would have booked me.'

'Not him. He's a toff. Looks after his own blokes like a father,' commented the able seaman.

I discovered that the Navy men on board were all survivors of battles in the Mediterranean and all had an intense hatred of Jerry dive bombers, although they admitted grudging admiration for the German pilots.

That evening, the RAF was allowed to entertain Navy and Army personnel of all ranks in the Sergeants' Mess, normally out of bounds to other ranks. The displeasure exhibited by some of the Army sergeants only helped to consolidate the bonhomie that existed between the other two services. As the drinks flowed, this fellowship steadily increased, even between different ranks.

Next morning at boat drill there were many grey faces and thumping heads, and the officer I had whacked on the shin came over to me and with a chuckle remarked, 'The price of victory is often painful, is it not?'

Lifting my head from my hands, I could only remorsefully agree. As the days passed, many were heard to say that there were worse ways to spend a war than cruising in a luxury liner, but there were men on the ship—the PoWs—who were less happy.

Joe and I were detailed to do a stint of guard duty on the entrance to the deck where the prisoners were kept, and the heat was stifling. The Italian prisoners seemed reasonably cheerful and delighted to be on their way to South Africa, away from fighting. Joe was in his element, having picked up a smattering of Italian from a family in Liverpool. He soon had quite a collection of badges, including German ones, which he was swapping for cigarettes—mainly a cheap brand named Springbok that he did not enjoy.

'Just wait till my bird sees these,' spoke Joe. 'She'll swear I'm a hero, and I'll have her knickers down in no time, especially when I give her a pair of those new nylon stockings.'

I laughed. 'What if she's a good girl and refuses to part with her virginity?' I asked.

Joe studied for a moment. Then an evil grin appeared. 'In that case,' he replied, 'I'll give her one stocking the first night and promise her the second the following evening if she ceases to be a good girl.'

Shortly afterwards, we were relieved by a pair of air gunners, and Joe bade a cheerful farewell to the prisoners, who seemed genuinely sorry to see him go. 'So long, see you after the war,' shouted Joe.

About this time, the ship's swimming pool was opened for our use most afternoons. Our foursome was glad to enjoy its coolness after the heat on deck. The evenings were spent playing tombola, also known as housey-housey (more commonly known today as bingo). This was the only service game where gambling was allowed.

Durban

About a week later, it became markedly cooler. As the South African climate was entering the cold season, we guessed that our destination was not far away; the guesses proved correct. On the following Saturday, the ship docked in Durban. After a warning to abide by what to us were strange laws on fraternising with coloured people, the troops were allowed ashore.

The welcome was like something out of a fairy story. As we came onto the docks, large cars, mostly open, were lined up, each with a pretty female behind the steering wheel who offered to drive into town.

After parting company with Joe, our Liverpool cabinmate, Arnie and I realised that we were almost broke, as usual. Assuming the cars to be taxis, we were walking past them when a feminine voice hailed us. 'Get in, you two, if you want a lift.' We looked round to see a very attractive girl holding open the door of a car. 'Come on, get in. It's free,' she insisted.

This latter remark decided the issue and we needed no second bidding. The girl drove with skill, and, without asking us where to go, she took us to a palatial house and invited us to join her for tea.

We were soon greeted by the girl's mother, a charming lady who, after hearing Arnie and I speaking together, twigged us about our Yorkshire accents. At a moment when the conversation lagged, she said to Arnie, 'Pass 't butter, lad,' and grinned at him.

Arnie's look of surprise caused her to chuckle, and in her more polished accent, she explained that she had been born in Wakefield and had come to South Africa after her marriage twenty years previously. Later in the evening, the girl, named Margaret, took us in the car to an open-air dance hall where we had a splendid time, but we had to cut short the fun in order to return to the ship by 11 p.m.

The following morning, we were once again met by Margaret, accompanied by her father. During a long and scenic drive, the father floored us with a suggestion. 'Why not let the ship sail without you? I can easily arrange for you both to disappear until the war is over and then fix you both up with better jobs than you will get back home.'

The offer was tempting, but Arnie and I had little difficulty in turning it down.

'No thanks, we're not heroes,' said Arnie with some sharpness. 'We have been trained to do a job, and we'll do it. And anyway, I couldn't look at myself when shaving if I was hiding here while my pals were flying and probably dying.'

I nodded assent.

The girl's father was quite unconcerned. 'Didn't really expect any other answer, but it was worth a try. No hard feelings?'

Arnie, who seemed to have adopted the role of spokesman, assured him on that matter and asked the question both he and I had been puzzling over. 'Why do you want men to desert here?'

Margaret's father was silent for a while, and when he spoke it was with a seriousness neither of us had heard in his voice before. 'There is a political struggle going on here between the English and Boer people, the details of which need not concern you. Suffice it to say, we will need all the help we can get.' He then added with a smile, 'We also need husbands for our daughters.'

By this time, the car had arrived back at the house and Margaret's father got out. 'See you later boys, and good luck. Margaret will take you back to the ship. You'll be sailing early tomorrow morning.' With a wave, he was gone.

The girl seemed quite unconcerned by all that had taken place, but Arnie and I were disturbed to think that a civilian knew when our ship was leaving; if one knew, so did others. Many South Africans were hoping for a Nazi victory, and ships were sunk periodically by German U-boats offshore.

The car stopped at the dock gates. We were rather rattled when we alighted; after thanking our charming driver, we set off for the ship. Our last view of Margaret and her car was of her holding open the door for two sailors to get in.

I turned to Arnie. 'Wonder if her father will have more success with those two?'

'Don't know, but I'll tell you what, it's a beautiful country with enough for everybody, but there is real tension under the surface,' commented Arnie. With a laugh, he added, 'It'll be good to get back to an uncomplicated war where we know who the baddies are.'

Cape Town

The timing of our departure, as forecast by our host of the previous day, proved almost correct, for when we awoke the next day we were well out to sea. Nearly 1,000 miles later, the ship docked in Cape Town. For me, seeing Table Mountain as the backdrop to the sweep of the bay was almost like being back in the geography room at school. The picture on the school wall did not do justice to the majesty of the real thing.

I did not have long to admire it, however, before transport arrived and took all the aircrew to Pollsmoor Transit Camp at the foot of the mountain I had so recently been admiring.

Contrasts seemed to be the order of the day. After the relative luxury of the *Nieuw Amsterdam*, bell tents were now our accommodation, and as it was the wet season, mud was everywhere. Needless to say, we, the inmates in this tent city, were wet and woebegone in a short time. There was one redeeming feature to the camp which was soon discovered, though. The Sergeants' Mess was a treat, with South African champagne at five shillings (25p) per bottle.

We spent the first evening in camp in the company of Americans and South Africans consuming quantities of the champagne and having a glorious binge. We ended our impromptu party by singing the usual indecent barrack room ballads. The damp clothes and blankets were only minor annoyances when we finally fell into our beds.

Apart from looking at the noticeboard each morning to see if we had a ship, our time was our own, and the delights of Cape Town were soon being explored by one and all. The kindness of the people was outstanding and indeed became almost embarrassing, as RAF men were not allowed to pay for a thing. The reason for the generosity, we discovered, was that we were the first aircrew seen going back to Britain, so we were regarded as veterans. Our lack of operational experience we kept to ourselves.

Arnie and I were becoming rather blasé about the noticeboard, as morning after morning we regarded it, only to discover that we had not been given a ship. So, it was with mixed feelings one morning that we saw a list of names, including Arnie's but not mine, to be transported aboard the former Cunard liner *Samaria* back to the UK. The hope of crewing up together now seemed dashed. I was genuinely sorry to see my pal depart on the *Samaria* while I remained behind.

Sailing to Liverpool

In due time, I was listed to sail aboard the *Nieuw Holland*. My spirits rose as I imagined it to be the sister ship of the *Nieuw Amsterdam*. When I finally went aboard, I found out just how wrong I was.

The only thing the two ships had in common was the name 'Nieuw'. Where the previous ship was spacious and modern and I had been in a cabin with three other chaps, the present ship was narrower-beamed and ten years older, and the accomodation was in the hold of the ship divided up with rows of wooden bunks. After stowing what kit I retained, I went on a tour of the ship and was not impressed, but after a day or so at sea, I discovered that things were not too bad.

Most of the troops were Army types being sent home to convalesce, many suffering from battle fatigue. As a result, there were few drills and I could relax. The small number of aircrew were given various duties. The wireless operators were detailed to serve a watch in the radio room from time to time, but as only a listening watch was maintained I had plenty of opportunity to talk to the ship's radio officer when it was his turn on watch. The radios were much bigger than the Marconi sets in the Wellington, and the radio officer was only too pleased to impart lessons on the theory of wireless telegraphy, which stood me in good stead later.

I was pleased to receive the instruction as my wireless training had been very sketchy on the theory side. I had been assured by the instructors that the wireless mechanics would maintain the sets on a squadron, while the aircrew were only there to operate them. The sets in this ship made the neat little 1082s and 1083s on which I had trained look like toys.

Time began to drag as the ship continually altered course to deter any U-boats that may have been around, but one night the boredom was broken. Many of the men, me included, were now sleeping outside on the deck to avoid the heat of the ship's hold. Having been lulled asleep by the vibration of the vessel tearing along at top speed, we were jolted awake in the early hours one morning by a shot fired across our bow by a nearby ship. Our ship halted. An Aldis lamp started blinking away, and I read, 'What is your destination?'

Looking towards the wing of the bridge, I also read the reply, but it was in code—a group of four figures that I memorised. My reason for doing so was the sweepstake being run on the ship regarding the port at which we would dock. Consequently, on my next watch in the radio room, I looked up the code in the destinations book and read 'Liverpool'. I staked my last five shillings with the ship's purser as soon as my watch ended and hoped not many of the other W/ops had read our ship's Aldis lamp.

Next morning, the coast of Ireland first came into view, and from then the ship was within sight of land all day. The green fields were beautiful. Everyone was excited, and at 10 a.m. the following morning the lines were cast ashore, the gangway went down and the troops prepared to disembark—at Liverpool. I was £5 better off than I had been the previous day.

Back in the UK and on Leave

The aircrew were assembled on the dockside. After customs, which was merely a formality, the usual RAF three-tonner appeared and whisked us off to Wilmslow, Cheshire.

Travelling to Wilmslow was enjoyable. The day was warm and sunny. England in July 1942, even in wartime, was infinitely better than many places on the Earth. Entering the camp gates eventually, we, the occupants of the three-tonner, were in the best of spirits, looking forward to leave and reunions with families and girlfriends. The RAF did its best to curb this exuberance, in the shape of the disciplinary flight sergeant who stood to the rear of the wagon as the good-humoured aircrew 'debussed'—a word only the military mind could have conceived.

'Shut up you, and listen!' he barked. 'You will be marched to Stores and kitted out. Go to the Station Sick Quarters for jabs and an FFI. From there make your way to Accounts for pay and finally to the Orderly Room for leave passes.' 'FFI' meant 'free from infection.'

The flight sergeant regarded us with disgust, not without reason, for we were in varying stages of dishevelment. Looking straight at me in my khaki shirt and trousers, topped off with my blue battledress blouse, he wrinkled his nose and grunted, 'My god, you look like a turd in tapes.' The stripes on a sergeant's arms were often referred to as tapes.

Of my original kit, I only possessed a battledress blouse, one vest, one pair of underpants, one shirt, socks, and shoes. The stores sergeant regarded me with suspicion. 'Where's the rest?' he asked. I gave the sergeant a resume of my operational career, brief as it was. As the sergeant still wavered between belief and disbelief, I produced a chit signed by the adjutant at Malta. After reading it, the sergeant's attitude changed. 'We might as well start from scratch, all bar the shoes,' he offered, whereupon two airmen were detailed to assist. They commenced by re-kitting me with two blue banded kit bags and a parachute bag; this was finished with a 'housewife', a small cloth container holding needles, thread and wool for running repairs.

Leaving the kit in Stores, I was cleared at the Station Sick Quarters. I collected my pay and finally my leave pass, which gladdened my heart by having no return date on it. 'You'll receive a posting to a unit while on leave,' explained the corporal on handing me the pass.

Gathering my kit from stores, I set off on leave, feeling like a beast of burden. After a tedious journey, I finally arrived home to the obvious delight of my parents and sister Sheila. After the initial excitement, I told them I was going the next day to see my girlfriend who was in the Auxiliary Territorial Service and stationed near Goole. A silence occurred. Sensing something was wrong, I gazed at Dad questioningly.

He looked at me with obvious concern. 'I'm sorry, lad,' he said quietly, 'Dorothy was killed a week ago in an air raid on Hull.'

Without a word, I rose from my chair, went out the front door, through the gate and onward to the nearby woods. In a daze, I sat under a tree. My dog Toby, accompanying me, sensed something was not right and, with a low whimper, slowly licked my hand. The gesture released my emotion, and, throwing myself on my face, I sobbed into the grass until my initial anguish was spent.

The dog, meanwhile, had been attempting to give me its affection. Sitting with my back to a tree, I placed my arm around the dog and hugged the animal to my chest. 'Sometimes, Toby, I think animals have more sense than do human beings,' I sighed. Now being more composed, I arose and made my way back home with the dog chasing imaginary rabbits, well pleased that her master was himself again.

What I had been anticipating, a long and enjoyable leave, now became a period of mild boredom. My parents were out all day on war work, so I only saw them at the evening meal, such as it was. The frugal rations were in marked contrast to the fare I had been enjoying in Egypt and South Africa. Although the Navy seemed to be getting the better of the U-boats, nevertheless, the enemy submarines were making their marks on the convoys with a consequent reduction in rations to the population of Britain.

Most of my pre-war pals were away in the forces and I found that I had little in common with the few who were still at home because of ill health or reserved occupations. When the July 1942 telegram came posting me to RAF Burn, I was pleased to be returning to a way of life in which I felt more comfortable.

3

The Gauntlett Crew Forms Up at 1653 Conversion Unit

Arnie and I Arrive at RAF Burn and 1653 Conversion Unit

Meeting up again with my mate Arnie Bridgman while stepping off the train from Leeds to Selby was an added bonus to my new posting. We agreed that if the situation warranted, we would crew up together. We were soon to learn what the next few weeks held in store for us.

As we stepped forward from the train, the driver of a 15-cwt gharry spied our uniforms and pulled up. 'You two sergeants for Burn?' enquired the driver, a typical motor transport operator in a battered forage cap, greasy tunic, and dusty boots. On receiving confirmation, he merely pointed a thumb in the back of the truck and lit a cigarette while we tossed aboard kit bags, parachute bags, gas masks and side packs. As it was summertime, we were in quite a lather when we finally climbed aboard.

'What squadron is here?' shouted Arnie above the noise of the Bedford.

'No squadron,' answered the driver. 'A training unit.' We were curious about our new opportunities, even in another training unit, though we were itching to get into the action.

The truck soon turned off the main road and down a narrow lane between hawthorn hedges. Through a gap in the hedge we saw the airfield and on the far side some large four-engined aircraft in the standard camouflage of the time: olive green and dark earth on the upper surfaces and matte black underneath. We were not familiar with the aircraft, however, and could not identify them.

The truck pulled up in front of the Guard Room, and we went in. Seated at a plain wooden desk was a corporal in the RAF Service Police, while behind him stood the smallest warrant officer we had ever seen, no more than five feet tall. He held the position of Senior Warrant Officer—better known as SWO—at RAF Burn, and, although a keen disciplinarian, he went out of his way to be helpful when called upon to do so, as we soon discovered.

After checking our documents, he ran his finger down a list. 'Hut 14,' he bellowed, in a voice which shook the building. 'Driver, take these men to Hut 14. Show them the Sergeants' Mess, then come back here. Be quick about it!'

To say that the words made the driver jump would be an understatement; he set off as if his life depended upon it. Waving an arm in the general direction of some trees, he shouted, 'Sergeants' Mess,' slid around a corner, skidded to a halt, was round the back of the wagon heaving out our kit, and then was off again, all before we had gathered our wits.

Leaving our belongings in the pile where the driver had tossed them, we went inside to inspect our billet. It was a typical wartime building, built of breeze blocks and cement rendered, but it had not been standing for long as it smelled of damp plaster. Painters were still working on the next block.

On entering, we were surprised to find that we were the first occupants. Immediately inside were two small rooms, one on each side. On the left was storage for cleaning materials, while the room on the right, disused at present, was normally the living quarters of a corporal in charge of other ranks occupying the block. Arnie, myself, and our cohorts, however, were of a higher rank; thus, there would be no corporal overseer for our lot.

Being no longer 'sprogs', or new RAF recruits, we proceeded into the body of the building and chose two beds midway between the door and the first stove, about five feet inside the building. Experience had taught us that beds near the stove were used by one and all as seats during the incessant card games that seemed to form an essential backdrop to wartime barrack room life. They were also used as seats on which to sit while making toast by sticking slices of bread on the sides of the stove; a slice was toasted when it fell off.

After a short examination, we went outside, picked up our kit, dumped it on the beds of our choice to register ownership, and made our way to the Sergeants' Mess. The entry to the Sergeants' Mess was the standard type: a small porch entered by double doors and, a short distance within, another pair of doors. The two sets of doors were designed to maintain a blackout in the event of an air raid. Through the second set of doors was a larger hall with a noticeboard on the right, on which were displayed Daily Routine Orders, better known as DROs. Arnie and I approached the board with mild interest and noticed the heading, '1653 CU.' Noting our curiosity, an Aussie flight sergeant who had just entered volunteered the information, '1653 Conversion Unit. We're all here to convert to Liberators.'

The shapes we had seen on the far side of the aerodrome now sprang to mind. Liberators, so far as either Arnie or I knew, were long-range machines solely used on Coastal Command for anti-submarine work, but what was puzzling was that all coastal aircraft were finished matte white on the undersides, whereas the Liberators we had seen at Burn were finished matte black underneath, as on Bomber Command.

Turning back again to the board, we noticed that there was an announcement of a parade for all aircrew next morning at 8 a.m. in the road outside the Mess. 'Oh well,' grinned Arnie, 'I suppose all will be revealed tomorrow.' On that note, we turned into the room on the left, which was the dining room. Inside were seated approximately thirty aircrew NCOs who scarcely noticed us as we took our seats for tea. We were both agreeably surprised by the meal that, although rather plain fare, was cooked well and cleanly presented.

'Always did like Welsh Rarebit, and this is a really good example,' murmured Arnie between mouthfuls.

'Agreed,' I said. 'If all the grub is as good as this I'll not complain.' To round off the meal, we had pieces of apple tart and large mugs of tea. 'Now what?' I asked. 'Think we should get sorted out in the billet?'

'Why not?' answered Arnie. 'We can come back later when the bar opens and meet one or two of the others.'

On returning to the billet, we were surprised to find how many beds had become occupied in our absence and were inwardly pleased to have had first pick of the beds. As we entered, a corporal and two airmen were in the process of distributing three blankets and two sheets to each bed.

Three small straw-filled square mattresses, called biscuits, had already been positioned on each airman's iron-framed bed. We quickly made up our beds in the approved RAF manner and then stowed our kit in the wooden locker provided beside each bed-space. The revolvers and parachutes we left in our parachute bags until such time as we could deposit them in the Armoury and Parachute Sections respectively.

On completing these tasks, we sat on our beds and regarded the other occupants of the hut with mild curiosity. The men who were the object of our study were a mixed crowd, and the first ones to catch our attention were four air gunners, obviously brand new with their almost incandescent stripes to go with bright, clean AG brevets. They were trying hard to appear experienced before the critical gaze of other members of the hut but were only successful in displaying their inexperience.

Their first mistake had been in selecting the beds near the stove. Then their way of talking shop, with much reference to the flak over Brest, only confirmed their recent completion of the last stage of their training at an Operational Training Unit, where the final flight was usually to the submarine pens at Brest or St Nazaire to give a sprog aircrew its baptism of fire. The other members of the hut were a mixed crowd: two French Canadian navigators, one small Scottish pilot, one Rhodesian pilot, and two English navigators.

Arnie lay on his bed and addressed the ceiling. 'You bods had better get a move on if you want to eat. They finish serving in ten minutes.' Within seconds, the hut was empty, except for Arnie, myself and the Scottish pilot.

'Ate in York,' said the Scotsman, a sergeant, without looking up from the book he was reading. 'Between trains,' he added, after a pause.

'Have you had a long journey to get here?' I asked.

'Inverness,' came the reply, 'real bind of a journey, had to stand most of the way.' He spoke with that soft lilt of the Highlander, which made his speech much more attractive than our own flat Yorkshire accents. It transpired that he had transferred to the RAF from the Army immediately after Dunkirk and had only recently completed his training on multi-engined aircraft.

'What mob?' I enquired with some curiosity.

'HLI, the Highland Light Infantry. Bloody shambles,' replied the pilot.

We three carried on a conversation mainly about our experiences to date. The hut slowly filled up with fellow airmen as the evening wore on; in time, it was lights out. We would bless the bar in the Sergeants' Mess another evening. The following day would bring new beginnings for us all.

Parading outside the Mess the next morning was a motley crowd of NCO pilots, navigators, wireless operators and straight air gunners. Surveying us from the height of the two steps to the Mess was the same tiny station Senior Warrant Officer Arnie and I had briefly encountered upon arrival at RAF Burn. We had discovered the previous evening in the Mess that off parade, the little SWO was a very likeable man, but on parade, what he lacked in inches, he more than made up for with strict discipline. As a result, he was much respected and earned the nickname 'the Big Man'.

Dead on 8 p.m., he pulled himself to attention and roared, 'Quiet!' The sound of that enormous voice emanating from such a tiny frame immediately quelled the hubbub. In a more reasonable voice, he instructed us to assemble in a large building all had seen on entering the camp, so in an untidy gaggle we started to move towards it.

The voice came again: 'Come back here, you sloppy lot!'

When once more assembled before him, the SWO stabbed out a finger at a tall Canadian. 'You stand there as marker. The rest of you fall in, in threes.'

When we were assembled to his satisfaction, he beamed, 'That's better. Now we'll march off smartly, not stroll along like a bunch of pansies. Left turn, queeek maach! Ef oi, ef oi, ef oi!'

Our Crew Takes Shape

Approaching the building, he gave the command, 'Squaaad halt!' but he did not immediately dismiss us. 'Get in there and sort yourselves out into crews: two pilots, one mastermind as navigator, two wireless operators, three gunners. Right, squad, 'shun! Deesmiss!' On completion of the command, he marched back to the Mess like a miniature guardsman.

We entered the building, which we guessed was the Parachute Section from the height of the ceiling. In the low light, officers were observed on a bench at the far end. All were either pilot officers or flying officers, so they were likely as raw as the majority of the NCOs. Somewhat embarrassed, the occupants of the room milled around, usually in pairs like Arnie and me. We had taken seats in a strategic area, the better to observe the other members. It was crowded.

'We must look like a couple of debutantes sitting here,' observed Arnie.

'Wouldn't know,' I replied, 'I was never invited to their parties.'

Idly glancing around, I saw the Scottish sergeant pilot from our billet in an animated conversation with a tall, well-made pilot officer. As I was looking, the Scotsman pointed straight at me. I nudged Arnie, 'Eyup lad, I think we've clicked.'

With studied casualness, the two pilots strolled across. The Scotsman spoke: 'You two crewed up yet?' The question was superfluous, as all four knew, but it opened the bidding. Cagey about committing ourselves, we two wireless ops shook our heads.

'How about flying with us?' asked the pilot officer.

Speaking for the two of us, Arnie asked, 'What is your level of flying experience?'

With a rueful grin, the tall pilot officer answered, 'No. 22 OTU at Wellesbourne, and then a Wellington delivery flight from the UK to Egypt, via Gibraltar and Malta. I'd transferred to the RAF from the Army several months after Dunkirk.'

'You did too, didn't you?' asked Arnie of the Scotsman.

'Aye,' he replied, 'I fancied sleeping in sheets at night.'

'Well Arnie, I'm game,' I laughed. 'If we get shot down these two can show us how to fight our way out.'

'OK,' said Arnie, 'I'm in.'

Now being half-complete, our crew still needed a navigator and three gunners, so we started searching together in the crowd. With the noise, the dim light and the sea of uniforms, our pilot officer at first failed to recognise a navigator with whom he had already flown from Blighty to Egypt, and whose abilities he readily admired.

By chance, however, my attention was focused upon this same navigator—a most peculiar airman sitting on a chair the wrong way around, reading a paperback and seemingly taking no interest in what was going on. His tunic buttons and shoes were badly in need of a clean and he required a shave, but the thing which interested me most was his half-wing brevet. He wore the 'O' brevet rather than the more commonplace 'N', while on his shoulder was the word 'CANADA'. The 'O', or observer, badge he was wearing marked him as a man whose training had been more comprehensive than that of airmen who wore the more recently inaugurated 'N', or navigator, brevet. Then, the pilot officer's eyes and the observer's eyes met, followed by a dual flash of recognition and broad smiles which exuded mutual respect and admiration.

'Sir!' barked the observer, with mock formality, 'I can't believe I missed you in this zoo! I didn't know you were here!'

'The same goes for me, you old goat!' kidded the pilot officer. 'Say, we're in need of a navigator. Fancy joining us?'

Feigning indifference while looking back down at his book, an obvious put-on, the Canadian replied, 'Guess so.' Then, he grinned while remarking, 'Right place, right time!' With that, we had scored us our navigator. He later told us that he had appeared in his untidy state to deliberately deter what he referred to as 'bullshit crews'. While pretending to read, he had sized up his options and had turned down three crews before fortune came knocking.

The problem of selecting the gunners solved itself. Our group, now expanded to five, was outside at the NAAFI wagon having a cup of tea when the pilot officer was approached by a tall sergeant air gunner. The sergeant was the opposite of the Canadian. He gleamed. He even saluted the officer before he spoke.

'Excuse me, sir,' he said.

'What do you want?' replied the pilot officer.

'Wonder if you are fixed up for gunners yet, sir, and, if not, would you take us three?'

The other two air gunners stood some distance behind him, pretending to be indifferent.

'What training have you had?' asked the pilot officer, who was already assuming the mantle of skipper.

'Straight from gunnery school, fifteen hours flying time each,' came the disturbing answer.

Turning to the rest of his newly formed crew, the skipper raised his eyebrows questioningly.

Receiving nods of assent all round, he turned to the spruced-up sergeant and replied, 'OK, you're in. Be at the bus stop tonight at seven, all of you. We'll have a piss up in Selby and get to know one another, alright?'

By such haphazard means was our crew formed, and if an element of luck played a large part, it must have been all good because we became an excellent team and comrades in the truest sense of the word.

Socialising as a Crew at The Friendship in Selby

Promptly at 7 p.m., eight of us, comprising a new bomber crew, were standing at the bus stop a little self-consciously when the Big Man pulled up before us in a three-tonner. On learning our destination, he told us to climb aboard. We gladly accepted. The journey was not a long one, and my crewmates and I were soon exploring the market town with interest. The medieval Selby Abbey caught our attention, and its sense of permanence made our existence as wartime aircrew members seem very fragile.

By this time, some of us were interested in thirst-quenching matters, and one of the gunners who was walking some way ahead turned and indicated to the others to follow him. He then disappeared into a public house. When the rest of us walked in, he was in the act of ordering eight pints of mild beer. As if anticipating a difference in the order, he announced that when he was in the chair, everybody drank mild ale—it was cheaper.

Although it was only late July, the evening had quite a nip in it, so the sight of a good fire in the grate pleased us. When we were comfortably seated around a table, the pilot officer opened the conversation.

'My name is John Gauntlett, and I am to be the captain of the aircraft. I was born in 1917 outside of Regina, Saskatchewan, Canada, where my English-born father was a prairie minister. In the winter of 1930–1931, my parents, two sisters, and I moved to the UK, and here I've been ever since. The war broke out in the third year of my schooling at Bristol University, and I felt compelled to join the Army, where I somehow attained the lofty rank of second lieutenant in the Royal Artillery.'

He continued, 'My ideas on discipline were not in harmony with those in authority, so that in 1941, when some of us were given the opportunity to volunteer for aircrew training in the RAF, I jumped at it. I hoped to fly fighters but ended up here with you. I dislike bull, and in the air, I demand cooperation. That way we might, just might, live to become grandfathers. If any of you don't feel happy with me as skipper, you can leave the crew without any hard feelings, OK?'

He looked at each of us in turn. 'By the way, the name is John when we're together and no saluting. Got it?' This was said with a glance at the tall air gunner who smiled a trifle sheepishly and nodded.

The next to speak was the small Scottish pilot. 'Name's Blue, William, but most folk call me Ben. After leaving school, I did various musical jobs and ended up playing clarinet in Teddy Joyce's dance band in London. Was called up as a militia man, went in the Highland Light Infantry, and was in France until being kicked out by the Germans. Saw the same call for volunteers in the RAF that John spotted and here I am.' He then added, 'My parents died when I was in my teens. I lived a spell with my darling grandmother.'

Seeing the rest of the crew regarding him with curiosity, he then murmured something about more drinks and went to the bar. We all agreed that Ben was going to be quite a character with his experience with the upper crust life in London and his skill on the clarinet. 'Carry on', said John, nodding to the Canadian.

Before he could start, however, Ben returned from the bar with eight whiskies and half-pints of beer, to the consternation of all. None of us had experience in drinking spirits, with the exception of John, who was a shade older than the rest of us, but in order not to hurt Ben's feelings, no one said a word. Raising his glass before us, Ben tossed back his drink. 'To us,' he said. As Ben looked around we, in turn, raised our glasses, and with a mumbled 'To us,' one and all attempted to down the tot of whiskey in one go, as Ben had done, but with varying degrees of success. Arnie and I, in particular, ended up coughing and spluttering for a moment or two, much to Ben's amusement. He was later to show that he could drink prodigious amounts of Scotch without any apparent effect.

The Canadian observer had been patiently waiting to speak while the rest of us were trying to appear unconcerned about our lack of experience with the Scotch. He now spoke. 'Name's Hartshorn, H. T.,' he said. 'Call me Harry. Born in Preston, Ontario. Pop has a shoe last factory. Sent me to high school to become the family genius. Mildly successful. Joined the firm but felt bored and so became a member of the RCAF as an observer. You are now lumbered with one who had all the makings of a first-class Canadian playboy. I did some flying as John's navigator at 22 OTU and then on our Wimpy ferry flight to the Middle East—and we're still alive, so both he and I must have done some things right.'

While speaking, he had been lolling back in his chair with his forage cap on the back of his head, eyes closed, and feet resting on a buffet. Opening his eyes, he regarded Arnie and me. 'You two guys from Yorkshire?'

Arnie nodded, 'Yes, we live about 30 miles away. Why?'

The Canadian smiled as if he had found two long-lost friends. 'My grandfather is a Yorkshireman. Originated in a place named Sowerby Bridge, but he emigrated to Canada before the First World War. Guess I'd like to see it sometime. Maybe you'll help me find it?' Arnie and I agreed to do so at some future date, and Harry, the observer, seemed well pleased.

John looked at me. 'You next,' he said. Slightly nervous, I then said my piece. 'My name's Bill Kirkness. My father's a signwriter with his own small business, which he started when the firm he worked for closed down in the Depression. He has been employed of late in the nearby Avro factory, in support of the war effort. Growing up, life was a bit rough at times, but we managed, and eventually I went to grammar school on a scholarship. I worked for my father until I was eighteen, then I joined the RAF. I hoped to be a pilot, but, being too short, I was offered a choice of navigator or wireless operator. As you can see, I chose to be a wireless operator.' Looking at Harry, I added with a grin, 'I think I chose wrongly.'

There being no comment from Harry, I continued. 'I'm a natural on the wireless, but the RAF insisted that I also qualify as an AG. Glad to have obliged by winning an air gunner's rating. So far my extracurricular flying also includes a Wimpy ferrying run from the UK to Egypt.'

Arnie spoke up next. 'Arnold Bridgman, born in Yorkshire of Oxfordshire parents. After leaving grammar school, I got a job in a mill near home, and after night school I ended up as a carpet designer. I joined up the same day as Bill, and we trained together as wireless operators and air gunners. I confess to having a hankering for firing my weapons, so being primarily an air gunner would suit me just fine. Have done my Wimpy ferrying from the UK to Egypt, too.' Quietly, he added, 'I've lost two brothers, one a non-combat death in the Army, the other gone missing in the fall of Singapore.'

From that evening onwards, every member of the crew respected him. His dark good looks and quiet manner were the outer signs of a person of great integrity and unassuming courage, and as time elapsed, his popularity increased with us all.

The gunners were the last to introduce themselves; the dapper one was the first to speak. He was tall and well-built, with hair brushed straight back with a centre parting much favoured by some of the sleeker film stars of the day.

'Fred Rozee. Born and bred in Canning Town, London.' His accent was unmistakably that of a Londoner as his pronunciation of his place of birth came out more like 'Cannin' Tarn'; when we all knew each other better, we would often pull his leg about his origins. He continued, 'When I left school, I did various jobs, such as working the markets, and at one time I was employed as a lighterman on the Thames. Fancied the idea of being an air gunner, so I joined the RAF nine months ago and met these two at gunnery school. We've been together ever since.' He pointed to the two other air gunners, who would speak next.

Having concluded his introductory speech, Fred downed his drink and sauntered across to the bar to order the next instalment of liquid refreshments. He sensibly bought half-pints all round, as some of us were not accustomed to heavy drinking so early in the evening.

Returning with the drinks, he sat down, placed a drink before each of us, looked across the table at one of the other two gunners and nodded. 'Get on with it, Chalky,' he urged. 'Don't keep us all in suspense! Let's hear the thrilling story of your young unsullied life.'

The remark was made in a bantering tone, but it succeeded in stinging Chalky out of his obvious shyness. It soon became clear that Fred's time spent working the markets had not been wasted, for it had furnished him with a quick wit which was an invaluable asset to the air gunner.

The man addressed as Chalky coughed nervously. 'My name is George White. For obvious reasons, my nickname is Chalky. I have lived in Hertfordshire all my life and after leaving school worked for Addis brushes. I was training to be one of their reps but was getting bored, so after seeing a recruiting film for the RAF, I decided to become aircrew. The quickest way into action was to become an air gunner.' He gave a nervous laugh. 'Not very thrilling, was it?' he asked the others.

There was a murmur round the table and John spoke up. 'Don't worry about that. Before this lot is over we'll have more thrills than we want!'

He looked enquiringly at the remaining gunner. 'Let's have it, then we can all get to know each other.'

The gunner looked up from his beer and glanced around with a slight frown. 'Not much to tell, really. My given name is Cyril Kirby, but in the RAF, I'm known as Bill. Born and bred in Warborough, Oxfordshire and on leaving school did a variety of jobs, mainly in agriculture. Had a short spell in the Cowley Works in Oxford, but I wasn't happy indoors. I left and made a pound or two by poaching.'

This last remark was made with a grin as though he expected us to be shocked, but we showed only a mild interest in the comment so he continued. 'I've always been keen on guns, and the idea of firing off those Brownings appealed to me, so I joined the RAF. And here I am.'

While he was speaking, I studied the gunner with some interest. He was the complete opposite of Fred Rozee. Where Fred was tall, straight-postured, and smartly attired, this other air gunner was more hunched and broad-chested, with puglike features. His battledress looked as if he slept in it, while his pleasant Oxfordshire accent was a counterbalance to Fred's London voice and the flat Yorkshire vowels of Arnie and me.

Bill Kirby turned out to be a man with a great sense of humour; no matter how much his leg was pulled, he would give a slow chuckle and usually turn the tide on his tormentors. If they could not take it, he would rib them even more until they had had enough. He rarely lost his temper, and if at times the rest of us felt protective towards him, we need not have worried. He was more than able to look after himself and the rest of us at times, too.

Becoming Enoch

As the gunner finished speaking, the skipper cleared his throat. 'It would seem we have a small problem, having three Bills in the crew. That makes for a might bit of confusion in the air, and in an emergency confusion leads to heartbreak. Let's try to eliminate some of the confusion right now.'

Continuing, John added, 'William Blue is easily dealt with. He's told us his friends call him Ben. Therefore, in the future, Ben it shall be. OK?' There being no dissent, John regarded the two remaining Bills—Cyril 'Bill' Kirby and myself—with a speculative frown. Then, Bill Kirby piped up. 'Back home I'm known as Willy, if it helps,' he offered.

In response, John smiled enthusiastically. 'It does indeed,' he said. 'It does indeed. From now on you'll feel quite at home, for you'll be known as Willy to us, too.' Cyril 'Willy' Kirby beamed as if he'd received an honour.

'What about you?' queried John of me. 'We could leave you as you are, but then there's the danger that if I say Bill, you or Willy, or both, might answer. Not good! Have you a nickname?' I blushed and shuffled my feet. Looking downward at them, I nodded.

My embarrassment was eased slightly by a guffaw from Arnie. 'His name at OTU was Enoch,' Arnie announced, 'because he impersonated the Enoch character on BBC Radio.' Arnie referred to *The Happidrome*, a popular programme. Voiced by comedian Robbie Vincent, Enoch's radio catchphrase, delivered in a broad Yorkshire accent, was 'Let me tell you!'

The rest of the crew grinned broadly, and the Londoner, Fred, gently chided me. 'Go on, Enoch, let's hear it.'

'I only do it when I'm pissed. Feel a right Charlie afterwards, too,' I answered.

'Alright, Enoch it shall be from now on,' said John. 'The reason for this naming ceremony, if such it can be called, is to prevent confusion in the air. On easy trips like cross-country exercises you can use the names decided upon tonight, but in serious stretches on ops you will call each other by your respective crew positions, such as rear gunner to pilot or wireless operator to navigator. Got it?' We all nodded and were happy with this arrangement, which stood the test of time remarkably well.

During the entire evening, Willy had had an unlit fag end stuck to his lower lip. Out of curiosity, I handed my cigarettes round and was amused to see Willy remove the fag end, carefully inspect it and return it to its previous place in the corner of his mouth. He accepted the offered cigarette and meticulously placed it in the edge of his forage cap.

By now, the pub was filling up with the evening's regulars, all civilians who kept casting curious glances at our crew. Feeling the time had come for another round, I went to the bar and ordered eight pints of mild. The drinks I had consumed and the large coal fire were beginning to have their effect, and I was feeling mellow when I returned to the table with the drinks. I noticed, as well, that the initial inhibiting shyness between new crewmates had evaporated.

Sitting down, I beamed at them all in turn, and like the strident voice so well-known on the radio I gave forth my best impersonation yet. 'Let me tell you!' I barked. 'You'll do for me, rough as you are!' There was a hush in the pub, then a general burst of laughter all round.

'I take it you're pissed then,' mused Fred.

I regarded him solemnly. 'Just gently, Fred,' I admitted, 'but I don't think I can handle much more, not tonight anyway.'

The pub was not on the main street of the town, nor was it a hostelry in which the local talent performed. The beer, however, was good, as was the welcome, the warmth of which was exceeded only by the great coal fire. When we finally departed that night, our eyes caught the pub's sign: 'The Friendship'. To our small band of aircrew, it seemed most appropriate. The bus taking us back to camp echoed to the strains of 'Nellie Dean' and less wholesome songs. The seed was beginning to germinate; its name was comradeship.

4

Initial Training at 1653 Conversion Unit

Getting Down to Specialty Training

The fresh westerly wind sweeping across the airfield was pushing drizzling rain and low scudding clouds before it as the Gauntlett crew—our new identification—paraded outside the Mess with the other fresh crews. The day matched our moods; most of our crew were unaccustomed to the quantity of drink we had consumed the previous evening. For the most part, we were silent on the parade, hoping to be dismissed in order to go back to our billets and lie down.

Only Ben seemed unaffected. On the contrary, he was bouncing with energy and was enjoying the misery of the others. 'Lovely breakfast this morning,' he chuckled as he surveyed his new gang. 'Soggy porridge with large lumps followed by greasy fried bread and beans.'

Willy slowly closed his eyes. His usually ruddy face took on a look of great suffering. 'Stow it, Ben. I feel ghastly. Don't speak of food, especially RAF food.'

He was saved by the appearance of the Big Man at the top of the Mess steps. 'Sharrup, the lot of you and listen. You trainees...'

He was interrupted by angry shouts from a bunch of Australians. 'Trainees be buggered!' one Aussie barked. 'Some of us have already done a tour in the Middle East!'

The SWO regarded the speaker with mild amusement. 'Well, good on you, Blue. I don't care if you captured Hitler last night. On this camp, while you are learning to fly the Liberator, you are trainees.' All this was said in a mock Australian accent, which was so bad everyone started laughing.

Scowling at the men before him, he continued, 'Pilots to the Crew Room, navigators to the Instrument Section, wireless ops to the Radio Section, gunners to the Armoury. Deesmiss!'

There was some confusion for a time among the navigators as to the reason for them being detailed to the Instrument Section, but eventually, they set off in a loose gaggle towards the place.

The Big Man appeared like the Fairy Queen in pantomime. 'Come back here, you scruffy lot!' roared the voice. 'What did I tell you yesterday? On this camp you march, not slouch. Fall in, tallest on the right, shortest on the left. Quick about it! That's better. Roiiight tan, queek maach! Ef oi, ef oi, ef oi! That's better!' Beaming to himself, the warrant officer disappeared back into the Mess. Taking the hint, the wireless ops formed up our group and marched off to the appointed destination.

Arriving at the Radio Section, we were met by a sergeant wireless mechanic who, with the assistance of half a dozen wireless mechs, proceeded to instruct us in the operating procedures on the radio equipment installed in the Liberator Mk II. The main transmitter and receiver were Bendix; to Arnie and me, they looked enormous after the Marconi equipment we had used in the Wellingtons.

The tuning of the sets took longer, but one useful piece of equipment was a wavemeter that, when meshed to a set of calibrations supplied with it, enabled the operator to tune the radio to the exact frequency without recourse to tuning back to the ground station. This piece of equipment was most beneficial in the Far East when problems with signals fading due to skip distances at extreme ranges sometimes occurred. All the main radio signals were in Morse Code, and the set proved reliable and pleasant to use after some practice.

The next sets we were shown were three small transmitters and receivers for the use of the pilot when speaking to the ground. By throwing a switch, they could be used for CW (Morse) transmissions in an emergency and were neat sets. The last piece was the radio compass, and it was useful in ways not intended by the RAF.

The radio compass was a refinement of the direction finding (DF) loop, the latter being a circular aerial on top of the Wellington that could be turned by hand inside the aircraft. When minimum signal was heard, a reading could be taken from the DF loop's base and the bearing of the transmitter of the signal read off. It was a tedious business made more difficult by the fact that there were two minimums, and it was not always easy to differentiate the weaker signal of the two.

All this was unnecessary with the radio compass. One had merely to tune in the required signal and read off the bearing from a dial resembling a clock with one hand. If the needle was pointing to the twelve o'clock position, the aircraft was flying directly towards the signal source.

Another improvement was the trailing aerial, which was raised and lowered by merely throwing a switch, as opposed to the Wellington, where it was raised and lowered manually. I soon discovered that I could match the aerial to the desired wavelength by depressing my Morse key and lowering the aerial until I had maximum signal strength on the requisite dial.

The last piece of instruction we received was on the inter-communication system, or intercom. At each position in the aircraft, there was a small square box into which a crew member plugged the lead from his helmet containing earphones and microphone. Each box had a switch with which members could select any of the following:

1. R. Compass, already described. This position was mainly used by the crew for listening to dance music on long trips.
2. W/T. Only the wireless operator used this, and he was not in contact with the rest of the crew when he was listening to the main radio.
3. Command. Mainly used by the pilots, this operated the three sets used when communicating with the ground.
4. Intercom. This was the main position used by the crew to speak to one another.
5. The last position was spring-loaded. When held down, it enabled the user to cut into any other position and was mainly used to wake up the wireless op.

Apart from a break at lunchtime, we were hard at it all day, so it was not until tea time that our crew could compare notes. As Arnie was keener on gunnery than I was, by mutual consent, I was made our crew's first W/op and Arnie was 2nd W/op. This meant that Arnie was primarily a beam gunner, but he could work the radio equipment as needed. Later, in India, Arnie flew as an air gunner on ops, except once when he filled the W/op position. The gunners, too, had sorted themselves out, with Fred being elected rear gunner, Chalky as mid-upper gunner, and Willy as a beam gunner.

I asked Harry why the navigators had been sent to the Instrument Section. 'Got to learn about a new bomb sight, and there is only one on the camp,' replied Harry. He continued, 'The Libs here still have the standard British sight, so I reckon I'll worry about it when we get one in our own kite.'

'Is that the one the Yanks say can put a bomb in a pickle barrel from 15,000 feet?' asked Willy.

'Yeah,' replied Harry with a grin. 'But who the hell wants to bomb pickle barrels?'

A Night in the Sergeants' Mess

After the previous evening, none of the crew felt energetic enough for another heavy night in Selby. We were content to sit in the Mess doing some quiet drinking until Harry spied a poker game and joined in before the rest of us missed him. Poker was a mystery to us. We were more accustomed to pontoon and brag, so it was with only mild interest at first that Arnie and I watched the action. All the participants were Canadian, and as the stakes mounted, so did the tension. What could have become an awkward situation was nipped in the bud by the arrival of the Big Man.

Without hesitation, he went straight to the table and placed a hand on the money in the middle of the table. In an authoritarian voice, he commanded, 'There will be no gambling in the Mess. Sort out the money in the kitty among yourselves or I'll confiscate it, and it can go into the bar fund.'

One Canadian, a little less overawed than the rest, asked what the bar fund was. Immediately, the little SWO picked up the money, walked across to the bar, and gave it to the barman. 'Drinks for these lads,' indicating the bemused ex-poker players. 'If there's anything left I'll have my usual.'

The audacity and speed with which the Big Man had carried out the move left most of us speechless, but he further confused us by taking the poker players' order and then carrying the tray of drinks over to them. Lifting up a large whiskey, he beamed at us all and downed it in one go. 'Cheerio,' he uttered, while looking straight at the man who had asked about the bar fund. 'That's what the bar fund is, laddie. Any more questions?' Dumbly, the man shook his head. Sitting himself at the table, the Big Man spoke seriously. 'If you must gamble, do so in your huts. Not in here. Got it? Right. There may be a little left in the fund. Who's for another?'

One or two shook their heads. 'Thanks, sir, but I'm broke,' said one. 'Can't stand my corner.'

Regarding the man with mock sadness, the SWO snapped his fingers to the barman. 'Same again, corporal,' he ordered. With alacrity, the corporal brought another round to the table and stood undecided beside it. 'Something wrong?' queried the Big Man.

'Yes sir, I need another three bob,' answered the man.

Silently, the SWO took a ten-shilling note from his wallet, gave it to the corporal, finished his drink, and went to the bar for his change. Without a backward glance, he walked out of the Mess, formally, as if he had just bought the King a drink.

'Well, I'll be buggered,' said one. 'What do you make of him?'

'Shrewd operator, keeps you off balance all the time,' answered Harry. 'Not a bad guy though. Put us in our places good and proper without even raising his voice. Think I'm going to like the chap.' There were murmurs of agreement round the table, and one by one the men drifted off to their billets.

Idly, I went to the noticeboard and called Arnie over. 'Think we'll be flying tomorrow, Arn?' I asked.

On the board was a list of duties for the following day. Heading the list was the order: Plt Off. Gauntlett and crew to the Flight Office at 8 a.m.

'Might be,' answered Arnie. He continued, 'We'd better turn in if so, although I should think we'll get something of the layout of the aircraft taught to us on the ground first.' With feelings of mild excitement, we turned in, glad that tomorrow we would likely be in the air again after our long layoff.

The Gauntlett Crew Is Introduced to the Liberator

The following morning was a beautiful one, and the first member of the crew Arnie and I sought out was Ben, who, together with John, had received dual instruction on the Liberator the previous day. 'What are these kites like, Ben?' I asked.

Ben gave his usual grin and remarked, 'Fundamentally similar to other aircraft. Fuselage onto which are stuck a high aspect ratio wing and a tailplane at the rear with two enormous fins and rudders. Oh yes, they also have four engines. Anything else?'

Irritably, I griped, 'You know what we want to know. How do they handle? What was your general impression of them?'

Thoughtfully, Ben replied, 'First impression good. The first take-off and landing were a bit dicey until I'd mastered the tricycle undercart.' Ben grinned at me and said, 'I'm no wireless operator, but from what I've seen I'd say that there are more than enough toys in one of these kites to keep you happy.' After the previous wireless instruction Arnie and I had received, Ben's remarks caused no undue panic. With suppressed excitement, our crew mounted the truck taking us out to the airfield. The driver of the truck pulled up with the usual lack of warning, tumbling us in a heap onto the floor of the wagon.

Willy was most upset as he had lost his dog-end. 'Bloody drivers, I've shit 'em,' he quipped. While speaking, he busily searched his battledress pockets for another Woodbine. Making various rude comments about the driver's parentage, the rest of us climbed out, dusted ourselves down, and glanced around. We had been deposited outside the Flight Office, before which stood John and two leading aircraftmen (LACs).

John, grinning at us, asked, 'Do you always arrive like that, or was today a special effort?'

Ben looked at John and with eyes twinkling said quietly, 'Just a small display in honour of our illustrious skipper.'

Indicating the two amused LACs, John informed us that they were to take us to a nearby kite to point out the positions of various pieces of equipment. Nodding to Ben to follow him, John informed us that we would learn the intricacies of transferring fuel from the outer wing tanks to the inners. Apparently, in the Mk II Liberator, this had to be done by manually altering U-tubes.

Walking out to the aircraft behind the two LACs gave us all a good chance to see the lines of the machine, for which we all would form an almost affectionate regard as our flying hours steadily increased. On the ground, the aircraft was something of an ugly duckling when viewed from certain angles. An elegant glazed nose led back to quite a respectable-looking cockpit, but the beauty stopped there. The rest of the fuselage was box-like with a mid-upper turret atop the fuselage coincident with the trailing edge of the wing and above the second of two bomb bay doors. The rear end terminated in a four-gun Boulton Paul turret.

Twin side-by-side .303-inch Browning machine guns protruded from each beam hatch position in the rear fuselage, behind the wings, while the tailplane was mounted on top of the fuselage, forward of the rear turret. At each outer end of the tailplane was an enormous oval fin and rudder. The wing was mounted in a high shoulder position, and immediately below the wing were the forward and rear bomb bays. The two separate bomb doors were unique in that they did not open outwards, as in a conventional bomber, but by sliding up the sides of the aircraft.

Entrance into the fuselage was through the bomb bay onto the catwalk, or, in the rear of the fuselage through a hinged floor hatch. When closed, the hatch could hold a .303-inch Browning machine gun in a ball socket for use in fending off attacks from below. One traversed the bomb bay across a narrow catwalk about a foot wide, with a rope down one side to hold onto.

Standing beneath the elegant wing, one of the LACs pointed to the four engines and informed us that they were Pratt & Whitney R-1830 Twin Wasps of 1,200 horsepower at sea level. He then indicated the rubber de-icing boots on all the leading edges, which were a marked improvement over the paste that was smeared on the Wellingtons.

After entering the Liberator and moving forward, the LAC showed Arnie and I the auxiliary power unit, or APU, on the left, under the flight deck. It would be the job of a wireless operator to fire up this petrol-driven two-stroke charging unit before the pilot attempted to start the main engines; the engine start-up task took an immense pull on the batteries, which first required a boost from the APU.

Stepping up onto the flight deck, we were agreeably surprised by its relative comfort compared with a typical British aircraft. The pilots' positions had adjustable seats to suit the contours of each man's body, an important perk bearing in mind the huge flying range of the Liberator. Behind each of these positions was a sheet of armour plating and then the positions for the navigator and wireless operator.

The navigator, seated facing outwards towards the port engines, had a good-sized chart table upon which to work while the wireless operator sat facing the starboard engines with his back to the navigator. The W/op also had a table upon which his receiver and log stood. His wireless transmitters were standing in the corner off to his right, while the Morse key was conveniently placed at his right hand.

At first sight, the Bendix wireless equipment was rather awesome in its sheer size, but it lost its terror with use. I soon enjoyed using these sets and gained a reputation as a quick operator. Being left-handed, I could write in my log while operating the Morse key with my right hand. The radio compass was situated in a position where it could be operated by either the navigator or the W/op.

The crew was next shown a highly amusing piece of equipment conveniently situated near each position. This was a black funnel about three inches across the top and attached to a piece of rubber tubing that led outside the aircraft. An LAC nodded towards one of these objects. 'Piss tube,' he said as he made ready to lead us through the bomb bay, but Fred, collapsing in laughter with tears streaming down his face, restrained him.

'Cor mate,' spluttered Fred, 'the geezer who designed that had never seen Willy's willy!'

Looking with mock seriousness at Willy, Fred murmured, 'Yer going to have to be a pretty piddler then, especially if we're at icing altitudes.' Willy snorted, but he was having difficulty trying to look annoyed.

Here, the LAC intervened. 'Always keep on the right side of your ground crew,' he lectured. 'They have been known to tie a knot in the tube.' With mock solemnity, he patted Willy on the shoulder. 'Could have horrible results for a lad like you.'

Indicating for us to follow, he stepped down into the bomb bay. Among other things, he showed us the location of the hand crank for manually lowering the landing gear, including the nose wheel, in case of hydraulic failure. The crank could be reached from the forward end of the catwalk. Proceeding along the catwalk posed no problem so close to the ground, but I foresaw a time when I would have to cross it at altitude and did not relish the idea.

We were pleasantly surprised at the rear fuselage's spaciousness. Forward of the beam guns large yellow cylinders strapped to the upper fuselage perplexed us until we were informed that these were oxygen bottles for the low-pressure American system; we were accustomed to the small bottles of the high-pressure system found in British aircraft.

As those of us with gunnery training were familiar with the armament and turrets, the only things we had to be shown were how to work the cumbersome dual .303-inch beam guns and how to remove a .303-inch Browning from storage on the side of the fuselage and position it in the closed floor hatch. Little more than a prop to scare the enemy, the floor gun was not of much use as a weapon.

Having completed his part of the conducted tour, one of the LACs stepped out of the aircraft and onto the tarmac. As if on cue, the NAAFI van pulled up beside the bomber, and a very attractive girl flung up the sides to reveal the usual tea urn and a pile of the typically rock-hard rock cakes. What was unusual, however, was the sight of about a dozen donuts, which looked as if they didn't belong in the van.

The girl, it soon became obvious, was well-known to the LAC. 'Where did the donuts come from, Jean?' he asked.

The girl simpered, 'Made them last night, Nigel, just before I went off duty. I know you like them, so I put them in a tin in the van, ready for this morning.'

Nigel, the LAC, blushed scarlet seeing the aircrew grinning at him. 'Oh, er, thanks,' he mumbled. 'Better give me two then.' The girl slid two over the van counter to him, and he prepared to pay.

'It's alright, love. They're on me,' she offered. She gave him a look that she had seen Lana Turner use the previous week at the local cinema. It was wasted on the LAC. He was too occupied with looking for somewhere to sit before eating this modest bribe from the love-sick girl. He disappeared inside the bomb bay and sat on the catwalk.

With the LAC's departure, the girl's attitude changed. 'Next!' she snapped, and Fred stepped up to the van.

'Tea and a donut please, darling,' he ordered.

She put a mug of weak tea in front of him and then yelled, 'You want any more, Nigel?' Receiving a reply in the negative, she slapped a donut down in the pool of tea she had made on the counter and held out her hand. 'Tuppence.'

Fred gave the girl the money and smiled at her. 'Don't worry,' he said, 'I'll put a word in for you with Nigel.'

For the first time, the girl looked at Fred. 'Ooh, would you? I've tried to get him to take a bit of notice but without success.'

'Good as done,' replied Fred as he wandered off to join the LAC in the bomb bay.

When all had been served and were sitting in a line on the catwalk, Fred cleared his throat. 'Reckon you're onto a cert there, Nigel boy. Lucky feller,' he said.

'None of your damned business,' growled Nigel. He continued, 'Anyway, I've never touched her. She scares me off.'

'Well, I reckon someone ought to, before she gets much older,' mused Fred, winking at the LAC. The conversation faltered, and they went some distance from the aircraft and lit up their cigs. 'Want to take the mugs back, mate?' asked Fred of the LAC.

With obviously faked indifference, the LAC brought the mugs back to the van, which departed shortly afterwards, and he returned with a broad grin on his face. 'Says she'll see you tonight at the camp entrance at 6 p.m.,' he smirked at Fred. 'I've been trying to get her off my back for ages. Tit for tat, wouldn't you say?' Fred's face was a picture, but whatever thoughts he had, he kept to himself.

Eventually, a wagon arrived and took us back to the Mess for lunch, and there we met Ben, who had been called off on other duties with John. Ben informed us that we would be flying as a crew for the first time at 3 p.m. that day. This resulted in an immediate, mad post-meal scramble to ensure that our flying gear was in order. Arnie and I realised suddenly that our parachutes had not been checked since we had departed 15 OTU. The fact did not alarm us, but we wondered what John would have to say as he seemed keen on details concerning flying safety.

While waiting for transport to the aircraft, Ben told us some of the good and bad points of the Liberator. It was quite docile on take-off and handled well in the air. 'George', the automatic pilot, was reliable. The aircraft should not be overstressed in a bank or dive, and the US Army Air Forces reported that the wing was vulnerable if the main spar was damaged.

The Gauntlett Crew's First Liberator Flight

When the NCO aircrew arrived at the aircraft, we found John and another officer pilot, Flt Lt Evans, awaiting us. Evans, not John, would be the aircraft commander, while Ben observed from the flight deck. We wore the issue Irvin jackets made of sheepskin reaching to the hips. The complete flying rig also included a pair of trousers made of the same material, but they were seldom worn on training flights as their bulk restricted movement. Also, on these flights at this time of year, the aircraft seldom attained an altitude where they were necessary.

Operational flying was a different matter, especially in climates where temperatures aloft were severe. These trousers were useful in other ways, as they could be zipped wide open and used as good bed quilts on cold nights. Ben and I eventually found another more amusing use for them in India, but more on that later.

Arnie and I still retained the old-style flying boots, also fur-lined, which resembled shoes with canvas calf-length uppers. Each fastened just below the knee with a buckle. The leather soles could be repaired, and if a man was shot down over enemy territory he could cut off the canvas upper lengths and be left with a respectable-looking pair of shoes. The rest of the crew wore the newer-issue suede boots, which were much looser-fitting and always fell off if the wearer had to bail out.

Over our shoulders, we each carried a leather flying helmet and sometimes the parachute harness, with the parachute pack itself carried in the other hand. The pilots were the only ones to wear the seat pack parachutes and always entered the aircraft wearing them.

Fred, who seemed to have appointed himself leader of the gunners, always carried a spare cocking lever stuffed down one of his flying boots, much to Willy's disgust. Willy never used a cocking lever, preferring to cock his guns with his forage cap, which he carried under the shoulder strap on his tunic.

Completing our apparel, we each wore a Mae West life jacket in case of ditching. Attached to each of these vests was a tiny bottle of compressed air that, when a lever was pulled, would inflate the life jacket rapidly. The jacket was also lined with kapok in case the wearer was unconscious on entering the water.

Harry, our navigator, was further encumbered by a large green canvas bag containing his maps and charts, compasses and various other impedimenta, not forgetting a rubber to correct his mistakes. If the flight was at night, Harry also had to carry a sextant for astro shots.

As wireless operator, I was similarly laden. I carried a bag containing my log, flimsies showing codes and frequencies, letters of the day for recognition purposes and the Syko card for that day. The Syko card, when slotted into a machine about the size of a small portable typewriter, enabled the user to decode any messages he received. I usually got Willy to carry this machine for me.

The pilots entered the aircraft through the bomb bay followed by Harry as navigator and myself as first wireless op, while the gunners entered through the rear floor hatch. After we had been sitting for a time, Flt Lt Evans, the pilot occupying the skipper's port seat, turned around to me and asked, 'Do we sit here all day?' I regarded him with puzzlement and did not answer. 'The APU, old boy, the APU,' spoke Flt Lt Evans.

Suddenly, I remembered that my first duty upon entering was to start the auxiliary power unit. Blushing deeply, I shot under the flight deck and pulled the starting cord. The engine did not fire. For what seemed an age I pulled and tugged, and finally, to my relief, it started. With a sheepish grin, I returned to my seat at the radio; with mock courtesy, the pilot thanked me.

When all four engines were running to the skipper's satisfaction, he called up the control tower and received permission to taxi out to the runway. With a slight lurch, the bomber was moving, and to me, standing with Ben between the two sheets of armour plating behind the pilots' seats, it immediately became apparent that the tricycle undercarriage improved forward visibility when taxiing in comparison to the conventional tailwheel type of aircraft.

The Liberator's tricycle landing gear also made a level wireless operator's table possible while on the ground. My logbook now stayed put on the table top; it slid off towards the rear on taildragger aircraft.

As the throttles were opened up against the brakes, the whole bomber vibrated, and the noise was awe-inspiring, even with our helmets on. Releasing the brakes caused the Liberator to surge forward and advance down the runway with ever-increasing speed. An initial wiggle of the nose was evident as trim was set by the skipper to counter the torque of the turning props, keeping the forward momentum on the centreline of the runway.

I watched the air speed indicator steadily move towards the magic take-off speed of 120 mph. When attained with plenty of runway to spare, and with only a slight backward movement of the control column by the skipper, the aircraft lifted smoothly into the air. After retraction of the undercarriage and the flaps, the Liberator was clean and settled down to a steady climb to our cruising altitude.

As the exercise was only local flying, Harry had gone under the flight deck and was map-reading in the glazed nose. I decided to join him, having completed the simple radio exercise I had been assigned by the signals officer. Taking my logbook with me, I crawled forward past the retracted nose wheel and found Harry on his stomach, looking through the large glazed nose. The view was excellent, and after plugging into the small control box and selecting W/T, I settled down to enjoy the flight and improve my map reading skills with Harry.

The skipper was following the river Ouse. By the time I had joined Harry, we were flying over the outskirts of York. The minster looked like something out of a child's fairy story with the sun bathing the stonework in a golden glow. With the river running through the city, nothing could have looked more peaceful.

We were enjoying flying as a team for the first time that day, and the fact that we were training to be killers never entered our thoughts.

Tapping Harry on the head, I indicated that I was going back to the flight deck. Upon receiving an acknowledgement, I gave Harry's helmet lead a tug to remind him to plug into the control box. Receiving a two-fingered salute from Harry, I struggled back to the flight deck and tuned in to some dance music on the radio compass.

I informed the rest of the crew but received no word from any of the gunners. Thinking they were not plugged in, I went through the bomb bay to check. All three were sitting on the floor playing cards.

Plugging Willy into the command box near him, I selected radio compass and saw his face beam. Indicating to Chalky to plug in also, Willy waited until they were hearing the same programme, then took him by the hand and did a shuffling imitation of a waltz. Shaking my head, I went back to the flight deck.

We had been airborne about two hours, and it soon became clear that we were losing height while preparing to land. Skimming over the railway line just beyond the south-east end of the main runway, the aircraft touched down smoothly, and we taxied in, well satisfied with our first experience with the Liberator Mk II.

On Base Having Fun

In the Mess that evening, the crew discussed the performance of the aircraft, mostly in terms of approval, although Arnie tended to think it appeared flimsy in construction compared with the geodetics of the Wellington. He had just started extolling the virtues of the Wimpy when, breaking off in mid-sentence, he turned towards the bar and said in a loud voice, 'Liverpool, what a dump.'

A broad but slightly round-shouldered figure slowly turned around with a face like thunder and came menacingly in the direction of the crew's table. It was Joe, the air gunner from Liverpool. As he came closer, his face changed to one of delight as he recognised Arnie and me, his cabinmates on the *Nieuw Amsterdam* cruise from Egypt to South Africa not long past. 'Now then, whackers, how long have you been here?' asked Joe.

Without waiting for an answer, he sat down and informed one and all that he had arrived that afternoon and was waiting to be crewed up. Looking at me, he asked somewhat wistfully, 'Suppose you've got a full crew. Haven't got a slag in your lot you'd like to dump?' Receiving a reply that our crew was complete and unified, he dropped the subject and regaled us all with the experiences of his leave.

I asked, 'How about the nylons, Joe? Did your scheme work of rationing them to one per night?'

'Work?' Joe roared with laughter. 'I had her sister as well before the leave was up.' With a pensive grin he added, 'Good job I ran out of nylons. I'd have been too pooped to fly otherwise.'

It was at this point that I noticed Fred's absence and asked Willy where he was. In a huff, Willy removed his usual dog-end and scowled, 'Gone out with that NAAFI bird. Smelt like a pox doctor's clerk when he went out.'

In the days that followed, the crew was kept busy on ground instruction and much local flying, the latter mainly for the benefit of the pilots. Often only Harry and I were carried as crew. Consequently, Arnie and the gunners had plenty of time off and spent it exploring the surrounding countryside on bicycles, with the result that they were remarkably well informed as to the whereabouts of the best local pubs, ATS camps (billets for Auxiliary Territorial Service women), and 'Waaferies' (billeting Women's Auxiliary Air Force personnel).

The end result of all this local knowledge was a crew that appeared on parade some mornings somewhat the worse for wear, but with smiles on our faces.

5

A Weekend Pass at Home

In Horsforth and Leeds with Harry and Ben

After being on the camp for several weeks, the crew was given a long weekend leave which extended from after lunch on Friday until 8 a.m. Monday morning. Fred, Willy, and Chalky squared things with the guard room and were out of camp immediately after breakfast, headed south. Unfortunately, John was flying in the morning and was unable to get away early, but I took the opportunity of inviting Harry and Ben to spend their short leave with me. Obviously unable to go home, both accepted.

Thus, Friday afternoon found the three of us hitchhiking to Leeds, and we arrived at my parents' residence at tea time. Mum was at home, and her reception was a mixed one. To have three young men suddenly added to the ration strength in wartime Britain was a worry to her until we each produced an emergency ration card and allayed her fears. Sleeping was no problem as there was plenty of floor space and a liberal supply of blankets.

Once the initial shyness had gone, she could not do enough for our guests, while my sister Sheila, aged fifteen, showed Ben an almost embarrassing amount of attention. Mum drew Ben into the kitchen and asked, 'Who is this Enoch you speak of? I'm a little confused.' He laughed and explained the reason for the nickname. With a prim look, she informed him that what I was called in the Air Force was not her business, but at home I was, and always would be, Bill.

About 6 p.m. Dad arrived home from the aircraft factory where he worked, and his delight was obvious on being introduced to Ben and Harry. When tea had been cleared away, Harry regaled us with stories about his home and its many differences to the English way of life.

Suddenly, Dad asked me, 'Think your pals would like to meet your maternal grandmother?'

Ben and Harry looked a little nonplussed when I eagerly agreed; meeting a man's grandmother was the last thing they had in mind. Shortly afterwards, however, they found themselves ambling up the road behind the older man, if not with enthusiasm, then at least without complaint.

After a short walk, Dad led the way into an old and attractive public house, The Queens Arms, and Ben perked up immediately. The hostelry had been built in the seventeenth century and was all beams and low ceilings. Originally, it had an island bar, but over the years walls had been built on two sides to form a small, comfortable room aptly named 'The Snug'.

Standing behind the bar was a dumpy older lady about 5 feet tall with a face that reflected the hard life she had endured. Her stern countenance hid from the world a warm and affectionate disposition which only emerged when she smiled, as she did when Ben approached the bar. From the angle of the bar, only Ben was visible to her, and seeing the wings on his chest, she said with obvious pride, 'My grandson's flying, but he isn't a pilot. Think he does something with a wireless. What would you like, luv?'

Realising immediately that he had been led on by father and son, Ben looked round to see Harry, Dad, and me having a quiet chuckle. Without a word, he turned back to the bar and ordered four pints of bitter. When the fourth was being placed before him, he gave the landlady a wicked grin and said, 'Your grandson's paying for them.' She seemed puzzled for a moment but then shot from behind the bar, saw me, and planted a smacking kiss on my cheek to my obvious embarrassment and her equally obvious delight.

After the inevitable questions had been answered to her satisfaction, we took our drinks into The Snug, where Harry sat back with a sigh of contentment. 'Boy,' he chimed, 'I sure picked myself a wizard wireless op. His gran keeps a pub!' Meanwhile, Gran could be heard telling anyone who would listen that her grandson was in The Snug with his crew, and what grand lads they seem to be, one coming all the way from Canada.

Soon, drinks kept appearing on the table from unknown sources, with Gran bringing them in on a tray, with a beaming face and the name of the latest donor. In the meantime, the pub had filled up and a piano was tinkling away in the room opposite. Ben, onto his usual tipple and desiring to sing, wandered off to see what was happening.

Shortly afterwards, we heard 'Loch Lomond' being murdered by Ben. He then went to the bar and insisted on buying Gran a double brandy and drinks for the few at the bar. It was obvious that Ben's bedtime had arrived, although he took some convincing. Harry and I were not too steady on our feet, either.

Dad had been drinking in a more modest fashion and remained behind as we three inebriated crewmen steered an erratic course for home. As there was no moon and the blackout was in force, the journey took considerably longer than on the outward leg, with the result that we were reasonably sober when we arrived at our destination. Mum was not too pleased, but she fussed around getting blankets. When she took one pile into the front room, she found Ben already asleep on the settee.

Harry accepted the blankets from her with a hesitant smile and moved to cover Ben with a couple, but with a sigh of mock exasperation Mum pushed him to one side. With surprising tenderness, she carefully covered the prostrate pilot.

'You should be ashamed of yourselves getting this lad into such a state,' she admonished. 'It's obvious he's not accustomed to drinking.'

Harry and I exchanged glances but said nothing, not wishing to bring more verbal fire down on our heads. With a hiss, Mum thrust blankets into our arms and was gone.

Bedding down quickly on the floor, we were just nodding off when Dad arrived home to receive his wigging for not taking better care of 'them young lads in t'other room!' The tirade did not last long, however, and shortly afterwards, the entire household was at rest for the night.

Saturday morning was beautiful, and in turn Ben, Harry, and I awoke. To the exasperation of Harry and myself, who were both very much under the weather, Ben could be heard whistling in the bathroom, and he then appeared in the room freshly shaved with his towel round his neck.

Seeing his two crewmates still lying about in our blankets, he began whipping us with the towel. 'Come on, you lazy sods,' he teased, 'hands off your cocks and on with your socks.'

With these words, Ben departed into the kitchen and reappeared with a note in his hand. 'Your parents have gone to work, Enoch, but your mother has left the makings of breakfast ready for us. So get your fingers out and let's eat. I'm starving.'

Harry stood up and groaned, 'I could kill that bugger being so cheerful first thing in the morning. It's not natural.'

Pulling on his trousers, he picked up his kit and went upstairs to shave. I heard the murmur of voices and remembered that my sister Sheila was also in the house. I shot into the kitchen to warn Ben to watch the language, but with an airy wave of his hand he grinned, 'Don't worry, I'm a proper gentleman when young ladies are around, especially very young ladies.' He then resumed cooking the bacon and eggs for four.

When ablutions were completed, we sat down to a surprisingly well-cooked breakfast. Sheila was displaying signs of puppy love for Ben, but he treated her with great kindness and consideration. Alternately, he indulged in childish gossip, and in the next breath, he spoke to her like an adult. Harry and I were impressed. The boisterous Highlander of the previous evening had been replaced by a courteous and thoughtful young man.

Sitting round the table smoking Harry's Sweet Caporal cigarettes, Ben asked me what the programme for the day was to be. 'I'm going for a walk to clear my head,' I replied. 'You're welcome to come if you wish.'

Ben and Harry stood up, and the three of us set off down the street. We were saved from being accompanied by Sheila by the arrival of one of her friends bearing two bananas, which the girl's father, a member of the Merchant Navy, had brought home on his last trip.

The nearby woods were pleasant, with the glorious sun filtering through the leaves and my dog Toby picking up scents and racing away after long-gone rabbits. Unconsciously, I led them to the tree I liked to sit under, and Toby promptly flopped down panting with a huge grin on her face. Ben and Harry took the hint from the dog and were soon full length on their backs on the grass, Ben with his eyes closed and Harry chewing a piece of grass.

Sitting down beside Harry, I was idly petting Toby and watching a couple of chaffinches busily flying to and from an old tree in which it was fairly obvious they had some young.

Ben said quietly, 'The war seems an awfully long way away just now.'

For a moment no one spoke, then Harry, equally reserved, replied, 'Yeah, and so does home.'

Realising Harry was feeling homesick, I asked him, 'What would you be doing right now if you were back home, Harry?'

There was a pause before the reply came. 'Well now, let's see. Saturday morning. I know, I'd be up at our lodge with my grandfather. It's about 200 miles north of our home on the edge of a lake where we have a canoe, and we would spend days like this fishing for trout. The stillness of an evening can almost be felt. Boy, it's great.'

With sudden vehemence, he said, 'Wish we could get on with this bloody war and we could all go home!'

Ben, who had remained hushed while Harry and I were talking, rolled over and looked at Harry. 'Don't rush your fences, Harry. We'll get to the action soon enough. In the meantime, just enjoy each day as it comes. That's my philosophy, because some of us are never going home.'

As the conversation seemed to be taking a sombre tone, I suddenly said to Harry, 'Fancy a game with my old bitch?'

Harry looked startled. 'Let's not introduce vulgarity into the proceedings.'

Suddenly realising that Harry had not grasped what I said, I stood up and told him to watch, while commanding Toby to sit. The dog was immediately alert, but obedient, as I ran off alone into the woods. After a time, I whistled lowly, and Toby shot off like an arrow from a bow. Ben and Harry heard the dog bark, and shortly afterwards, Toby and I came trotting together through the trees.

Sitting down slightly out of breath, I told the pair of them that the next bit was more difficult. Turning to the dog I said, 'Right, Toby, off you go,' and away went the dog. In a short time, after hearing one bark, I set off in search of the dog. After a slightly longer period of time, dog and owner returned together.

By this time, Harry's interest had been aroused. 'Say Enoch, how do you locate the dog?'

Chuckling, I replied, 'It's not too difficult really. She gets so excited, and she whimpers when she's in the bracken. The more you pretend not to see her, the more she whimpers. Fancy a go?'

Harry's melancholy mood had by now largely disappeared, and after telling the dog to sit, he set off rapidly through the woods. The dog heard the whistle and looked at me. 'Go find him,' I urged, and the dog was off with a delighted yelp. After quite some time dog and man reappeared, with Harry grinning all over his face.

'What kept you?' asked Ben.

Harry laughed. 'Thought I'd be a really smart cookie and climb a tree. Thought the dog would find the tree, but not finding me, I expected her to then go chasing off elsewhere. She didn't! She just lay down under the tree, and I had to come down eventually.'

Leaning down, he patted the dog affectionately, and she responded by trying to lick his hands and face. Ben next had a turn at trying to find Toby, and he, too, came back having obviously enjoyed the simple game. Had anyone suggested that we had been acting like young boys let out of school, we would have been most offended, but then, we were little more than boys anyway, despite our military trappings.

As our appetites told us it was time to eat, we made our way back to the house feeling fit and hungry. The midday meal, made by Mum once home from the armaments factory, consisted of plenty of Yorkshire pudding and potatoes to fill us up, but the meat ration was sparse.

Harry had expressed a desire to see the city of Leeds. Shortly after the meal was eaten and Ben and Harry had washed up the plates, the three of us were soon on the top deck of a tram heading towards the city centre. Harry had never travelled on an English tram before, and the ride to him was something of a novelty. He insisted on sitting in the front seat as the tram swayed, rattled, and clanked along.

His exuberance overflowed when the conductress came for their fares. 'Tuppence please,' she uttered. The young woman handed Harry his ticket and held out her hand for his fare without a smile. Harry, a little flustered, turned in his seat to look at Ben and me sitting farther back, assuming we had paid his fare. Ben looked straight back at him stone faced, while I gazed hard out the window at nothing in particular.

'Tight sons of bitches,' muttered Harry as he fumbled in his pocket for the required two pence.

The conductress, who had been standing with what looked like diminishing patience, suddenly cracked and started laughing. 'Don't worry, luv. They've paid,' and spotting Harry's 'CANADA' shoulder flashes, she added, 'You don't want to let them make fun of you.'

Sizing up the situation, Harry looked at her like a lost spaniel. 'They're always doing it. Dropping me in it right and left.' With extreme seriousness, he looked at the girl. 'Say, honey, at what speed does this thing take off?'

Puzzled, the girl looked at Harry and then at Ben, who with a sorrowing gaze at the conductress, raised his hand, and gently tapped his head. Giving Harry a look halfway between pity and anger, she moved rapidly downstairs as the tram pulled up at a stop.

When the tram eventually arrived at the city centre Harry pressed something into the girl's hand—a packet of Sweet Caporal cigarettes. She smiled with real pleasure. 'Eeh, ta luv,' she responded with glee, 'cigs are real hard to come by. Why give me 'em?'

Harry grinned, 'Just to prove to them two I'm not as barmy as they are. I was going to give that packet to them.' She giggled and dinged the bell, and as the clanking monster moved off, she leaned out and blew a kiss to Harry but thumbed her nose at Ben and me.

The shops had a dowdy air with many of the display windows painted over, except for a tiny area which could be blacked out without painting. Thus, it was still possible for passers-by to window shop, except that none of the shops had much to show in the third year of the war. Harry remarked how small everything seemed after Canada, and in particular, the road vehicles and railway rolling stock, but when Ben and I reminded him of the differences in size in comparison to the vastness of his own land, Harry acknowledged his comprehension. He told us of riding for three days on the train and seeing nothing but trees when he crossed Canada to come to Britain.

The few civilian cars which were around also puzzled Harry by each having a white line about one-inch wide painted around the edges of the mudguard and things like large bean tins on the fronts of the headlights. Patiently I explained that these were to prevent the lights being seen by any German aircraft in the event of an air raid, and the white line was to give pedestrians some chance of seeing the car in the dark.

The streets were quite busy, it being Saturday afternoon and many civilians were getting their weekly rations. Indeed, many women could be seen clutching their precious ration books as they looked in various windows hoping for that little extra to help eke out the normal ration.

Most young people were in uniform, and there were also the uniforms of continental countries to be seen. Ben remarked that he thought if a German officer walked by, the man would simply be saluted, not arrested.

All in all, the city had a jaded look with most of the property badly in need of a coat of paint. Even the buses, normally quite jaunty in their vivid liveries, were now all the same dreary grey to make them less conspicuous from the air. Citizens seemed to move with a grim doggedness in war-challenged Leeds.

After some aimless sightseeing, during which we toyed with the idea of going to a cinema, we decided to return to my parents' home after a supercilious RAF service policeman demanded that we show our leave passes to him. Producing the passes, which were in order, obviously disappointed the SP. He tried to find fault with our appearance but was put firmly in place by Ben, who made the man address him as sergeant and stand at attention when speaking. No doubt the policeman regretted picking on someone with an Army background.

After returning home in the late afternoon, I detailed the evening's programme to the other two: visit a big and brash pub with Dad, have a drink each and then, leaving Dad behind, size up the local talent at an attractive nearby dance hall. 'Sounds fine to me,' said Ben as he spruced up his buttons and shoes.

The evening turned out to be a success, much to my satisfaction, as I wished to give my pals as good a time as possible. Dad was a mate of the pub's landlord, and we three airmen were made most welcome. Its main attraction was a large lounge comfortably furnished with green leather seating and thick carpets. At one end sat a grand piano, at which the landlord, Alex, seated himself and proceeded to play with great skill.

There was also an amusing rubber-faced comedian who, seeing he was making a great hit with Harry, commenced addressing all his jokes directly to him. This made Harry laugh even more, and soon the surrounding company was infected until Harry finally fell off his chair and staggered in to the other bar to calm down.

Ben, in the meantime, was making good progress with a blonde Auxiliary Territorial Service girl with sexy eyes, which she was using to good effect on him. The girl's companion, also in the ATS, was dark and displeased not to be receiving the same attention as her companion, but Harry's re-entry solved that. He went immediately to sit beside the girl, who brightened up considerably.

He informed Ben and I that there was no bar in the dance hall and that they had better be moving because its owner allowed no one in after 10 p.m. In reply, Ben nodded and winked back at Harry. We three crewmates bade goodnight to Dad and were walking through the doors when Harry looked round at the two girls.

'Coming?' he queried. As they hesitated, he shrugged his shoulders and followed Ben and me into the night. For a moment or two we stood still; the blackout rendered us blind until our night vision reasserted itself. After a brisk walk, we reached the dance hall and entered without any difficulty just on the stroke of ten.

The interior surprised Ben and Harry. Far from being the little village dance hall that they had been expecting, it was almost palatial. Downstairs were cloakrooms and toilets, while upstairs, the hall itself was tastefully decorated with a sprung floor and a better-than-average band. Across one end of the room ran a balcony with cinema-type double seats, which were being used by couples to further their amorous inclinations. Occasionally, the owner would walk on this balcony and tell the more adventurous pairs to cool it, much to their annoyance.

Shortly after arriving in the hall, Harry nudged Ben and nodded towards the entrance. There stood the two ATS girls we recently left in the pub. Strolling over to them, Harry, with his most disarming smile, took the brunette's arm and proceeded to waltz her round the floor. As the band was playing a foxtrot at the time, his efforts at dancing were not too successful, so Ben took the blonde's arm and, as if to show Harry how it should be done, went around the hall expertly two or three times until the tune finished. He brought the girl back to Harry and me and then went straight up to the band leader and tugged at his sleeve.

After a brief conversation, Ben was observed climbing onto the small stage and taking the clarinet from one of the bandsmen. The band then struck up a languorous slow foxtrot. At an appropriate moment, the leader nodded to Ben, who proceeded to give a solo on the instrument to such good effect that the crowd on the floor slowly stopped dancing and stood swaying in time to his playing. When the melody finished, the crowd clapped with enthusiasm, so different from the cursory applause which typically heralded the end of each dance.

Handing back the clarinet, Ben shook hands with the leader, who thanked him publicly on the mike and asked him to play again, but Ben shook his head and rejoined his friends.

'Not bad, Ben,' said Harry.

The blonde was almost drooling over Ben. 'You're a smashing player!' she exclaimed. 'I love the sound of a well-played clarinet.'

Ben merely grinned at her and said, 'I play several instruments. I'll tell you about them on the way home.'

The girl smirked at her friend who had tried to dance with Harry, but before either girl could speak, Harry intervened. 'Do you live near each other?' he asked. 'If so, we may as well go home together, the four of us.'

The dark girl seemed quite pleased with this arrangement and nodded her assent. I asked the girls where they lived, and receiving a reply to the effect that their homes were not too distant, I wished my pals luck and gave them directions to reach home later.

I then looked around for a girl for myself, but as the dance was nearing its end, most of the good-looking ones had been claimed. I ended up dancing with a nondescript mousey-haired girl, but on learning she lived 3 miles away, I lost interest and set off for home alone.

Arriving to find my family in bed, I had a cup of tea and then bedded myself down on the settee and was quickly asleep. I was awakened by titters and giggles from my two pals at about 2 a.m. Pretending to be asleep, I was having difficulty not laughing out loud as I listened to them. It was apparent that their gallantry in escorting the girls home had been rewarded. Slowly, we all settled down, but Ben continued to chuckle to himself for a while longer. He had thoroughly enjoyed his Saturday night. Soon enough, we were all asleep.

Sunday morning was grey and drizzly, and the household was slow to awaken, but eventually the smell of frying bacon roused the three of us into sitting at the breakfast table. In answer to Mum's questions as to our adventures the previous evening, Ben's highly coloured accounts amused us all, though some of his white lies caused me to splutter into my tea. His description of walking the girls home would have done credit to a Methodist minister.

Although the weekend pass allowed us to be out of camp until Monday morning, we three decided to return to camp that Sunday afternoon rather than to madly rush the following day. After a brief visit to Gran, not to mention a slippy drink with her, we collected our gas mask packs, which contained only our small kit. As the regulations stated that an individual must carry a gas mask at all times, each of us was obliged to carry the haversack-type container, but the mask itself was back at camp while the sand-coloured pack was perfect for carrying small kit. We had decided long ago that the risk of a gas attack was minimal.

Back to Camp

The return journey to RAF Burn was a repeat of our earlier trip in the opposite direction, and we were lucky enough to hitch a lift on a builder's wagon going all the way to Selby, reaching the camp in time for tea.

Later in the evening, Arnie arrived and seemed reserved. He announced quietly that he had become engaged over the weekend and hoped to marry the girl in the not-too-distant future. We were slightly taken aback as it seemed a bit too serious a step to consider, but after some leg-pulling, we wished Arnie luck and left him alone to contemplate his fate.

Fred and Chalky arrived in the Sergeants' Mess together late in the evening, both looking tired out despite sleeping on the train. Having been 'up west'—in the West End of London—Fred told us of its delights, but he was annoyed because the Yanks were getting all the best birds.

When Ben was asked by Chalky how he had spent the weekend, he replied that he'd had a quiet weekend in the country with my family. The tone of voice used by Ben caused Chalky to eye him quizzically, but no more was said, and the five of us turned in for the night with Willy still missing.

6

Flying Continues and Tragedy Strikes

Back to Business

At breakfast the following morning, our worry intensified as Willy was now AWOL and could end up in trouble if caught, especially as we were detailed to fly at 10 a.m. Fred, in particular, was concerned as he seemed to take a fatherly interest in the shapeless but likeable Oxfordshire man.

'The silly sod,' commented Fred, 'if I'm not around to wipe his backside, he's arseholed.'

Standing outside the Mess as 9 a.m. came and went, we gazed with increasing apprehension down the road. Finally, we could delay no longer and went to our billet for our flying gear. I was in the process of donning my parachute harness when a battered cigarette came around the door; immediately behind it, a crumpled but beaming face was attached—Willy was back.

'Come on, you gormless blighter, we're flying!' I exclaimed. 'Where the hell have you been?'

Without speaking, Willy shuffled off to get his gear and appeared outside with the rest of us. In answer to our questions, he removed the unlit cigarette from his mouth and smiled at us all in turn. 'Got back to town last night and had a great night in Selby,' he said.

We were stumped, and he enjoyed keeping us in suspense. 'Know that NAAFI bird o'yours, Fred?' asked Willy. 'I met her, and we had a drink, and she said she was lonely, so I spent the night with her. Couldn't let her be lonely, now could oi?'

There was a note of affection in Fred's voice as he gave Willy a mock blow on the chin and murmured, 'You old bastard, Willy, you old bastard.'

While we were speaking, the 15-cwt gharry arrived, and in it was John, the skipper. 'My god,' he said, 'what a woebegone lot you look! Come on, let's get off into the wild blue yonder and clear the cobwebs away.' We never did discover where John had spent his weekend.

It was good to be together again. Arriving at the aircraft, we were surprised to see John and Ben climb aboard without a seasoned 'screen' pilot to oversee them at the controls, and we rightly presumed that John must have been passed as qualified to fly as the Liberator captain. Having learned from my initial Lib flight what my first duties were, I made no mistake this time and went immediately to the APU to start it. Although I pulled and pulled until I thought my arm would drop off, the two-stroke motor refused to even cough. Being left-handed and having to pull with my right, I was unable to get a really good yank on the cord.

I was cursing the recalcitrant engine when I felt a tap on the shoulder. Willy did not say a word but motioned me up onto the flight deck. As I made room for him, Willy grinned up at me, saying, 'You need more Yorkshire pudding.' He gave a tug on the cord, which almost removed the unit from its mounting. Within seconds, it was purring away and supplying the aircraft with the necessary voltage to start the engines, which John proceeded to do. Willy came up to the flight deck and shouted into my ear, 'That's after a night with the NAAFI bird. You Yorkshiremen are bloody soft.'

I turned as if to throw the logbook at Willy, but he had already disappeared through the bomb bay. The weather was perfect for flying with good visibility and only the odd cumulus cloud in the ice blue sky, which, as we climbed higher, became the colour of deep sea blue.

The flight was an exercise for Harry in using bearings on the radio compass and drifts from the rear turret. To obtain a drift for Harry, Fred would centralise his rear turret and look through his illuminated sight with the guns pointing towards the ground. When an object passed through the centre of the sight, Fred would track it with the sight until he no longer had to move his turret to keep the object central. He would then look at the rim of the turret to his left or right and give Harry the reading—so many degrees red or so many degrees green—thus revealing the amount the aircraft was drifting to port or starboard. Harry, in turn, would give a correction to John on the course he was steering.

The flight was uneventful, and Ben was given the privilege of landing the aircraft, which he succeeded in doing without bending anything. The ensuing time at Burn was a busy stretch for our crew, and we were in the air practically every day on one exercise after another. One aircraft which we used had not yet been fitted with a rear turret, and the fuselage ended in a large hole. Willy, wishing to relieve himself and not choosing to use one of the tubes provided for the purpose, strolled to the rear and proceeded to spray Britain from a great height. He was hanging onto the top of the bulkhead with one hand and laughing over his shoulder at the other two gunners sitting against the side of the Liberator.

All went well for a time, but after about twenty seconds the drag of the aircraft caused some of what he had parted with to come back at him with a rush. The sudden shock caused him to let go of the bulkhead, and he almost went out through the hole. The other two could not have helped him as they were too far away, and anyway, they were helpless with laughter. They made Willy sit well away from them for the rest of the trip.

About this time, Arnie was nominated as our fighter controller, which meant that during a fighter attack he stood with his head in the astrodome and instructed the pilot on when to turn into the attack, thus spoiling the enemy pilot's aim.

Other crews, too, were working up to readiness to join a squadron. One such was the crew our mate Joe had elected to become part of, as the rear gunner. They seemed a competent lot, and Joe, with his larger-than-life approach to anything, was soon informing anyone within earshot that he was a member of the best crew on the unit. This remark was said half-jokingly so that no one could take offence, and his popularity soared among his peers.

The Loss of AL588: 5 August 1942

On 4 August, there appeared on the Daily Routine Orders a list of two crews detailed to carry out fighter affiliation exercises the next day with a Spitfire from a neighbouring unit. Each crew would take its turn in Mk II Liberator AL588, starting from and then returning to Burn aerodrome. Noting that our crew was scheduled to participate, I looked forward to the event with mild excitement.

On the afternoon of the 5th, we were the first to take on the Spitfire in the mock aerial combat, which would benefit all involved by yielding practical experience in a controlled setting. With John at the helm and Ben beside him, AL588 taxied out and took off *en route* to the exercise area over Rufforth 15 miles to the north of Burn and due east of the RAF aerodrome at Marston Moor.

When both the Liberator and the Spitfire were in position, John came on the intercom and told the crew to prepare for the exercise to begin. The Spitfire was observed on the port beam flying a parallel course. Harry fired a green Verey cartridge, and the mock attack was on.

Manning the port beam gun, I fully expected the Spit to come straight in towards me. I was puzzled when it proceeded to climb rapidly and cross from port to starboard, where I lost sight of it. Meanwhile, Arnie had picked it up from his vantage point in the astrodome and was giving a running commentary to John.

The fighter was by this time slightly behind and above on the starboard side, still flying parallel to the Liberator, and the pilot, at first, seemed content to stay there. Suddenly, he dipped his port wing and came hurtling in towards us.

'Turn starboard, go!' came Arnie's slightly excited voice, and I felt the aircraft bank towards the attacker. This was done to try to force the fighter pilot to tighten his own turn and, thus, give him a more difficult shot. The Spit pilot knew his stuff and went sliding past the rear turret, offering Fred only a minimal target to aim at as the fighter passed through his gun sight too fast for him to apply the rules of air gunnery.

'Rear gunner, where the hell is he now?' queried John from the cockpit.

'Dunno, skip, he disappeared underneath,' answered a clueless Fred.

'Beam to captain, oi gottem,' came Willy's unflappable voice. 'He's climbing back up to attack from underneath.'

'Tell me when he looks like attacking,' said John. 'Keep up the commentary and try passing him from one gunnery position to the next.'

The fighter was now preparing to attack from below—the Liberator's most vulnerable position. Our only defence underneath the aircraft was a single tunnel gun that Willy had removed from stowage on the starboard wall of the fuselage and inserted through a ball socket in the centre of the closed belly hatch gun framing. For Willy, awkwardly sitting on the floor trying to aim the weapon, visibility was negligible. In this instance, however, he caught a glimpse of the fighter's nose lifting in preparation to attack. He barked the order, 'Dive, dive, dive!'

Instantly, and aggressively, John dropped the bomber's nose to alter the fighter's angle of attack. The Spitfire pilot, realising that he had lost this chess move, promptly abandoned the attack.

Seeing that the fighter was preparing to make another concerted attack from a different direction, John proceeded to fly the aircraft on a corkscrew course which made aiming extremely difficult for the fighter, but which was quite strenuous work for John and Ben in the cockpit.

The Spitfire pilot pulled up alongside, waggled his wings to signify the end of the exercise and joined up on the Liberator's port wing. After removing the tunnel gun from its socket mount and stowing it back in its secure position, Willy stood with me at the port beam hatch marvelling at the eye-pleasing Spitfire in flight.

The Liberator and the Spitfire landed back at Burn. With the engines still running, the Gauntlett crew exited AL588, replaced in a flash by a crew of ten skippered by a Welshman, Sgt Bryn Williams, and including an Air Gunnery Instructor and a fitter/armourer ground crewman along for the ride.

Before entering the aircraft, Sgt Edward Thorley, a wireless operator, affably greeted Arnie and me, saying, 'See you tonight in the Mess! I have a parody on "Poor Little Angeline", and I'm singing it.' Very quickly, the Williams crew and the Spitfire were airborne at 4.30 p.m. to do round two of the fighter affiliation exercise.

The airspace where the training would be conducted was too far away for our crew or anyone else at Burn to see what transpired next. Later, I heard an account from the Spitfire pilot. From the start, said the fighter pilot, it was obvious that the second Liberator crew was intent upon showing him how it should be done. Thrown around like a fighter, AL588 was being flown by Sgt Williams beyond its recommended stress limits. There could be no denying, however, that Sgt Williams and his second pilot, Sgt Alan Bell, were giving the fighter a difficult time. In reviewing the exercise with me, the Spitfire pilot later expressed admiration at the skills of his compatriots.

Then, tragedy struck at 5.15 p.m. As the fighter prepared to make a mock attack from below, the Liberator went into the standard evasive action by entering a dive. The dive was steeper than the one John had made when similarly 'attacked' by the Spitfire, and the consequent pull-out was more abrupt. As the pull-out was almost completed, at 2,000 feet, the entire starboard tailplane, still attached to its oval fin and rudder, parted company with the aircraft. Uncontrollable as a result, AL588 immediately proceeded to dive towards the ground.

'Get out! Get out! Get out!' instinctively screamed the Spitfire pilot to the crew of the doomed bomber, but he could not be heard. Survival was hopeless, as the height at which the Liberator had been flying left the airmen no time to escape.

The doomed machine impacted the ground and burst into flames in a field on the outskirts of Tockwith village, half a mile east of Marston Moor aerodrome. Ironically, the separated tailplane, fin, and rudder unit took almost five minutes to reach the earth, silently fluttering over and over like a huge kite at the end of a broken string. At last, it landed near the Station Sick Quarters on the aerodrome.

The accident stunned everyone who witnessed it, including many at RAF Marston Moor. After transmitting the news to the Burn control tower, the Spitfire pilot continued to fly backwards and forwards over the blazing wreckage, so badly shaken that he failed to realise that his actions served no purpose. The thick column of black smoke, which had followed the sounds of impact and explosion, alerted all in the vicinity to the precise crash point. Eventually the pilot, recognising the futility of his overhead vigil, broke away and returned to Burn.

Word of the crash rapidly spread round 1653 Conversion Unit. The aircrews were treated to sincere consideration by the sympathetic ground crews, who also grieved the loss of one of their own. Not much was said as my crew drove back to our living quarters. Each man sat with his own thoughts. Arnie and I, in particular, were sunk in gloom, having lost a close friend in the accident. Even the stoical Willy was shaken to such an extent that he absentmindedly handed his cigarettes around, something he had rarely done before. The gesture, however, went unnoticed at the time, as his crewmates, too, were hardly aware of the surroundings.

Each realised the obvious: had we gone second in the exercise, it very well may have been the Williams crew grieving for us. We wondered how close we had come to dying, as the first to be airborne in AL588, especially had the tail unit been damaged or weakened to begin with.

The returning fighter pilot seemed to blame himself for the accident. Taken immediately to the Station Sick Quarters, he was given an injection by the doctor to calm him down. Later, after the initial shock had worn off, he was able to describe the sequence of events that had transpired late that afternoon. He stayed the night at Burn and, with the doctor's approval, returned to his home base the following day.

It was learned elsewhere that four bodies had been recovered quite easily from the rear fuselage, where there was no fire, but the removal of the last six bodies was hampered by flames and heavy wreckage. Five were recovered after the blaze had been mostly brought under control, and a Coles crane had been brought into use, but darkness halted the work. The final body was found and removed the following day. The remains were brought to the Station Sick Quarters at RAF Marston Moor and prepared for coffins.

The atmosphere in the Sergeants' Mess back at Burn on the evening of the crash, contrary to what one would imagine, was unusually boisterous as a kind of tribute to the ten men who were no longer with us. During a lull in the noise, I spoke to Fred and Chalky, saying, 'They're in good company, you know.'

The other two looked at me as though I had gone off my rocker. 'Where they crashed, Marston Moor,' I explained. 'One of the bloodiest battles of the Civil War, almost three hundred years ago.'

Fred was not impressed. 'I'll bet most of those poor sods were not fully trained, either,' he countered.

The next morning, volunteers were requested to act as pallbearers; members of the Gauntlett crew stepped forward. Two days later, Sgt Edward Thorley was laid to rest in his hometown of Manchester. With arms linked across one another's shoulders, Arnie and I helped carry our friend's coffin for burial. Ben was among the other pallbearers.

A fine trickle of sand from the coffin settled on our shoulders as we slowly moved to the grave. After the service, we each noticed the powdering on our tunics, and with a kind of studied nonchalance we brushed it off with our hands. 'Sand. It's sand,' offered Ben.

We knew it had been added to weigh down the coffin because there could not have been much left of our friend. We three crewmates said nothing further but just stood and looked at each other.

7

Finishing Up at 1653 Conversion Unit

Another Leave in Horsforth

The loss of one Liberator and ten men did not stop the relentless training required to prepare our crew for operational action against the enemy. Weather, however, could alter plans in a pinch. Fog, combined with a forecast of bad weather, caused the cancellation of flying on Saturday morning, 8 August, followed shortly afterwards by the announcement of a stand-down until Monday morning.

I invited the entire crew home, including John, who, being in the Officers' Mess, was not a regular member of our social forays. Mum was startled to suddenly find eight young men on her step, but after the initial shock, she hastily collected all of our ration cards and bustled off to do some shopping.

The weekend was almost a repeat of the previous visit by Ben and Harry. The only worry was caused by Willy, who had not arrived at my parents' home on Sunday morning following dance hall fun the previous evening, but he was eventually found being well-looked after by Gran when we all called to say 'cheerio'. Apparently, Willy had lost his way after leaving the dance hall and found himself outside the only pub he knew in the district. Gran had taken him in and put him up for the night. He was no fool, our Willy.

The visit was enjoyed by all and repeated on other weekends. We were highly regarded young men. So much so that Alex, the landlord of the large pub with the grand piano, made quite a fuss over us whenever we appeared.

Sitting in Gran's pub on one visit and with each of us in a mellow mood, we were somewhat surprised when she began to ask where our airfield was and how to get there. Receiving the necessary information, she said quite calmly, 'Right, then, I'll pop over and see you all one day.'

We all smiled politely and dismissed the matter, thinking she was being motherly and perhaps a little squiffy due to the brandies Ben had insisted on buying her all evening. I was not too sure. I knew my grandmother could handle her brandies and that she could also be a very determined lady when she wanted. What the Air Force would make of this tiny widow I could not imagine.

An Evening out in Selby with Gran

We found out about a fortnight later. John and the rest of the crew were sitting in the sunshine outside the Flight Office when the tannoy clicked on and a sharp mechanical voice ordered me to report to the Guard Room immediately. Turning to John, I raised my shoulders with outspread arms in the universal signal of befuddlement and set off to the Guard Room.

On entering, I saw the corporal behind his desk and another RAF service policeman in the corner, and seated with her back to me was Gran. Each of the SPs was holding an issue pint pot, and I was confused as it was too early to be brewing up tea. I quickly realised, however, that Gran had been dispensing her usual liquid hospitality—that is, brandy—after the corporal greeted me with unaccustomed bonhomie.

Gran, spying me, gave me another embarrassing and mighty kiss. 'Come on, luv, I've come to take you out for the day,' she said, in a voice that brooked no argument. She was a little confused when I said that I could not leave camp until after 6 p.m. and also that I was flying that afternoon.

Puzzlement on her face gave way to pleasure. 'Eeh, that's grand. Can I come for a ride?' she asked. Patiently, I tried to explain to her the workings of the RAF mind, but it was all too complicated for her.

Eventually, she decided to make the best of a bad job and told me to meet her in The Londesborough Arms hostelry in Selby at 7 p.m. that evening, together with the rest of the crew. 'I'll treat you all to dinner, so tell 'em all to arrive hungry,' she offered.

I promised to carry out her wishes. Bidding her goodbye, I asked the SPs to look after her. They both eagerly agreed to do so. For my efforts, I received a look of withering scorn from Gran and an admonition not to be late, and anyway, she needed no looking after. She'd been taking care of herself quite nicely, thank you, for many years.

Beating a hasty retreat, I returned to my crew and gave them the news, which was greeted with enthusiasm. Eating out in wartime was a fairly frugal affair, but it would be a change from Mess food. With the thought of a night out pleasantly in our minds, we climbed aboard the Liberator to do a radio exercise.

This practice for landing in blind conditions required close cooperation between pilot and wireless operator. It was known as a ZZ landing procedure and commenced when the wireless operator transmitted INT QGX in Morse. On receipt of QGX, he then held his key down. The ground station took a bearing and then transmitted a course to steer, together with a height to maintain. As the aircraft neared the ground station, cross-bearings were taken, and the heights given were lowered accordingly. This was before the days of radar approaches, and although primitive, it was a great help to crews struggling to land in bad conditions.

The aerodrome where we were to do the practice was at Linton on Ouse, 22 miles to the north of Burn. The orders were to descend to within 30 feet of the runway and then climb before repeating the exercise. John had to watch the instruments, but Ben was free to look outside the bomber in case of emergencies.

The practice commenced and was carried out successfully, there being only one slight hitch. The runway on which the controller was lining us up was still being constructed, with many men working upon it. As the large four-engined aircraft swept down upon them, the workmen received quite a shock and scattered in all directions. By the time of the third pass, the men realised, or had been informed, that no landing would be attempted, and they casually waved to the aircraft as it swept past them. Willy waved back with enthusiasm.

Following the satisfactory completion of the exercise, the short trip back to base was achieved without incident. By now, John was quite skilful at landing the Liberator and always tried to touch down in the 'pancake,' the circular patch at the end of the runway. This flight was no exception. As we approached the runway, however, a passenger train was passing along the line immediately in front of the runway. Standing between the two pilots, I could see white faces looking at us from the coach windows, and then we swished over the carriage roof and touched down dead on the pancake.

After taxiing back to dispersal, we finally climbed out and sat on the grass awaiting transport. Grinning at John, Arnie commented, 'Bet you cured the constipation of one or two on that train, skipper.'

John, who was lying on his back with his head on his parachute and his hat over his eyes, spoke without moving. 'Got to take care of the health of the nation in wartime, and anyway, the civvies need a little excitement in their dull lives just now, poor sods.'

A Chevrolet truck soon picked us up and took us back to our respective Messes. John was first to alight from the truck, at the Officers' Mess. Before the truck pulled away, however, he held up an admonitory finger. 'Make yourselves presentable for this evening. Get your buttons cleaned on your best blues and shine those shoes. Let's put some bull into it this time.'

I was impressed. 'Thanks, skipper,' I said, 'I appreciate your remarks.'

John looked at me pityingly. 'You miss the point, Enoch. You be as smart as the rest of 'em, and Willy, try, just try, to look like an airman and less like a sack of Arran banners. Let's make Gran proud to be seen with us.' He tapped the side of the wagon and the driver set off with the usual jolting start.

The rest of the afternoon was spent cleaning shoes and shining buttons on our best blue tunics. Usually, we went out in our battledress, which had concealed buttons and did not require any effort apart from the occasional press. The best blue was the standard RAF tunic and trousers. Although smarter, it required more effort, in that we also had to wear a collar and tie, whereas when in battledress, we usually wore the issue white sweater. Pressing our trousers was accomplished by leaving them folded under the biscuits—our mattresses. The weight of our bodies kept a presentable crease in them. Fred was the exception, having an electric iron which he used regularly; consequently, he was always immaculate when he went out.

Willy was grumbling away as he borrowed shoe polish, Silvo button polish, and shaving cream. 'Bet old Gran won't even notice. What do you think, Fred?'

Fred, sitting on his bed, looked up from the immaculately shining shoe in his hand. 'Come here, Willy,' he said quietly.

Willy complied, and Fred looked him over from shoes to cap badge. Standing up, he picked Willy's hat from his head with his thumb and forefinger and eyed it distastefully. 'Ugh, you disgusting, horrible man! Take my towel and wet it,' scolded Fred. He continued, 'When you return we'll try and restore some shape to this thing.' As Willy used his cap to cock his guns, it was of undefinable shape and rather greasy.

While Willy went to dampen the towel, Fred collected Willy's best blue off his bed. Making an ironing pad from a blanket, he laid the trousers on the blanket as Willy returned, dripping water on Fred's bed-space. Fred snatched the towel from him and flicked him with it before laying it on the trousers. Willy grinned good-naturedly as the wet towel stung his ear. 'You're a toff, Fred,' he sniped.

Ironing away, Fred snorted, 'Remove that cap badge before I iron it, and clean the back of the bloody thing. I'll bet it's green mouldy.' Willy did as he was bid and proved Fred right. Puffing and blowing, he steadily brushed away the accumulated old filth and tarnish on the badge. Fred did his best with the cap but to little effect, and finally he tossed it across to Willy with a look of disgust. 'You should be put down in the interest of hygiene,' Fred spurted. 'Let's have a look at your tunic.'

Willy meekly handed over the uniform requested, and Fred proceeded to press it while Willy cleaned the two small buttons on his cap. As he was doing so, he caught my eye, gave a hearty wink and nodded towards Fred's bent back. For a moment, I was confused, but then I realised what Willy meant. Fred was quietly being conned into cleaning Willy's kit. As I polished my shoes, I grinned at Willy and gave him the thumbs up to indicate my approval.

In due time, we were at the bus stop when John arrived. Looking us up and down, he grunted his approval. We were all standing somewhat self-consciously awaiting the bus when joined by the Big Man. He gave us a cursory glance and then did a rapid double-take. 'Hellfire!' he exclaimed. 'What's wrong! Don't tell me I'm finally getting through to the scruffiest set of aircrew on the station!'

Harry explained the reason for our pristine appearance, and the SWO regarded us with fresh interest. 'I met the lady in question this morning,' said the SWO. 'She seems a most persistent person. I'll look in later to see that you're acting in a manner conducive to good order in the RAF.'

The arrival of the bus terminated the SWO's remarks, and shortly thereafter the crew entered the lounge of The Londesborough Arms to find Gran comfortably seated near the window and wearing a smile which lit up the rather dim room.

'Sit yourselves down, lads. I've ordered the drinks,' she chimed. 'Saw you coming from the window. By gum, you look real smart! Looks like you've been getting toffed up for tonight.'

I smiled at my grandmother. 'John said we had to. We don't usually wear this sort of uniform.'

Gran looked at John and said quietly, 'Thank you, young man, that was kind of you.' John waved a deprecating hand and was spared further embarrassment by the arrival of the drinks.

As the crew was on its best behaviour, the conversation was somewhat stilted, and we were all pleased to go in for the meal that, although modest, was well-cooked and quite enjoyable. Gran was in her element. The other diners were perplexed at the sight of this diminutive lady in charge of eight young airmen, and she constantly glanced round the room with a look of sheer pride.

To round off the meal, she ordered brandy and cigars for each of us. Seeing the obvious distaste with which I sipped the brandy, she reached over and took it from me. 'I think this will do me more good than it will you,' she insisted.

Without another word, it went down the hatch, and she proceeded to collect her bag. With a final beam around the room at everyone, she nodded to the crew to follow her and went back into the bar where we had first met her.

Ben went up to order another round, but with surprising speed, Gran was at his side to tell him in no uncertain terms to sit down. 'My treat tonight, Ben, and no arguments,' she said. 'Go sit down, and we'll all relax and enjoy ourselves.'

The meal had produced a mellowing effect on us all, and with the consumption of more drink, Gran was soon being regaled with descriptions of some of our less hectic escapades. When Willy told her of his attempt to relieve himself through the rear of the aircraft lacking a turret, she burst into peals of laughter.

I had noticed that Gran was having her fair share of brandy and thought she must have booked a room for the night, so I did not worry unduly until suddenly she turned and naïvely asked me to find her a taxi to Leeds. In a quandary, I tried to explain the wartime restrictions on taxis to her. She listened and groused, 'You young 'uns, no initiative at all. I'll sort this out myself.'

Luck or fate stepped in at this moment in the shape of a short, pudgy man who had just entered the bar. Seeing him, Gran's face lit up. 'Frank,' she called out, 'come here, luv. It's grand to see you. Sit down, and what are you having?'

The man, obviously delighted to see Gran, stepped over to join our party. He gave her a tremendous hug and sat down behind the drink she had ordered. 'Eeh, Minnie,' he said, 'it must be five years since we met. What are you doing here?'

After explanations and introductions all round, Gran and Frank were soon in deep conversation, and I saw quite a pile of petrol coupons given to him by Gran. I was slightly shocked by Gran's obvious involvement in things shady, but I chuckled with resignation when she gave me a colossal wink and a thumbs-up sign.

When she started collecting her belongings, it became obvious that she was leaving. 'Come on, Frank, time we were off,' she commanded. Addressing the bemused crew, she smiled. 'Thanks, lads, I can't remember when I've had a better day out. Don't forget to come and see me next time you're with Bill in Horsforth.'

For one moment, she looked at John solemnly and spoke. 'Bring these lads home safe and sound, luv,' she begged.

Embarrassed, John could only nod and smile encouragingly. With a wave she was gone, and, sadly, for some of my crew it was the last time they spoke to her. Shortly afterwards, we were posted to Lyneham in Wiltshire to collect a new machine and fly it out to India to join a bomber squadron.

Flying over Gran's Pub and Sowerby Bridge

On one occasion, the crew did see her from a distance. One of our last flights from Burn was an exercise in transferring fuel, and we made it a pleasure flight. Sitting at the port beam hatch, I recognised Leeds, and John came on the intercom to explain that we were going to say cheerio to Gran. In no time at all, our Liberator was skimming over Gran's pub, and she was clearly seen waving a tablecloth. After a final pass, John waggled the wings and climbed to a safer altitude.

'Steer 220,' directed Harry. His voice on the intercom was flat and noncommittal.

John dutifully set the aircraft onto the new heading and followed Harry's instructions to orbit a small town shortly after overflying Halifax. Bewildered, I went forward, only to meet Harry on his way aft with the camera. Retracing my steps back to the beam position I'd vacated, I watched in silence as Harry methodically set the camera in position and commenced taking photographs. Thinking it was some exercise for Harry, of which I was not aware, I showed only mild interest.

Finally putting the camera on the floor, Harry sat beside me, pulled out a pack of Sweet Caporals and handed them round to the assembled gunners. He had a look of satisfaction on his face. Patting the camera, he shouted above the noise of the engines, 'Granpop will love these,' and seeing the mystified expressions on our faces, he laughed, 'That was Sowerby Bridge, his birthplace. Now I can truthfully say I've been there.'

As the pilots were map-reading their way back to base, Harry and I stayed in the rear of the aircraft until we joined the circuit to land. We then went forward onto the flight deck to restore the aircraft's trim prior to landing. We had broken many of the rules with our low flying and photography but were not unduly worried, as we would be posted to 1445 Flight at RAF Lyneham before any complaints could be lodged. It was late September 1942 as our tenure at 1653 Conversion Unit concluded. The following morning saw us away on two weeks' leave.

8

RAF Lyneham

Leave in Horsforth Before Departing to RAF Lyneham

Arriving home on leave with all of my possessions packed in two kit bags and a parachute bag, I flopped into a chair to a look of astonishment from my father. 'What the hell have you got in the bags?' he asked me.

'Just my usual kit, plus my flying gear,' I replied. 'I've been posted to a new station when my leave is up.'

Dad looked apprehensive and asked quietly, 'Starting on ops in these Liberators?'

Sensing the tension in my father's voice, I answered equally quietly. 'No, Dad, we're going to a station down south to collect a new aircraft, and then we'll be off to the Far East to bomb the wily Japs.'

Hearing the end of the conversation, Mum asked hesitantly, 'Will you be away a long time?'

Not wishing to upset her more than necessary, I answered nonchalantly, 'No more than six months, I should think.' I did not tell her that we had been briefed before coming on leave that single men were expected to do four years in the Far East, and married men three years. To young men, it sounded like a life sentence.

Within four or five days, the same restlessness I had felt on my last leave returned, so it was with delight that I answered a knock on the door one afternoon to see Ben with all his kit. 'Got brassed off back home,' offered Ben, 'so I thought I'd finish my leave with you, if you have no objections.'

I was delighted, and the rest of the leave went pleasantly, but all too quickly. Among other things, we spent time with Gran at her pub, where we were always at the centre of attention.

To RAF Lyneham and Waiting for a Liberator

When the day arrived for us to catch the train to Lyneham, neither Ben nor I was eager to leave. We departed at the last possible moment. Arriving at the large RAF aerodrome at Lyneham in darkness, we were shown into an empty hut. We were glad to climb into our beds after a long and wearying journey.

Up early next morning and walking to the Sergeants' Mess for breakfast, we were somewhat awed by the size of the camp. We observed at least eight different types of aircraft in the circuit. The Mess itself seemed to be packed with aircrews. It was with some difficulty, then, that we rounded up the rest of our crew, all bar John, who was in the Officers' Mess. When we were finally able to get to the noticeboard, we found that the Gauntlett crew was to report to the Flight Office.

John was there when we arrived. 'Thought you lazy sods would show up eventually,' he teased. 'Got some good news and some bad news. Good news, 1445 Flight hasn't got a kite for us yet, but we are to remain as a crew, although we will be split up to do various jobs. I have been put in charge of the Communications Flight with Ben to assist me. Harry and Enoch are to do loop and compass swings on Bisleys and Albemarles, and the rest of you are to make yourselves useful in the Armoury. Bad news is, it may be some time before we get a new Lib.'

The news was received with mixed feelings by the crew. Fred, in particular, was impatient to get on with the war, if only to put a stop to the raids on London. Willy, in his easy-going way, took everything as it came, and having seen many rabbits on the aerodrome, he was looking forward to shooting them rather than the Japanese.

Within a week of arriving, Ben had organised all of us except John into the same hut, which also held some more Liberator airmen, but not bomber crews. These men were members of 511 Squadron, a transport unit that sent its aircraft to all parts of the world on a varied assortment of duties.

My crew soon became accustomed to the disappearance of one or more of the other crews for periods lasting up to a fortnight. No one asked where they had been, but shrewd guesses could be made as to their likely ports of call by the goodies they returned with. American cigarettes, nylons, and cosmetics indicated a trip westward, while bananas, oranges, and French perfume pointed in the other direction. One crew perplexed everyone by returning with cases of vodka. Ben, Harry, and I considered applying for a transfer to 511, as the perks seemed more appealing, but the thought of splitting our crew deterred us.

The new duties were not difficult, and Harry and I usually finished by about 4 p.m. Ben frequently assisted us with performing compass swings, as he had little to do on the Communications Flight because John hogged most of the flying. When Ben helped, Harry and I finished even earlier. As Harry stood outside holding up large numbered cards to indicate the heading on his hand-held compass, Ben would rev the port or starboard engine and turn the aircraft onto the same heading and make a note of any deviation showing on the aircraft's compass.

Meanwhile, I would take bearings on a radio beacon with the DF loop and also mark any deviations. Back in the hut, I plotted them on a graph and usually ended up with a line like a letter 'S' on its side. This I then stuck to the base of the loop inside the aircraft to enable the wireless operator to make the necessary corrections.

After the sophisticated radio compass in the Liberator, the old-fashioned DF loop seemed primitive. None of us liked the Bisley, an offshoot of the Blenheim that seemed to have lost the Blenheim's character in the development process. There was not a lot of room inside, and there seemed to be bits of metal sticking out everywhere. These were the source of much cursing whenever I banged myself on them.

The Albemarle was a peculiar aircraft. Designed to be constructed in case of an aluminium shortage, it was built largely of wood and was fabric-covered. Standing on a tricycle undercarriage, it was not inelegant, but speaking to the crews who had to fly the Albemarle, it was obvious that its performance left much to be desired. One of its peculiarities was the way it corkscrewed through the air instead of flying straight and true, and this fault was cured by doping a short length of cord down the trailing edge of each of the two rudders.

Girls

If Ben, Harry, and I were finished early enough, a quick spruce-up was in order, followed by a short train ride into the bright lights of Bath. The first port of call was always a pub, The Half-Moon, where we would stay a while eyeing the talent. Ben, with his worldly approach, was most successful when it came to chatting the ladies up, and he was usually the one to get us dates. Then, it would be off to a local dance. When luck was with us, this would be followed by a spot of romance in the park, a quick goodnight, and a mad dash for the last train back to camp.

After about a month on the station, our crew was becoming well-known to some of the permanent staff, particularly the WAAFs. Suddenly showing great concern for his crewmates' safety, Ben began taking our parachutes, one by one, to the Parachute Section for airing and repacking. Perplexed by Ben's lengthy absences, Harry and I decided to take our own chutes for repacking, partly through curiosity about Ben and partly to satisfy ourselves that nothing would be amiss should we need to use the chutes.

Entering the building, we were awed by the scene before us. Elongated parachutes, like long white chrysalis pods, disappeared upwards into the gloom. As we stood hesitantly inside the doorway, a pleasant enough corporal approached us. Beckoning over his shoulder, he led each of us, in turn, to a long table. Pointing to the rather scruffy packs on the table, he looked at us and sadly shook his head. 'How long since these were last tested?' he asked. After much shuffling of feet, Harry admitted one check, while I had to confess that mine had never been checked since its issue to me at OTU. Muttering to himself on the insanity of all aircrew, the corporal pointed to Harry's chute. 'OK,' he said, 'pull the D-ring.'

Harry stepped forward and gently pulled at the indicated ripcord. Nothing happened. The corporal snarled his exasperation. 'Pull the bloody thing. It's not your dick you're pulling.'

Harry gave the ring a sharp tug, and silk shot out in a cascade onto the table. With a smile and a nod of satisfaction, the NCO swept the parachute to the end of the table and prodded me to tug at my ripcord. The result was dramatic and unexpected. Instead of a pleasant swoosh of silk, the pilot chute shot out, instantly followed by a veritable snowstorm of tiny pieces of silk.

A look of horror spread across the corporal's face. 'Where the hell have you had this thing?' he asked.

'Malta and the Middle East,' I answered with a sickly grin as the implications of what had just occurred dawned on me. While I had been answering, the rest of the packers had gathered round, mostly WAAFs, but when the corporal retrieved a dead mouse from the pack, they hastily retreated.

'Well, sergeant, looks like you owe the RAF quite a lot of money. Don't come cheap, these parachutes.'

Seeing the crestfallen look on my face, he grinned and patted me on the shoulder. 'Don't worry,' he said. 'I can put it down to battle damage, but in future keep it well away from battery acid. That's what caused the rot, but the mouse must have been an international hitchhiker.'

I breathed a sigh of relief. 'Thanks, corporal, I'll buy you a drink in Bradenstoke one night.'

'You'll buy him two,' said a familiar voice from behind. It was Ben, accompanied by an attractive WAAF. 'Alright, you nosy pair of buggers,' he added. 'Meet Thelma. That's why you are here, isn't it?'

With some embarrassment, we confessed that we thought Ben was hiding something, and we thought the answer lay in the Parachute Section. Never one to be taken aback for long, Harry turned to the girl named Thelma and poured on the charm.

'Can you fix Enoch and me up with two of your pals, and we can all go out together?'

Thelma readily agreed, and the following evening saw Ben, Harry and I in the little pub in Bradenstoke, which the crew used as its local. Needless to say, the rest of the crew were not far behind and were just as inquisitive as to what the 'flight deck bods' were up to as Harry and I had been about Ben.

At the pub with the girls, the drinks began flowing freely, and Willy suggested that we introduce the WAAFs to Cardinal Puff. Curiously, the girls watched Willy.

The idea was to drink a toast to Cardinal Puff with a long, complicated ritual. If successful, his health was then proposed for a second time, and the ritual had to be gone through twice, and two pints downed. If no mistakes were made, his health was proposed for the third and last time, whereupon three pints had to be consumed and the ritual repeated three times. When the participant made a mistake, he or she was compelled to start again at the beginning. Needless to say, it resulted in early intoxication for Willy, much to the amusement of the rest of the party and the few regulars in the bar.

Much to everyone's surprise, Thelma said she would like to try so it was agreed she could, but she need only drink half-pints. As predicted, she also failed to complete the course.

By closing time, our whole crowd, well under the weather, tottered back to camp. Prior to reaching our destination, however, the three couples—Ben and Thelma plus Harry, me, and our dates—temporarily disappeared into a field while the 'arse enders', as Ben called them, rolled up the road to the strains of ribald songs. We all reached camp safely, and our smiles more than hinted at the good times we had.

RAF Lyneham was unusual in having a Red Shield canteen, in addition to the Officers' Mess, Sergeants' Mess, and NAAFI. Staffed by members of the Salvation Army, the Red Shield was open to all ranks. The tea and snacks were of good quality, and it was a useful meeting place, so it was not surprising that the crew and our WAAF companions of the previous evening gathered together the following morning. There were some sheepish glances all round, but it was fairly apparent that Ben and Thelma were becoming increasingly fond of each other.

As Ben's crewmates, we regarded the liaison with mixed feelings as he was good company for us all, not just Thelma. What's more, he always had the price of a night out when the rest of us were broke.

That is, almost always. He received an envelope each week that contained not a letter, but a crisp white fiver. Ben, however, reluctantly spent two evenings around the stove with us because of my absent-mindedness. After picking up the crew's mail one day—in this case only a correspondence with money for Ben and one letter for Fred—I stuffed them in my battledress pocket and promptly forgot to deliver them. I only discovered the envelopes a couple of days later when looking for a fag end. Ben had been temporarily denied his social stipend and two nights out became two nights in.

Converting to Halifax Bombers

After having been on the station for weeks, assigned to a ferrying unit with little to do, even the most complacent among us was becoming restive so it was with some relief that we greeted the news given us one early December 1942 morning by John. 'We're converting to Halifax bombers to ferry to the Middle East,' he told his crew.

'Here we go again,' I said to no one in particular.

All were agreed, however, that ferrying was preferable to the tedious hanging about that we had recently been doing, excepting girls and drink.

In converting to the Halifax, I was the only regular crewman carried, as a safeguard in case of emergencies. John, but not Ben, was instructed in piloting the Halifax by an affable Canadian, Stan Pettingale, who would eventually join us on a Liberator squadron in India in the summer of 1943. I was already familiar with the Marconi radio equipment. The apparent strength of the Halifax in comparison to the Liberator impressed us, and the easy camaraderie was evident whenever we were doing something useful, such as flying in a Halifax.

Teddy Tailers

Sitting in the leather chairs in the Mess one lunchtime before returning to the Flight Office, Harry and I exchanged glances when Ben gave a guffaw of laughter while reading the morning paper.

'Let's all share the joke then,' said Harry, but Ben, still chuckling, shook his head. 'All in good time, laddie, all in good time,' he said.

With this, we had to be content until a small parcel arrived in the post for Ben. Opening it, he removed some written instructions, under which were seven colourful enamel lapel badges. On each was the emblem of a mouse. Solemnly, he handed each of us a badge and then informed us that he had enrolled the entire crew in the Teddy Tail League. As this was a children's club organised by the *Daily Mail*, the rest of the crew were more than a little bewildered.

'Oh, it's just for a laugh,' grinned Ben. 'We'll greet each other with this comical salute, but I don't think we'll bother with the passwords, etc.'

By now, the humour of the idea was beginning to percolate through to each of us. Willy beamed as he fastened the badge to the whistle which he carried on his battledress blouse. He stuck his left thumb in his ear and chuckled as he waggled the fingers of his hand. 'Bloody good idea, Ben,' murmured Willy with a smile. 'Makes us rather special.'

We each fastened a badge in the same place on his tunic, and the lot of us sheepishly waggled fingers at one another, much to the amusement of the other members of the Sergeants' Mess.

Fred suddenly looked at Ben. 'What about the skipper?'

Ben looked slightly uneasy and then said somewhat hesitantly, 'Couldn't see John wearing the badge in the Officers' Mess, and I didn't want to embarrass him by offering him one.'

'Makes sense,' concurred Arnie, and the rest nodded in agreement.

For some days, the stunt was a novelty with much finger waggling, which had to be explained to John. Shaking his head in mock misery, all he said was, 'What a shower, what a bloody shower.'

Soon thereafter, and seeing him in conversation with another flying officer nearby, Willy nudged Chalky and nodded towards John. At that moment, John was obviously discussing the crew, but he had his thumb in his ear and was roaring with laughter.

'Looks like he approves,' laughed Willy.

The Gauntlett Crew Gets a Liberator, AL597

The conversion course on Halifaxes, in preparation for ferrying duty, was short-lived and all for naught. Again, we found ourselves playing the waiting game on 1445 Flight, without a Halifax to deliver and, more importantly, without a Liberator of our own to fly overseas to join an operational bomber squadron. With little flying on the cards, Lyneham was a dreary, bitterly cold prison, of sorts, in January and into February 1943. I was only able to fly three times so far in the new year aboard Airspeed Oxfords—twice with Ben at the controls and once with John. Total flying amounted to a mere two hours and fifty-five minutes.

One morning in late February, on the posted Daily Routine Orders, there was a note informing us that at long last a Liberator was available for the crew, but when Harry saw its serial number, AL597, he exploded. 'Hellfire!' he cursed. 'That's one of those clapped-out Mk II crates we were flying at Burn!' Comparing the number with past entries in our logbooks confirmed Harry's remarks.

'Things must be bad if they are sending us on ops in that old bugger,' remarked Ben. He continued, 'Things do not auger well for us, I'm thinking.'

Our initial pessimism, though, quickly mellowed. In truth, our first sight of the old kite pleasantly surprised us all. The repainted AL597 looked quite presentable, and much to our delight, four new engines had been installed.

On 24 February 1943, we took her up on local flying, and the two pilots expressed satisfaction. I was also content with my radios. After the frustration of the previous months at Lyneham, the crew unanimously agreed that now events would likely move at a much more purposeful pace.

One final month of preparatory flight exercises and tests remained on the agenda, all in AL597, before we would depart for overseas.

Final Leave to Horsforth Before Departure Overseas

Apparently satisfied with our progress, in mid-March, the powers-that-be despatched us on leave one last time. Arnie took advantage of the break to marry his sweetheart, Marjorie, back in Yorkshire. I had the privilege of being best man.

Halfway through the leave, Ben appeared at my parents' home. Although Ben and I went through the motions of enjoying ourselves, we knew that we might never be here again. On the last night, we were in Gran's pub with my parents.

Mum could not conceal her anxiety, causing the four of us to be somewhat sombre, a point not unnoticed by Gran. She disappeared for a moment and returned with a bottle of whiskey. She sat down at the table and spoke. 'Now then, you lot,' she said, 'I'm putting this on the top shelf of the bar, and it will be untouched until you lads return. On that night, we'll open it and sup it.'

It was a kind gesture but not too successful in lifting the gloom, and shortly afterwards we bade Gran goodnight and prepared to return home. As Ben and I were passing Gran, she seized our arms, and with an expression of extreme anguish on her face, she hugged each of us, in turn, with surprising strength.

'God grant we meet again,' she prayed. Turning to face Ben, she nodded over her shoulder at me. 'Look after each other,' she pleaded. 'Think on, look after each other.'

Far from being embarrassed, Ben quietly took her hands, and seeing the tears in her eyes, he squeezed. 'I'll do my best,' he said in a low voice. Quickly, he turned and went out of the door. Not wishing to prolong her obvious distress, I gave her a quick but sincere hug and followed Ben outside to see him putting away his handkerchief.

We agreed that it would be best to leave early next morning as hanging about would only protract the agony. After an emotional farewell, we were on our way back by 7 a.m.

After a long and dreary journey, having stood all the way on the train, we arrived back at Lyneham tired out. We went straight to bed, only to be awakened by Chalky at midnight rolling in far from sober.

Finishing up at Lyneham

A brief thirty-minute air test in AL597 brought the crew back into focus late the following morning. There were no surprises and we knew that we had truly gelled well as a team.

On tap the next day was a six-hour-and-twenty-minute cross-country petrol consumption test, the only highlight being that as we descended below cloud at one point, we found ourselves surrounded by American Army Air Force B-17 Flying Fortresses fortunately going in the same direction. The Liberator's sudden appearance from cloud could very easily have resulted in a catastrophic aerial collision or a squirt or two from trigger-happy Yank gunners.

Apparently setting off on a daylight raid, the Americans skittishly fired off Verey cartridges to challenge this strange Liberator which had appeared among them. Fearing antsy American gunners, John pulled back on the stick to regain altitude, and it was with relief that cloud enveloped the Liberator once again without one shot being fired at us.

The rest of the preparations for departure were accomplished without any holdups, and on 28 March, John informed us that we were to set off for Gibraltar that night. We had all been expecting the news; nevertheless, it came as a slight shock not only to us but also to the WAAFs with whom we usually spent our tea breaks in the Red Shield.

Ben's girl Thelma, in particular, having become quite attached to him, had to be consoled by the others. All the girls vowed to be at the edge of the runway when our bomber took off, but they were less than enthusiastic when informed that the time of departure was set for midnight. The early take-off into darkness would enable the Liberator to cross the Bay of Biscay without being seen by German Ju 88s, which regularly patrolled the area, and it would also ensure arrival at Gibraltar in daylight.

The rest of the day seemed to pass as if in slow motion so it was with relief that the Gauntlett crew boarded the bus taking us to the aircraft. Arriving at the Flight Office, most of us missed the petite figure hovering outside the door until it detached itself from the surrounding darkness and ran up to Ben. It was Thelma. How long she had been there we did not know, but her coat had a covering of sleet, and she looked frozen.

Ben took her arm and led her into the Flight Office, where she came to an abrupt halt on seeing the Commanding Officer. She need not have worried as the CO had seen many departures such as our own. He merely indicated a chair near the radiators, for which she was grateful, while the meteorological officer gave Harry the latest report and the signals officer gave me a flimsy on which were listed direction finding beacons, German as well as our own. He also gave me the colours of the day and the letters in case the Royal Navy challenged us at Gibraltar.

The weather outside was deteriorating by the minute, and the sleet was changing to snow. We fully expected the flight to be scrubbed, so it was with surprise when we heard the CO speak. 'Right, you chaps, time to go,' he said. 'I'd like to wish you all the best. You'll climb above this clag, and the met reports are for improving conditions all the way.'

Turning to Thelma, he offered her a lift back to the 'Waafery', which she was glad to accept. As she left the office, she turned to embrace Ben one precious, tender last time; each knew that the written word would have to suffice between them indefinitely. Adoring all of Ben's crewmates, every last character, she looked at us all in turn. 'Good luck,' she whimpered in a breaking voice, with eyes moist, and she was gone.

9

Onward to India and 159 Squadron

To Gibraltar

Boarding the Liberator, I took a failed stab at starting the APU, and as usual, Willy made it look like child's play. After the standard pre-flight checks, we taxied to the end of the runway. Upon receiving a green signal from the Watch Office, John opened the throttles. Quickly, the aircraft gathered speed, although we felt it hesitate as it hit patches of slush. Eventually, the bumping of the wheels stopped; with relief, we realised that we were airborne and on our way. It was in the first minute of 29 March 1943 as we took off for Gibraltar.

Shortly after retracting the undercarriage, Ben put the de-icer boots into operation. I was a little unnerved by the thumps of dislodged ice striking the airframe, but the CO had been right about the weather. Eventually we emerged into clear skies. Harry worked in the astrodome taking star shots, and I was pleased to see that the DF bearings I had been giving to Harry were pretty accurate when plotted.

Poking Harry in the back, I made a show with my hands to indicate that the bearings were good, but Harry also answered without speaking. He held his nose and made the action of pulling a lavatory chain. Then, as if regretting the action, he came on the intercom. 'I guess they'll do,' he said to me. As if to confirm the statement, he handed me one of his cigarettes, a Sweet Caporal.

Harry's parcels from home invariably contained Sweet Caporal cigarettes, together with luxuries long disappeared from British shops in the fourth year of the war. The crew had much appreciated these gifts from our generous navigator, and many an evening in the huts back in England had been improved by his distribution of cake, chocolates, cigarettes, and the occasional bottle of rye whiskey.

The flight proceeded without incident or concern. With the coming of dawn, the clouds over which we had been flying dispersed, and Gibraltar was visible from quite a distance. After being escorted onto the approach by two Grumman Martlets, John landed the Liberator without fuss. Upon taxiing to dispersal, the rather weary crew climbed out, seven hours and twenty-five minutes after departing Lyneham.

Standing beside the aircraft awaiting ground transport, our overseas trip almost ended there and then. As we watched, a Lockheed Hudson which had made a faultless landing suddenly collapsed its port undercarriage and swung towards us. We scattered madly, but our panic was unnecessary, as the Hudson continued to swing in a big arc and came to rest without hitting anything. Personnel ran towards it from all directions to offer assistance, but as the dust settled the crew climbed out unaided, with the Aussie skipper swearing so fluently he sounded as if he was speaking a foreign language.

Willy regarded the pilot with undisguised admiration. 'What a command of the English language,' he breathed.

It was obvious that the Hudson had been involved in a scrap as there were many holes in the aircraft not put there by the makers. John later informed the crew that the Hudson had been in action against a U-boat which stayed on the surface to fight it out with the aforementioned result. Gibraltar, Arnie and I agreed, was a much busier place than on our last visit.

To Egypt, Iraq, and Bahrein

We did not have long to absorb the bustling sights and sounds of Gibraltar, as two evenings later, on 31 March, we set off for Egypt. The Liberator seemed to bear a charmed life as the two pilots made the unforgivable sin of taking off with the cooling gills open, making the take-off slow and lumbering.

The pained take-off did not go unnoticed by Fred in the rear turret. 'What the hell are you silly sods up front playing at?' he asked bluntly. 'If you go any slower I'll have to get out and push, and if you go any lower I'll be able to do so.' John and Ben, who knew they were at fault, did not turn this into a pissing match, and Fred's point was made without repercussions.

After the brief excitement, the flight settled down to a rather boring trip of ten hours and fifty minutes, only relieved for me when I went to the rear of the aircraft to stretch my legs. Gazing out of the starboard beam hatch window, I was surprised to observe that we still appeared to be over the sea. I was nearly at the point of telling Harry, but thinking more about the baffling rigidity of the waves, I suddenly realised that they were made of sand. The sand sea had lived up to its name; we were over the desert.

The transit from the UK to Cairo via Gibraltar officially counted as the first two 'ops'—operations—of our upcoming tour of flying on an operational squadron. A 'tour of ops' for an airman was roughly set at thirty sorties or 300 hours of operational flying, whichever came first. These numbers were not always set in stone as we found out in India.

Touchdown near Cairo on 1 April was accomplished smoothly, and after a day of eating reasonable, but sandy, food we were off again in daylight the following morning on a four-hour-and-twenty-minute leg to Habbaniya, Iraq. There, we received a surprise as Habbaniya town was lush with green vegetation, fed by the adjoining Euphrates River; however, beyond the banks of the river, arid desert prevailed. The substantial RAF base even had a swimming pool and cinema.

The airfield had been the scene of fierce fighting the previous year. An attempted nationalist and pro-Nazi coup commanded by four Iraqi Army generals led to a siege against the British at Habbaniya, which was swiftly crushed by the resident British ground and air forces in May 1941. Defying the substantial Iraqi forces encamped on the plateau overlooking the airfield, the British launched pre-emptive airstrikes against the rebels. With British air superiority, the siege was quickly lifted when Iraqis retreated. Ultimately, the coup failed.

As in Egypt, it was a stop of only one day at RAF Habbaniya for the Gauntlett crew, during which Harry and I still managed to each have a kit bag stolen. On 3 April, we were off again on a three-hour-and-twenty-five-minute daylight flight to Bahrein Island, where the airstrip was only just above sea level.

Karachi, India

The following day, 4 April, we took off in the early morning from Bahrein Island to Karachi, India on a leg lasting four hours and thirty-five minutes. We were nearing our transit journey's end.

The crew's first impressions of India were mixed. We had been instructed to land at the civil airport as the facilities for servicing our aircraft were better. Consequently, all our meals were taken in the airport restaurant and were very good. We also had our first encounter with Indian bearers. Complete with turbans and smart uniforms, these men acted as waiters. Chalky, in particular, was tickled to death to be addressed as *'Sahib'* and to receive a bow each time he had reason to speak to a bearer.

Our next encounter of any significance was with an object with which we were all to become familiar during our stay on the subcontinent: the charpoy. A rather inelegant piece of furniture, the charpoy was the Indian equivalent of a bed, being a rectangular frame on four legs covered with what looked like a thin rope net. First impressions were not good, but Fred, the first to try lying down on one, exclaimed with some surprise that it was quite comfortable.

He was right, and we slept well that night, only to discover next morning that we had all made the acquaintance during the night of a well-known resident of India, the bed bug. To a man, we were covered in bites.

Ben suggested that we all go to the Station Sick Quarters to try and discover a remedy. This was provided in the shape of a half-gallon of paraffin dispensed to each crewman by a tired medical orderly who, with studied patience, told us to drag our charpoys into the sun and liberally paint the netting with the paraffin.

In our newly issued khaki drill uniforms, we were seen as obvious newcomers, and many ribald comments came our way as we patiently treated the charpoys. The effects were startling. Within minutes, bed bugs by the thousands dropped to the ground. An obvious old timer who was passing gave us a good tip for when we arrived at our permanent station: to stand the four feet of each bed in small tins of paraffin; it was a tip that we all observed.

Our first time into the city of Karachi was a bewildering experience. Never had any of us seen so many people. Beggars were everywhere, some horribly deformed and all wretchedly poor. Cows strolled about the streets, freely helping themselves to food on the kerbside stalls, but no one touched them as they were considered sacred. The only fat Indians were the ones who were obviously better off and had an air of contempt for all around.

Within a very short time, each of the crew had been approached by pimps offering lurid delights, but with the lectures on the dangers inherent in India still fresh in our minds, none of us accepted.

Tradesmen sat on the pavement. The shoemakers interested us, and we soon discovered that these men would make a pair of shoes to measure in one day for the equivalent of five shillings (25p).

The heat was a great trial for all of us, particularly Fred, who, with his colouring, was especially vulnerable. As the day concluded, despite wearing his topee, he was suffering mildly from heat stroke.

Allahabad, India

We endured a full eight days in broiling Karachi as we awaited permission to advance another step closer to our final destination. At last, on 13 April, we were on our way again, on another four-hour-and-thirty-five-minute hop, this time to Allahabad, India. Take-off was in the morning, when the relative coolness of the air acted like a tonic to all in the crew.

Allahabad seemed a pleasant enough place from the little we saw of it. The most lasting impression was the strong smell of jasmine that permeated the air as we walked through the streets in the evening. As Arnie remarked, 'Now it really smells right, fragrance of the East and all that. Wish I could bottle it and send it home to the wife.' He had been quiet all the way out but now seemed to be accepting the tour we had to do.

Willy, trying to cheer him up, remarked, 'As a married man, you only have to do three years.'

To us all, the length of the tour, three years for the married Arnie but four years for the others, seemed interminable, but, as Ben remarked, the war should not last that length of time. Even if it did, we were not certain to be around to see it. 'Live for the golden moment,' he chuckled.

As this philosophy seemed about the only solution to our present uncertainty, the crew adopted it, and we were not surprised to discover later that most other aircrews on our squadron also lived by a similar code.

To Salbani, India to Join 159 Squadron

The stay in Allahabad was brief. At 9 a.m. on 14 April, less than a day after arriving, we were off on the shortest leg of our entire journey, two hours and ten minutes to our final destination—Salbani aerodrome in West Bengal. Salbani was just over 65 miles west of Calcutta. From the air, the place looked disappointing. The overall colour was not the tropical green we had been anticipating, but a uniform red with a splash of green here and there, indicating the presence of a village.

Some of the larger hamlets were grouped around rectangular ponds lined with brick; these were known as tanks. Much of the life of the village took place there. Inhabitants laundered their clothes and bathed themselves and even their precious water buffaloes in these cisterns. There, as well, women filled brass water containers before walking with the full vessels on their heads. Their careful movement, to avoid spilling the water, presented a stately and elegant manner of perambulation. Over time, we discovered many more facets of Indian village life, but the initial impressions upon landing were not reassuring.

After climbing out of the aircraft at the indicated dispersal, we were met by a decrepit three-tonner to carry the crew to our *bashas*, as the living quarters were called. Puzzled by the lack of activity, John asked the driver of the vehicle about the squadron, No. 159.

'Welcome to the Forgotten Air Force,' replied the driver. This remark was said with a bitterness that surprised us all. 'We're at the end of the queue out here when it comes to supplies of any kind. Reckon we are the poor bastards who are having to carry the can for all the years of incompetent administration and penny-pinching by governments since the first war.'

'Where are all the aircraft?' queried John. 'Are they out on a raid?'

With a cynical laugh, the driver spoke. 'Sir,' he said, 'you have just increased the strength of 159 Squadron by twenty percent. With your addition, our grand total of Liberators now numbers six.'

Little did we know at the time, but within two weeks of our delivery of AL597 to Salbani, 159 Squadron's strength would be reduced to two flying Liberators. April 1943, in fact, was the worst month ever for 159 Squadron's aircraft.

The first loss of the month, actually, was AL585, which had been chosen to transport VIPs to and from a conference in the UK. On 12 April, having arrived in Karachi from Salbani, this Lib went unserviceable, never to return to 159 Squadron.

On the night of the 15th—the day after we arrived on 159 Squadron—AL564 was written off in a landing accident after the starboard main tyre blew out and the undercarriage collapsed.

On the 19th, AL560 departed for Karachi to replace AL585, but it, too, suffered a series of mechanical problems, which prevented its return to Salbani until the end of July.

In the early morning of 20 April Liberator AL544 crashed at Chittagong, across the Bay of Bengal. It was written off after an undercarriage collapse attributed to damage from enemy fighters while on an op to bomb Toungoo aerodrome in Burma.

Finally, on the evening of the 27th, AL550 crashed into an aircraft shelter with no brake pressure, causing serious damage. It did not fly again with 159 Squadron until 12 May.

The early months of 1943 saw the multinational Allied army and air forces in India and Burma hanging on with the barest minimum of equipment and supplies. Improvement, however, was only a matter of time, as reinforcements began to trickle through. My crew was part of that trickle, and it would grow into an unstoppable, victorious personnel and matériel pipeline.

So, the weather-beaten veteran AL597 was welcomed to 159 Squadron, known informally as the Pioneer Squadron—the first heavy bomber unit in India. At the end of the supply line in what had been a low-priority theatre of action, though, 159 barely qualified as a squadron at that point.

We were transported by truck to our quarters—first John to his *basha*, among fellow officers, and then the others the short distance to our NCO billet. During the previous conversation, the crew's spirits had slowly ebbed, and the first sights of our new abodes did little to uplift us.

Our *basha* was hardly an imposing building. Built on a concrete base, the sides were of rendered brick. The roof was thatched, and a veranda ran the length of the building. On the veranda were tin bowls for washing, and sitting on the ground at one end of the building was a skinny native pulling rhythmically and slowly at a rope which disappeared through a hole in the wall, into the *basha*.

It became obvious what the native's duties were. Slowly moving backwards and forwards was a pole about eight feet long suspended on rope from the ceiling. To the rope was attached a piece of carpet the same length as the pole and approximately two feet wide. As it moved, it had the effect of stirring up the torpid air to give some semblance of coolness. This was fine as long as the *punkah wallah*—the manual fan operator—was pulling, but he had a habit of falling asleep, which brought forth cries of, 'Pull, you lazy sod,' or similar profane and stinging cries.

Life on 159 Squadron

Slowly, the Gauntlett crew settled into our new life on 159 Squadron. Administratively, we were assigned to 'B' Flight, one of two Flights on the squadron, 'A' Flight being the other.

A great cause for complaint was the boring and unpalatable diet which we had to stomach. Yams, better known as sweet potatoes, looked something like elongated potatoes and seemed to provide a backbone to the meals, but they were anything but popular. They had a curiously indistinct flavour, which Willy likened to the taste of old wet flour bags. Vegetables were of the dehydrated variety and were quite unsavoury.

There seemed to be a lack of flavour in everything. Even the tea, grown on the Indian subcontinent, was hardly fit to drink. This was a bitter disappointment to us because delicious Indian-grown tea should have been readily available. Sugar appeared to be non-existent. If one held a piece of bread up to the light, weevils could be seen crawling around. The only food the cooks did not ruin were eggs, which were fairly abundant.

One delicacy that was universally detested was the soya link, provided in place of sausage at breakfast, dinner, and tea. Just the sight of unappetising soya links disgusted almost all in the squadron.

Some American car dashboards were allegedly manufactured with a soya bean content during the early part of the war. The look and feel of the product was similar to Bakelite. For this reason, our soya links were often referred to as Bakelite bangers. Fortunately, the *char wallah*—the native tea servant—toured the camp frequently and did good business with a variety of food and drink, including mugs of tea, sticky buns, egg banjos, and fruit like bananas and mangoes. In the evening, he hawked things called chicken cutlets, the contents of which would have defied description had they been analysed, but which were far tastier than the food in the Mess.

He was a Punjabi and, like many of his race, a big powerful man with a good sense of humour. On one shoulder, he carried his tea urn with its small fire in the bottom, and on the other shoulder, a tin trunk containing eatables.

When we came to know him better, we discovered that under the tray of buns he also hid erotic paperbacks, which he hired out to the sex-starved inmates of the camp. He granted credit freely and was never known to write anything down, but his memory was amazing and woe betide anyone who tried to cheat him. His cry was a mournful '*Char wallah, char wallaieee*,' and on arrival at a *basha*, he would squat down on his haunches and dispense his tea. A most useful camp follower, he was popular with all the aircrew.

He never seemed to sleep, and later, when we returned from an operation, he could invariably be found outside the Ops Room waiting with his tea urn. On one occasion when a crew failed to return, he had a look of real anguish on his face when he uttered, 'Good men, all gone, *Sahib*, oh dear, not good.' As an afterthought, he added, 'One man, he owe me two rupees,' and with a sad shake of his head he strode off into the darkness. Looking at his retreating figure, we were not sure which he regretted more: the loss of the men or the two rupees. Altogether, he was a most remarkable man.

Prior to arriving in India 159 Squadron had performed useful work aboard Liberators in the Middle East by bombing Axis shipping and ports of entry, mainly in North Africa. India, it was soon discovered, was a very different kind of war. Supplies of all kinds, not just aircraft and parts, were difficult to obtain, and the Indian bureaucracy had to be experienced to be believed until the name of the game was discovered. Its name turned out to be '*baksheesh*'—a bribe; wonders could be achieved by even a simple monetary bribe in the right hands.

To us young men, most with no prior knowledge of the world outside of our hometowns, India seemed a peculiar place, indeed. Salbani aerodrome, still in the course of construction, was a prime example. A small, skinny man in nothing more than a loincloth would lead three or four women in wraparound *sari* garments with baskets of earth on their heads to a point indicated by another, slightly more prosperous-looking man. At that spot, the baskets would be dumped. It seemed an odd method for building an airfield, but as there were hundreds of natives at work, the results were sometimes surprisingly good, and at least the poor Bengalis were getting something out of all the work involved.

Going on Leave with Prickly Heat

My crew and I found the heat a dreadful burden. This, allied with the intense humidity, soon had us all suffering from prickly heat, which resulted in an irritating rash all over our bodies caused by excessive perspiration. For some of us, especially the ground crew working on the aircraft in terrible temperatures, this rash sometimes turned septic. The victim usually regarded it as a mixed blessing, for although in distress, the more acute cases were sent to a hill station, where the air was cooler and a cure effected. Usually, however, the cure was only temporary, with the trouble recurring when the victim returned to the unit.

Tormented by a bad bout of prickly heat not long after reaching Salbani, I was one of the lucky ones sent on leave to the hill station at Darjeeling, high in the mountains. I never suffered badly from prickly heat again. Darjeeling was considered a heavenly relief from the heat of the plains. A long train journey brought me to a town at the foot of the mountains, but one more spectacular rail trip awaited me.

Alighting from my train, I transferred to a tantalising mode of rail transport for the journey up into the mountains: the Darjeeling Himalayan Railway. My new conveyance was positively tiny compared with any previous train I had seen.

In a short time, the odd train pulled out of the station, and I soon discovered with alarm the gradients the little train negotiated. So steep were they in places that the train did not go round such bends but proceeded up the mountain in a series of zig zags: forwards for so long, then in reverse up the next incline. The train went so slowly in stretches that I got out and walked beside it, and I even hiked directly up the mountainside in one short interval to await the train's laborious arrival at a higher elevation.

Steadily crawling along, my train stopped once on a loop to allow a downhill-travelling train to pass. Eventually we arrived at a station. After a quick transfer to a three-ton truck, my long journey from the discomfort of West Bengal to the cool magnificence of Darjeeling was completed.

While at the hill station's camp, I palled up with a Hurricane pilot who was convalescing after having been shot down by the Japanese. His face made it obvious that his kite had been on fire as his skin was badly marked apart from where he had been wearing his goggles; there his skin was clear. He had also been wounded in the belly and was suffering badly from constipation.

The toilet facilities were of the primitive type and were cleaned out each day by natives of the sweeper class who, being of that caste, were destined to unpleasant duties for the rest of their lives. The good thing about the toilet was its open-sided position, where the view from its seat was breath-taking. The hillside fell away for two or three thousand feet, and one could see hundreds of square miles on a clear day.

The Hurricane pilot made a regular visit to the site immediately after each evening meal, more in hope than in realisation, except for one memorable occasion. The occupants of the Mess saw him set off with his Tilley lamp, as usual, and wished him luck in various terms of good-natured vulgarity. Usually, he was gone for about fifteen minutes and would return and shake his head sadly when asked about his efforts, but in this instance, he was back quickly in a disturbed state babbling about a panther.

When he had calmed down a little, he told us what had happened. 'I was sitting all peaceful,' he recounted, 'thinking what I'd like to do to the bloody Jap who caused me all these shitty problems, when I sensed I was being watched. Looking up, I saw the blackest panther you can imagine sitting on its haunches calmly staring at me as if I was some sort of *hors* bloody *d'oeuvre*. I let out a yell and pushed the Tilley lamp towards it. It didn't seem unduly concerned but stood up slowly, and with a last look over its shoulder, it bounded down the hillside.'

We looked at the pilot and at one another, wondering if he was cracking up, for although panthers were caught sometimes in the area, they usually avoided contact with humans. 'Let's go and have a look. He just might be telling the truth,' suggested someone. Armed with nothing more lethal than lamps, we proceeded to the site of the reported interaction. Sure enough, there were pug marks of a very large cat.

'Bugger me, he's right. Let's go and buy him a drink. He'll probably need one,' remarked a real old sweat.

Back at the Mess, we plied the pilot with drinks to atone for our disbelief, and quite a party started. Suddenly, the pilot stood stock still with a drink halfway to his mouth and a look of bliss crossed his face. 'That cat did me more good than the quack. If I'd had my pants on, I'd have filled 'em. Hope he comes again tomorrow!' Unfortunately, the panther declined to appear again, but our pilot friend started to improve rapidly from then on.

Rejoining 159 Squadron

Shortly afterwards, I returned to 159 Squadron. Little had changed in my absence. Serviceable Liberators were still a scarce commodity, despite the commendable initiative of the sweating, and largely unsung, ground crews.

Many on the squadron were suffering from homesickness, and in our theatre of the war it was obvious that the Japanese, a formidable adversary, would keep us from returning home for some time yet.

The main reason for despondency was the length of the overseas tour, which applied to all in the RAF, not just aircrew. To young men, four years seemed to stretch to infinity. Some airmen secretly hoped that when and if they completed thirty ops or 300 hours of operational flying, they would be sent home to instruct new crews. Even that possibility, however, would be long in coming, because there were so few aircraft and plenty of aircrew.

With scarce recreational activities on the squadron, the amusements of its members took peculiar forms. It was not uncommon to see a bunch of men standing around a ring of blazing petrol, within which two scorpions were fighting to the death. To see the soon-to-be victor bring its stinger over and kill the other had a horribly fascinating effect on us.

Some had tame lizards that proved quite amiable pets as well as practical ones as they helped to keep down the insect population to some extent. This, however, was a well-nigh impossible task as insects appeared in droves around any light. As there was no electric light in the Mess or the billets, it was customary to place the lamp some distance away from where one was reading or writing home, in order to prevent being covered by all types of insects. A particular annoyance was a large beetle which would fly into the lights with a resounding thump. If one fell onto the table near the lamp, a lizard was onto it like a flash.

Sitting outside the Flight Office one morning, Willy wandered off to examine a termite mound. About six feet tall and constructed of mud, it was as hard as concrete, as Willy discovered when he tried to kick a hole in the thing. After hopping around for a time and cursing his own foolishness, he stopped and looked down with renewed interest. He beckoned to the rest of the crew to come over. 'There's a bloody war going on here apart from our own!' he cried. 'Come and look!'

Sure enough, he was right. The termites, similar to white maggots in appearance, were being attacked by swift-moving and fairly large black ants. The ground was littered with the bodies of termites and ants, and still they were fighting for no reason we could observe. Infrequently, however, an ant would emerge from the mud pillar with what appeared to be an egg in its claws.

Arnie, looking a little bemused, observed, 'Wonder if they have any more idea what they are fighting for than we have?'

Willy chuckled, 'Course they do. They're better off than we are. First of all, they don't have a four-year tour. Second, they go home to the wife at night, that's assuming ants have wives. And third, they don't have to live like sodding monks. When we get some leave in Calcutta, I'm going to get a bird.'

Coming from Willy, this was quite a speech, and it brought a sharp rejoinder from Ben. 'Suppose you get a packet from some infected bird. What then?' he asked.

'Go see Doc Kelly,' replied Willy.

'Suppose you're taken prisoner by the Japs. You'll get no treatment from them,' retorted Ben.

Willy looked thoughtfully. 'Hadn't thought of that. Think I'll stay celibate after all. 'Tisn't worth the risk.'

His reference to Doc Kelly amused us. The squadron medical officer was a popular member of the unit, but he was a fearsome man to encounter after sundown unless one had changed from shorts to slacks and long-sleeved shirts to minimise the risk of bites from malaria-carrying mosquitoes. He had caught Willy only a couple of days previously.

Nights were spent in the Sergeants' Mess, which had been made attractive by the members to resemble the interior of an old English pub. Bar stools were the stout cardboard containers in which the bomb fins were delivered. Apart from the bar with its somewhat bizarre range of drinks, the only other amenities were a shove halfpenny board, a dartboard, and a portable gramophone with one record, an old 12-inch of *The Nutcracker Suite*, which usually produced howls of derision whenever anyone dared to play it. Gramophone needles were no problem as thorns from the bushes nearby served perfectly.

The tedium of the place was getting Ben down and he started drinking heavily. The low point came when, during an argument with Chalky, he let fly with his revolver, upwards, not at Chalky. Promptly, Chalky asked for a transfer to another crew.

He was the first to go, but he need not have bothered. Shortly afterwards, Ben was taken out of the crew to fly as second pilot to Sqn Ldr Louis Massey DFC and Bar, one of the squadron's two Flight Commanders, and John was relegated to second pilot in our crew, now skippered by an experienced pilot, Fg Off. Jack

Evans. John's shift from skipper to second pilot was common practice with a new, untested pilot like him; an experienced operational pilot was invaluable in myriad ways.

After some practice flying together, the Evans crew was put on the operational roster in May 1943. Operations, however, were severely curtailed until October due to the onset of the lengthy monsoon season.

With the ever-growing heat build-up as the year advanced, work at the Flights became almost impossible in the afternoons. Consequently, the working hours were changed. The aircrews found themselves being transported to our Flight Offices in the early hours of the morning until tiffin (the midday meal), having the afternoon off, and then working again in the evening for a couple of hours.

Keeping a bomber squadron functioning called for hard work in any locale, but in the sometimes brutal conditions at Salbani, the effects of the climate could not be ignored. The poor ground crew, generally relegated to the bottom of the RAF hierarchy on base, suffered the worst, but still the weather as a factor in health and productivity was carefully considered by the CO. Later, in October, with the advancement into the dry season, afternoon work hours were changed again to take advantage of relatively cooler weather.

10

Bombing Operations Begin and the 1943 Monsoon Arrives

My Third Op (First on 159 Squadron): Heho Aerodrome, 13–14 May 1943

Having taken well to his new crew, captained by Sqn Ldr Massey, Ben started acting more like his old self. He again thoroughly enjoyed pulling the legs of his mates in the 'Teddy Tailers' and never missed a chance to rouse us.

The six of us who remained Gauntlett crewmates, intact for nearly ten months, were beginning to get something of a guilt complex over having done no operational flying. Willy and Fred, in particular, were receiving letters from pals with whom they had trained in England informing them of fellow trainees who had bought it over Europe. We did not wish to die, but we wanted to earn our corn, even though we were only paid a pittance. Soya links hardly qualified as payment.

Ironically, Ben had not yet flown an op on 159 Squadron either, but still he persisted with his teasing, even after we, his former crewmates, began our operational flights.

Finally, our green crew was detailed for its first op on 159 Squadron, aboard AL597, on the night of 13–14 May. Fg Off. Jack Evans would be our captain. On the morning of the 13th, the aircraft was taken up on an air test, a standard practice prior to any op. With everything being satisfactory, AL597 was given over to the ground crew to bomb up and fuel up before the gharry took us to briefing. Later, with experience, we endeavoured to find out, in advance, the bomb load and fuel amount we would be carrying, to give us a rough idea of the distance to the target. On this morning, however, we proceeded to the briefing in total ignorance.

In addition to Fg Off. Evans as skipper, the crew for the op would comprise the remaining core of the Gauntlett crew plus a screen navigator and a screen wireless operator. John, as second pilot, would be joined by his five regulars:

Harry (navigator), myself (second wireless operator/air gunner), Arnie (mid-upper gunner), Fred (beam gunner), and Willy (rear turret gunner). Fred and Willy would swap their normal crew positions.

Harry was well-trained and highly rated. On this flight, he was especially keen to perform his duties with precision and to impress as he was under the watchful and benevolent eye of the seasoned screen navigator, Flt Lt John 'Bunny' Moffatt.

I was lucky to have another Yorkshireman as my screen wireless operator, FS George Nixon, a Whitby lad who possessed a good sense of humour and was a popular member of the squadron.

The Briefing Room was a bamboo *basha* with a service policeman on duty outside the entrance. Beside him was the inevitable *char wallah*, complete with his equipment and his ever-present grin. In a way, he was a reassuring sight.

All three of the serviceable 159 Squadron Liberators—AL571, AL597, and the newly repaired AL550—were available for the evening's op. The nervousness of the uninitiated among our crew was not obvious to the other two aircrews operating that night. Most of the men sitting on the wooden benches were experienced, and I noted that the majority appeared to be bored with the entire proceedings.

Later, I was to discover that all present were apprehensive even before the curtains covering a blackboard were drawn back, revealing the target map. At our briefing, this was done by Wg Cdr Max Boffee, 159 Squadron's Commanding Officer, after which everyone saw that the length of red ribbon stretched from base to a spot in central Burma.

Wg Cdr Boffee spoke: 'Alright, you chaps, give me your attention, please. Your target tonight is Heho aerodrome. Photographic reconnaissance reveals that the Japs have moved in a substantial number of aircraft recently. We must try and knock out some of these machines.'

Someone muttered the words 'night fighters', and the CO, hearing the remark, replied, 'Yes, it's likely there will be some about, so keep your eyes peeled.'

Next came the meteorological officer, informally called the 'met man'. He assured us that the weather should be clear, but with the monsoon season imminent, we might encounter cumulonimbus clouds, which were to be avoided if at all possible. We had been warned about these storm clouds by some of our experienced squadron mates and hoped we would not encounter any *en route*.

Navigation and signals officers followed to brief the waiting navigators and wireless operators. Later Harry, Arnie, and I could almost recite these briefings by heart, but we absorbed the first one as if it was the Holy Writ. The armaments officer gave instructions to the gunners, and the CO closed the briefing by announcing the time of take-off (6.15 p.m.) and wishing us all luck.

Sleep was supposed to be taken in the afternoon, but it was impossible with so many conflicting emotions racing through our heads. Most spent the time reading or writing home. We took our evening meal in the Mess: bacon and eggs, almost a ritual for operational crews.

The gharry eventually took us and the other crews to our aircraft. On the ride to the Flights, Willy hummed his variation of the song 'Heigh-Ho' from Walt Disney's animated film, *Snow White and the Seven Dwarfs*: 'Heho, Heho, it's off to work we go'. One or two others took up the song. Most men, though, sat quietly in the wagon with their own thoughts.

Arriving at our Liberator, Willy performed his usual nonchalant start of the APU, following my failure, and the remaining crew boarded, carrying their gear over their shoulders. As it was so hot, only when the aircraft was in cooler air at about 5,000 feet did we don our parachute harnesses and Irvin jackets. We had to wear the flying helmets before take-off, however, as the earphones were built-in, causing much sweaty discomfort on the ground and at lower altitudes. We were all greatly relieved when later the squadron was issued with newer Mk III model Liberators, complete with American plugs and sockets, which enabled each crew member to wear earphones without the helmet and to communicate through a throat mike.

The 5,500 pounds of bombs swaying gently in the bomb bay did not look malevolent. On the contrary, they resembled rather large children's skittles, and they were not painted black, as I had imagined, but were a rather pleasant sandstone colour. Two metal containers, each holding twenty 4-lb British incendiaries, were carried on the catwalk as they could not be fitted to the American clips.

Liberator AL597 was the same aircraft on which most of our crew had trained in England and then flown out to India. Now, our experienced captain, Fg Off. Evans, stood on the brakes and opened the throttles, with John to his right. The Liberator vibrated in place. When the skipper suddenly released the brakes, the heavy bomber accelerated rapidly down the runway and was finally airborne.

Being the first time most of us had taken off in a bombed-up aircraft, the climb to 6,000 feet seemed to take much longer than usual, but we settled down to the business of getting our cargo to its destination. Willy in the rear turret gave drift readings to the two navigators. Compelled to maintain radio silence, I could only assist by giving intermittent loop bearings, which I ruefully admitted were not very accurate, and eventually, as we passed out of range of the beacons, I ceased completely. As navigation was by dead reckoning, Harry had to be on the ball all the time. His screen navigator, Flt Lt Moffatt, was impressed with Harry's ability to focus.

Our Liberator proceeded on its own course, independent of the other Liberators. That was how night flying was done—each aircraft on its own, with no formation flying possible. Each Liberator would make its bomb run or runs independently. The chance of collision or of being struck by bombs released by another Liberator did exist. It paid to keep a sharp lookout in the target area for other bombers, not just enemy night fighters.

By now, well into our flight over the Bay of Bengal, Fred was instructed to drop a flame float from time to time to enable Willy in the rear turret to take drift readings for Harry. As the British flame floats were rather large and cumbersome to slide into the flare chute, the request for one typically caused a string of invectives over the intercom. Although cumbersome, the floats burst into flame on hitting the water and burnt steadily for about fifteen minutes.

Occasionally, other flares were spotted below, having been dropped by the other two Liberators on the raid. They had the effect of making us feel less alone.

Willy's steady humming away on the intercom brought a smart rejoinder from the captain. 'Cut out the singing, rear gunner. We're approaching the enemy coast, and I want the intercom clear, OK?'

Meekly, Willy replied, and the intercom became silent. The words 'enemy coast' had jolted us out of the semi-hypnotic state we had all fallen into, caused, perhaps, by the beautiful moonlit night and the steady rumble of the engines.

The enemy coast passing beneath us was anticlimactic, with no flak, no searchlights, and (so far) no night fighters. Harry obtained a pinpoint on the coast and gave the skipper a new course direct to the target. The lack of activity seemed eerie, and by now, I could sense a knot in my stomach.

'Keep a sharp lookout, gunners,' cautioned the skipper. 'It's not like the Japs to leave us in peace forever. How long to the target, navigator?'

'Ten minutes, skipper,' replied Harry. 'Navigating in this bright moonlight is a piece of cake. I've been getting good pinpoints ever since we left the coast.'

'OK,' spoke the skipper. 'I can see someone else's flares going down now. Wireless op, remove the horseshoes from the bombs.'

I gave FS Nixon, the screen W/op, a puzzled look. FS Nixon, in return, stepped down into the bomb bay and beckoned me to follow. Between the bomb casing and the pistol fuse in the nose of each bomb there was a brass horseshoe-shaped piece of metal that prevented the pistol from being accidentally struck home, igniting the bomb.

Cautiously, the two of us went down the bomb bay and removed all of the horseshoes and then resumed our places on the flight deck. FS Nixon tapped the skipper on the shoulder and stuck up his thumb.

Fg Off. Evans said something to FS Nixon, who turned to speak to me. 'I'm going back on one of the beam guns,' Nixon said. 'You have to kick out the incendiaries.'

With that, FS Nixon disappeared through the bomb bay, and I followed him onto the catwalk and sat down beside the two cans of incendiaries.

As the bomb doors slid up the sides of the Liberator, I felt anything but happy as the only thing between the ground and myself was fresh air—6,300 feet, I later learned. When I realised that my parachute pack was up on the flight deck and well out of reach, I felt even more nervous.

Events now sped up, and I had little time to dwell on my nervousness. I heard the skipper tell Fred to drop two flares and was gratified to see them ignite below the aircraft, revealing in clear detail Heho aerodrome spread out below. Although we were too high to pick out any enemy aircraft, the runways were clearly visible.

The Liberator was now committed to the bombing run, and Harry could be heard giving corrections to the pilot. 'Left, left, steady, steady, steady,' he directed. 'Bombs gone, skipper,' reported Harry, and with a suddenness which startled me, about half the bomb load suddenly fell from the aircraft.

'OK, kick out the incendiaries,' ordered Fg Off. Evans.

Gingerly, I stepped onto the catwalk. Holding onto the rope down the port side of the narrow metal strut, I got my foot under each box, in turn, and nudged them off the catwalk. Falling below, they were whipped away by the slipstream, whereupon I resumed my squatting position at the base of the deck, which formed the beginning of the bomb bay.

Within seconds, I saw our bombs burst across the north end of the main runway but was disappointed not to see the incendiaries burning, as I felt as though I had a proprietary interest in them.

With a rumble, the bomb bay doors rolled shut as the Liberator was pulled around for another attack. I remained in the same position. The doors slid open once again as we lined up on a different heading for the second stick to be dropped. The incendiaries from the first run were immediately visible, and one seemed to have started quite a respectable fire.

Up to now, not a shot had been fired at us, but when Harry was halfway through the backward countdown from twenty, read out during the second bombing run up, there were bursts near enough to be heard in the aircraft. Plt Off. Evans did not deviate and maintained his straight-and-level flight, which was so essential for setting up an accurate bomb release.

Harry continued in a dull monotone, 'Nine, eight, seven, six,' but the Japanese were firing accurately, and the bursts were by now getting frighteningly close.

'Five, four, three, two, one. Bombs gone,' announced Harry. His voice was monotonous to the end.

I saw the rest of the load fall away. Immediately, the bomb doors were rolled shut, and I had difficulty resuming my seat as the Liberator dove and turned away; I was pressed down by the gravitational forces exerted upon me.

By the time I regained my seat on the radio, we had left the target and were beginning to settle down when Fred reported in a calm voice, 'Single-engined fighter preparing to attack from the starboard quarter up.'

Fg Off. Evans immediately started flying the Liberator in a series of swerves and swoops to spoil the aim of the enemy pilot. With no gun to man, I could only stick my head in the astrodome in a bid to see the enemy. I was lucky enough to spot him. The aircraft was a small radial-engined fighter, but what intrigued me was its fixed and spatted undercarriage. Codenamed 'Nate' by the Allies, the fighter was highly manoeuvrable, but when the mid-upper and tail turrets opened up, its pilot swiftly withdrew. We were not bothered again.

After crossing the coast, the atmosphere in the bomber relaxed markedly as sandwiches were eaten and coffee was consumed from the one-gallon flask on the flight deck. This coffee would always be a source of irritation as it was usually only tepid by the time we were on the way home, and like most drinks on the squadron, it was sadly lacking in sweetness.

Being by this time reasonably out of range of enemy fighters, it was considered safe for gunners to leave their turrets and stretch their legs. Exiting his rear turret, Willy moved forward for coffee. As he drew a beakerful from the tap on the bottom of the flask and then tasted it, he summed it all up. 'Witch piss,' he declared, and he promptly poured it down the nearest relief tube.

Willy sat down on the floor near the radio and tapped my leg. 'Not too bad, was it, our time over Burma?' he asked. I grinned.

'So,' I asked, 'did you get a squirt at that fighter, Willy?'

'Yes,' replied Willy, 'but I didn't hit him. He was out of range, but I bet I frightened him severely, 'cos when he attacked from astern and I couldn't get a gun on him, I threw a toilet roll at him. Bet he thought it was some sort of secret armament we were carrying.'

We were in high spirits, probably as a reaction to the tension we had been under. When Harry joined us, Willy slapped him on the back, saying, 'Not a bad dropping for a beginner, not bad at all.'

Harry gave his slow smile and retorted, 'Those bombs go off with a good crack, don't they? Almost as good as one of your farts, Willy.'

Accepting this as a compliment, Willy stood up, raised one leg and in an exaggerated pantomime pretended to deliver one of his more blistering efforts. With a laugh Harry shoved him towards the bomb bay, and Willy retreated to the rear of the aircraft.

Harry settled at his table and continued with his course corrections. As we sat back to back, whenever Harry wanted my attention, he nudged me in the back. Harry and I had worked together so long that I was reasonably sure what he wanted whenever I felt a nudge. When I received Harry's prod after about fifteen minutes, I called base and asked for a QDM—a course to steer. Base came back promptly and, after a while, gave me the required information.

Having heard the other two aircraft calling base, and having nothing else to report, I went to the rear of the fuselage to sit by the beam hatches. Looking out, I found the scene breath-taking. With the moon sinking low on the horizon, the sky was inky black and the stars were brighter than I had ever seen them. There must have been millions of them, and they reflected off of the Bay of Bengal's surface. The Liberator appeared to be stationary and suspended in the immensity of space. Even the noise of the engines with their steady rumble seemed to add to the illusion.

Nudging Willy and Fred, I pointed out of the port beam hatch and asked, 'Do you ever wonder what it's all about?'

Nodding slowly, Willy answered almost to himself, 'What we've been up to tonight looks a bit pathetic at the sight of that lot, doesn't it?' We were speechless, something that rarely happened. Fred moved forward for coffee and a yarn with

Harry up front. Even though he had already been airborne for six hours, Fred still appeared smart and unruffled.

Shortly afterwards, Arnie slid down from the mid-upper turret to join Willy and me. Arnie didn't say anything, but he lay down on the fuselage floor and went to sleep. I patted Willy on the shoulder and went forward to my radio, where FS Nixon, the screen W/op, was monitoring the set. On seeing me, he stood up to allow me to take over.

The Indian coastline at the upper reaches of the Bay of Bengal was useless for obtaining a visual pinpoint for navigational purposes as we crossed in an area known as the Sundarbans. This vast area of mangrove swamps was where the mighty Ganges reached the sea. The channels were constantly changing. Consequently, it could not be mapped accurately, but we were now within range of the medium frequency beacons, which were improving in signal strength as we drew nearer. I was thus able to pass accurate radio bearings to Harry.

Fg Off. Evans smoothly landed AL597 back at base without incident at 2.38 a.m., eight hours and twenty minutes after take-off.

Debriefing was fairly quick. Most of the talking was done by the more experienced members of the crew. I gave my two penn'orth and confused the intelligence officer by stating that the bombs had fallen in the exact opposite direction to the positions indicated by Harry. After some bewilderment, it was realised that in facing the rear of the bomb bay, I had a reverse view to that of the bomb aimer/navigator. The attack by the fighter was taken as a matter of no great importance, much to the chagrin of the gunners.

Immediately after the debriefing, we handed in our money belts and were allowed to go to bed. A money belt was a canvas strap, about four inches wide, divided into pockets and filled with silver rupees to be used for bribing the native Burmese into assisting an airman to escape, should he come down behind enemy lines. We each wore such a belt. The money belts were fairly heavy, and Harry had his own ideas about them. He thought they were designed to act as sinkers in the event of a ditching in the Bay of Bengal.

US B-24s Stage out of Salbani: 22–23 May 1943

The cumulonimbus clouds appeared much more frequently with each passing week, and everyone longed for the monsoon to break in the hope that the rain would cool things down a bit. Our main source of information on matters Indian, the *char wallah*, said it would arrive at a certain date, and the rains would start at 3 p.m. on that particular afternoon. He was only one hour out with his prediction as it started to rain at four. His accuracy was not due to clairvoyance, but to a shrewd analysis of All India Radio weather forecasts. He collected rupees from the more gullible who had placed bets with him.

On 22 May, the sound of many aircraft roared overhead as I lazed about in advance of my second op with 159 Squadron, laid on for that night. Going outside, I recognised the obvious reason for the noise. The sky seemed to be filled with Liberators. We were delighted; at long last, we were getting some replacements.

Sadly, our pleasure was short-lived. As the aircraft landed, we realised that these Liberators, an advanced model compared with our old Mk IIs, wore American markings, and they were crewed by Americans, too. Oh well, I thought, the Americans get the new bombers before we do, but I sensed that our time would come.

Soon after landing the NCOs among them appeared in the Sergeants' Mess, still in their flying gear. At first, they were somewhat reticent, but gradually they thawed and turned out to be not much different from their 159 Squadron brethren.

They stated that they were headed off on a coordinated 7th Bomb Group op as soon as the aircraft were bombed up. While two other 7th BG B-24 squadrons were releasing mines in the Rangoon River, they would be attacking land targets in Rangoon as a diversion.

From the conversations which ensued, it was obvious that undertraining was a serious issue at some crew positions. We heard that some of the navigators could only map read (not much use over the Bay of Bengal), and that their radio operators—the equivalent of wireless operators in the RAF—could only work Morse Code at five words a minute, whereas the standard speed in the RAF was eighteen. Learning of these inadequacies, we viewed our visitors with concern, and there was more than a little feeling in the 'Good luck!' with which we bade them goodbye when the American bombers finally took off.

Reflecting upon the episode afterwards in the Mess, Ben, with bitterness, said to no one in particular, 'Whoever sent those blokes on that raid should be tried for murder when this lot is over. Poor sods.' No one spoke, but from the murmurs of assent it was obvious that everyone agreed with him.

Later, the news filtered back that weather had defeated the Americans that night. Most of the 7th BG B-24s on the bombing force had turned back from their Rangoon targets, and all of the sea mines were brought back to base by the separate 7th BG squadrons tasked with the mining mission.

My Fourth Op: Rangoon (Burma Coast Road Bombed), 22–23 May 1943

Aboard AL597, we also faced the wrath of nature on the night of 22–23 May. The second 159 Squadron op for the majority of the crew taught us in no uncertain terms that weather in the Far East could be as formidable a foe as the enemy.

At briefing, we felt apprehensive when no other crews appeared, the other two aircraft in the battle order having been declared unserviceable.

Fg Off. Jack Evans would again be our bomber's captain, with John as his second pilot. Five of John's lads—Harry, Arnie, Fred, Willy, and me—would be aboard. For the second time Willy would take the rear turret, normally Fred's station, and Fred would man a beam gun. Arnie was our mid-upper gunner. Joining us would be two experienced air gunners, FS Hurring and Flt Lt Ashworth.

I noted with some vanity that both the screen W/op and the screen navigator who had been aboard as watchdogs on the crew's first in-theatre op nine days earlier had now been withdrawn; Harry and I were considered operationally competent.

Our assigned target, separate from any of the specific American objectives of the same night, was also in Rangoon, the main port of entry into Burma and a lucrative target for Allied bombers.

During the afternoon, ominous black clouds were all around the airfield. Frequent flashes of lightning punctuated the dramatic skyscape. Most of the crew were convinced that the trip would be scrubbed, as the cloud base was steadily lowering all the time. Our convictions were wrong, however. The Americans had departed without incident, and at 7.20 p.m., we were airborne once again on our one-aircraft operational flight.

Within minutes of take-off the Liberator was in cloud and remained there for a long time, until we eventually came out of the top. Whereas an hour before we had been cursing the heat, now we were feeling the cold, and the thin khaki drill trousers in which most of us were clothed offered little protection at this altitude. Most of the crew still had some basics to learn, one being the value in dressing appropriately for the conditions. At least our helmets and oxygen masks were keeping our heads and faces warm, and the insulation of fleece-lined Irvin jackets was a blessing. Being above the main clouds, however, was worth the chill as the altitude enabled the pilot to avoid the CuNims—the dreaded cumulonimbus thunderheads.

Even though we avoided the storm clouds, the aircraft was being thrown about in an alarming manner by atmospheric turbulence, and as fast as Harry tried to get an astro shot on a star, he was bounced around the fuselage so he had to give up in disgust. I endeavoured to help with the radio, but it was hopeless with all the static from the lightning. I was also half-afraid that the aerials would be struck by lightning. Eventually, I admitted defeat. We were flying by guess and by God's will.

All during the trip, Willy had been a model in maintaining silence on the intercom. Later he admitted he'd been too scared to sing. The crew on the flight deck had things to do, and thus we kept our minds occupied with our essential tasks, but the gunners could only look out on the meteorological violence around us. In a way, the brilliant flashes of lightning assisted the pilots by revealing the positions of the CuNims.

Harry and I were discussing the situation when the skipper called up, 'Pilot to navigator. Can you give me a course to the target?'

Harry replied to Fg Off. Evans, 'Navigator to pilot. Take your pick, sir. I've only a vague idea of where we are. Can't get an astro fix with the aircraft bucketing about like this. Can't get a drift, 'cos we can't see the ground, and the wireless operator's box of tricks is useless in all this electrical interference.'

Quite calmly, the reply came back. 'OK, navigator, don't worry. Give me an estimated course to the target. With a bit of luck, the Japs will shoot at us and we'll know we have arrived.'

Harry and I exchanged looks, then Harry answered, 'Navigator to skipper. Try 120 degrees magnetic. I suppose it's as good as anything else.'

'Roger, navigator. Hope you're right,' replied Fg Off. Evans. Feeling the aircraft swing onto the new heading, I tried to raise a broadcasting station on the DF loop, but the static nearly blew my ears off. With a shrug of apology to Harry, I switched off the equipment once again.

After some time, Harry called the skipper and informed him that we were in the target area. The bomber commenced to execute huge circles in the sky, while at the same time avoiding the electrically charged thunderheads. We were either miles off course or the Japanese were choosing not to betray their presence by shooting at the orbiting aircraft.

Finally, the skipper called up the crew to inform us that we were going home and asked Harry for a new course.

'Steer 310 until I tell you differently,' replied Harry. 'At least we're going in the right direction, and as we get nearer base the wireless op may be able to help. I hope.'

'Roger, course 310,' confirmed the skipper.

With those few words, we set off for home, but we had not been on the new course long when Fred piped up on the intercom, 'What stupid pillock decided we have to fly in this clag?'

Arnie, usually seldom heard in the aircraft, answered in a quiet but peeved voice, 'The RAF decreed that we would fly, and here we are.'

There was an angry silence, and then various comments not flattering to the CO, Wg Cdr Boffee, were expressed from various members of the crew. Willy had the best solution: 'We'll bring him with us on the next one, and…'

He was cut short by the skipper, who added, 'Let's get back from this one first, and then you lot can decide how to run the war. Navigator, let me know when we're over the sea and we'll dump the bombs.'

Since leaving the target, the pilot had been gently losing height, down to 3,000 feet, hoping for a break in the solid clouds. 'Should be near the coast now,' estimated Harry.

Then, a hole in the clouds opened, affording Harry at least a minor target of opportunity: the coastal road south of the town of Sandoway. It would be more than just a blind bomb-dumping exercise, after all.

'Wireless op,' commanded the skipper, 'go aft and remove the horseshoes. We'll drop them live. Navigator to the nose.'

Harry and I went to our respective stations. I hated this job when the Liberator was bucketing about in the turbulence, and I struggled to keep my balance on the catwalk. Gingerly, I removed the horseshoes and foolishly informed Harry while still on the catwalk.

Harry, eager to get out of the nose of the aircraft and back to the comparative comfort of the flight deck, immediately opened the bomb doors and toggled the 5,500 pounds of bombs in one stick. I grabbed one of the upright stanchions and hung on; I had no wish to go tumbling down.

My frights were not over, though. Harry had hardly uttered, 'Bombs gone,' when terrific explosions occurred beneath my feet.

'Hellfire!' I cried in exasperation. 'First the stupid sod tries to drop me out, then he attempts to blow me back in again!' The doors slid down and closed, and, slightly white around the gills, I encountered Harry after we had each returned to the flight deck. Having by then cooled down a bit, I twigged him more in fun than in anger. 'You silly bugger,' I chided, 'you nearly killed me back there!'

Harry looked much more shaken than I. 'Nearly blew us all up!'

During the entire episode, Fg Off. Evans had not said a word from the flight deck. Now he came on the intercom, and his words were blistering. 'Get your fingers out, you two back there, if you wish to see tomorrow morning! I know you are relatively new, but if you intend to become old start getting us back to base! *Jaldi*!'

'*Jaldi*' was an expression used when trying to make the natives move a bit faster, and Harry was not amused. 'Talking to us like we're bloody wogs now,' he griped. 'I'll bloody show him. Can you get me any sort of help from that bloody box, Enoch?' Whenever Harry was roused, the word 'bloody' figured prominently in his conversation. Meanwhile, the skipper wisely put the aircraft into a steady climb.

I pondered my options. 'Could try to raise base for a QDM course to steer, but it's a long shot with all the interference,' I offered.

'Do it,' suggested Harry. 'The Japs aren't likely to come looking for us in this shit.'

Cautiously, I switched on the transmitter and called up Salbani to establish contact. Initially, there was nothing. I then transmitted in Morse much more slowly and asked base to keep transmitting their call sign for two minutes. I strained my ears to catch it through all the static.

At first, I heard nothing and shook my head to Harry, but in a brief clearing in the background mush, I heard what I was desperately waiting for—our base call sign being repeated over and over again. Without moving from the set, I thumped Harry in the back and held up my thumb. As soon as the base station stopped, I called and asked for a QDM and held my key down to enable them to take a bearing on us. Then, I waited.

To my great relief, back came the answer, faint but audible: QDM 330. I called the skipper and gave him the course. Harry already had it as he had watched me write it in my logbook as it came in.

Getting cocky, I called Chittagong with the same request and was gratified when the answer came back much stronger: QDM 097. With an air of nonchalance, I passed it to Harry.

Seeing it, he beamed at me and promptly plotted the two QDMs. The Liberator should be where the two lines crossed. Although second class, the two plots gave Harry something to work on; as we continued to fly towards our own base, the signal strength steadily improved.

Knowing that we were now well clear of land, the skipper resumed his gentle let-down towards the sea, with a corresponding increase in turbulence, but he was hoping to find the cloud base. Unsuccessful, he eventually settled for a height of 1,000 feet as being both safest and of an acceptably comfortable level of turbulence. I could clearly hear signals from base now despite the mush caused by the electrical activity outside, and Harry was a much more confident man.

Approaching base, new problems arose in figuring out how to get the Liberator back down on the ground in one piece. I asked for and was given the height of the cloud base over the aerodrome, 150 feet. There was not much room for error. Discussing the problem with the skipper, Harry told him of the ZZ landings we had practised back in England. Unfortunately, Salbani did not have the facilities for us to carry out this type of controlled landing but did have DF facilities so we decided on a compromise.

We would come in on DF bearings lined up with the runway, and as the ground in the vicinity of our aerodrome was flat, we would let down gently to 150 feet and hope to then land visually. As the crew put this plan into effect, the tension in the aircraft rose, but fortunately, we got it right the first time and landed with everything intact at 5.30 a.m., after being aloft for ten hours and ten minutes.

At debriefing, where no mention was made of the fiasco with the bombs, a feeling of anticlimax set in, and all of us were in a foul mood when we sought out our charpoys.The next morning, Ben, who still shared our billet despite being in another crew, asked us how it had gone.

Arnie answered quietly, 'Thought my wife would have been a widow this morning at times last night.' Nodding towards Harry and me, he chuckled. 'Skipper says they didn't do bad for a couple of beginners.'

This called for an immediate response, and as Arnie was still in his charpoy, Harry and I strolled over and slowly emptied two large earthen waterpots over him. The others joined in, and in a short time, water was being hurled in all directions, to the amusement of everyone except the poor old bearer who had to refill the waterpots. As we appreciated his devotion to us, when we finally collapsed on our charpoys with the odd guffaw, Ben restrained the bearer, and we all, in turn, went and refilled our own water containers—probably the escapade helped release the tension within us.

The 1943 Monsoon Arrives

With the arrival of the monsoon in late May, operational flying on 159 Squadron all but shut down until October. Even training flights were severely curtailed by the weather.

The intense precipitation of the monsoon season changed the appearance of the whole aerodrome. The reddish-brown dust no longer rose in clouds behind the gharry on the journey to and from the Flights, the sunburned scrub became greener by the day, and flowers appeared as if switched on overnight.

Unfortunately, the insects also increased, and trying to write a letter at night became almost impossible. Strangely enough, insects were almost non-existent during the day. Those that did appear were speedily dealt with by the lizards.

One thing about the monsoon that we all enjoyed, apart from the drop in temperature, was the availability of a shower whenever we felt like it. One merely stripped off and then went outside in the rain. When wet enough, a man could retreat onto the veranda, soap himself, and then step outside again for a rinse.

Having been on the squadron since mid-April, our crew was settling in, even despite the paucity of both training and operational flights.

Calcutta Leave: Early June 1943

The kit with which we had been issued before leaving England had been designed for peacetime and was woefully inadequate for wartime use on the plains of India. The shirts and shorts were not too bad, and the stockings for use with the shorts were adequate, but the tunics were worthless as they were a khaki drill replica of the blue tunics worn in cooler conditions back home. The bachelor buttons, held on with split rings, would scratch our skin. As any minor cut could quickly turn septic due to the atmosphere in which we lived, after a very short time, no one wore them, and most were given away to the bearers.

Members of the squadron who had been in India for some time had equipped themselves with bush jackets and slacks in a lighter grade of material. Shirts were made to measure by the local tailor or were bought in Calcutta when on leave. One useful item of clothing with which all were issued were pairs of white woollen socks that, if looked after, saved many a man from foot rot. The newcomers were startled to discover how quickly materials either rotted in the humidity or were eaten by rats or insects.

The old hands had bought steel trunks in which to keep their gear. When the crew was granted a seventy-two-hour leave in Calcutta in early June, we all shared the same intention: to be as well-kitted out as the rest.

Older members of the unit gave us addresses at which to stay, and we took the gharry to Kharagpur railway station, 19 miles due south of Salbani, to start the 72-mile journey east to Howrah station in Calcutta. When our train arrived, we were surprised at the size of the locomotive, enormous in comparison with English trains.

The train compartments were comfortable, if one could ignore the heat, with bunks that could be lowered to form beds for overnight travel. There was also a fan in the room of the compartment, but it was almost useless. Later, we learned the trick of purchasing a large block of ice and placing it and its container directly under the fan; then, it worked remarkably well.

Most of the railway staff were Eurasians and good workers. We had a sneaking regard for them as they seemed to fit in with neither the British nor native communities. Many of these workers asked for the native Indian's displeasure because the Eurasians tried to be more British than the British did.

At every station, hundreds of hands appeared at the windows of the compartment with a plaintive cry, usually from children with pot bellies due to malnutrition. '*Baksheesh*, *Sahib*,' they pleaded, 'no papa, no mama, no *khana*. *Baksheesh*.' '*Baksheesh*' was money given as alms, a tip, or a bribe, while '*khana*' was a meal. At first, we gave a few annas to the nearest hands, but we rapidly learned that this only attracted urchins from the rest of the train. In time, the cries ceased to touch us.

We also learned to guard our possessions. Willy was sitting with his hand half-out of the window. The pen he was holding was whipped from his hand, and it was impossible to see the thief as the throng around the coach was so dense.

In the end, we pulled down the Venetian blind-type shutters whenever the train stopped at a station. Each window was equipped with three sets of covers—a normal glass one, a gauze protection against the insects, and one such as we lowered at the stations.

Arriving finally at Howrah railway station in Calcutta, we were in for more surprises as bodies seemed to be everywhere, but it was not the result of an air raid, as we first suspected. The bodies were Indians who lived on the station, having no other place to call home. Though periodically cleared out by the police, the squatters soon returned, and who could blame them? Willy looked around him. 'Poor bastards,' was all he said, but it summed up what we all thought.

While we were gazing around, our bedrolls had been picked up and were being carried to the taxi rank by natives wearing a cheap blue '*dhoti*' as a kind of uniform. A *dhoti*, worn chiefly by Hindu men in India, was a garment consisting of a length of cloth that was typically wrapped around the waist, passed between the legs, and tucked in at the waistline. Each porter wore a brass badge, upon which was a number. They were so desperate that they would often fight to be allowed to carry a person's luggage.

After paying off the porters, we piled into two taxis and gave the Sikh driver of the leading taxi the list of addresses given to us back at the squadron. After a cursory glance, he nodded and set off at a seemingly suicidal speed across the magnificent Howrah Bridge over the Hooghly River, and through the throngs of people, rickshaws, vehicles, and other impedimenta of the roads in Calcutta. To add to the driver's problems, the occasional cow would stroll across his path, but he was most careful to stop until the cow decided to move.

It always mystified us that the Brahman cattle, which were regarded as having religious significance, were treated with great consideration by the natives, whereas water buffaloes, which were used as beasts of burden, were subjected to callous cruelty by their drivers.

Passing the Maidan, a large open park-like area alongside Chowringhee Road, the main thoroughfare, we were intrigued to see Hurricane fighters parked at intervals, ready to take off in the event of a Japanese air raid. Radar had been activated only recently along the strategic approaches to India, so things did seem to be moving in the right direction, at long last.

The taxi deposited us outside a small and shabby hotel, which caused some misgivings, but we had little control of events, as our bedrolls had been carried smartly to the front desk by the hotel porters. The exterior did not do justice to the place as it was quite pleasant inside, and we were soon installed in two clean and airy rooms.

From our appearance at the dining table in our issue khaki drill, the helpful hotel manager summed us up, quite rightly, as recent arrivals to India. 'Hope you enjoy stay here, *Sahibs*,' he said. 'You want I get you tailor or shoe maker?'

Fred jokingly said, 'You can get me a bird if you like.'

Without a flicker of emotion, the manager bowed to Fred, 'You want woman, *Sahib*? Certainly. What kind you want? Anglo-Indian, Chinese, Indian, or European?' The directness of the questions amused the rest of us, but Fred was most embarrassed and told a regretful manager that he had only been joking. The disappointment of the man was due to his lost commission. Bowing again as he withdrew, the manager stated, 'Anything you are wanting, I get.'

He cheered up considerably when told to get a tailor for all of us. Within an hour, he had three on the premises, and we were all getting measured up for bush jackets and slacks at ridiculously cheap prices. Our pleasure at knowing we would at last be reasonably smart, as well as comfortable, was doubled when we were informed that the garments would be delivered the next morning.

Willy considered ordering a duplicate set immediately, but I was more cautious and advised him to see what the first ones were like. When, the following morning, we went down for breakfast, there were our new garments laid out with each man's name on its respective pile. Each set was beautifully made, and as we paid the manager, he beamed as each man ordered another set.

'You want mosquito boots, best quality, only eight rupees?' That was about 60p. The voice belonged to a shrivelled-up little man carrying a bag over his shoulder and a roll of leather under his arm. Again, the price was cheap, and Fred, as particular about his appearance as ever, agreed to have a pair made. Swiftly, the shoemaker removed Fred's shoe, drew round his foot onto a piece of paper and measured the broad part of the foot.

'Ready morning, *Sahib*,' he said. Sitting himself down cross-legged in a corner, he proceeded to cut out the leather. He worked quickly and hummed a weird tune to himself as he cut the leather with a knife, which had a home-made look about its string-bound handle.

After watching the shoemaker for a time, Harry, who always had itchy feet, said he was going to see what Calcutta had to offer, and all agreed to accompany him. The hotel was reasonably cool with its marble floors and the constantly turning fans, but walking outside was like entering a Turkish bath. Within minutes, the beautifully starched and pressed bush shirts were wet through and sticking to our bodies.

Stepping onto the Chowringhee Road sidewalk was like entering one of the termite mounds back at camp. It was impossible to stride out; all we could do was drift along with the throng. Matters were not helped by the sleeping forms on the pavement or the hawkers sitting on small squares of carpet and selling everything from razor blades to aphrodisiacs and repulsive-looking sweetmeats. I felt my fountain pen snatched from my top pocket but realised within seconds that I would never catch the thief in that throng.

Shaking my head, I grinned sheepishly at Willy. 'Snap, Willy,' I said, 'looks like we're both in the market for something to write home with. We'll see what's on offer from the next pen *wallah* who accosts us.'

Willy nodded gloomily. 'Don't talk about home,' he advised. 'It makes me brassed off.'

About twenty minutes later, a skinny-looking man in the usual white *dhoti* tugged at my arm and asked, 'You buy pen, *Sahib*? Very good pen, Waterman.'

I took the proffered pen to examine it more closely, and my jaw dropped. 'You thieving bastard! Hold him, Willy!' I barked. The man had offered me my own pen without realising he was selling back to the person he had stolen it from. He was a wily bird, however, and took off as soon as I opened my mouth. Getting over my indignation, I turned to Willy. 'Pity you didn't hold him,' I said. 'We could have got one for you.'

Willy gave an enigmatic smile and held out his hand. In the palm were three pens, and seeing my bewilderment, he let out a great guffaw. 'Lifted 'em from his *dhoti* as you were talking to him,' he proudly boasted, and raising up an admonishing finger, he laughed and added, 'When in Rome, Enoch. When in Rome.'

The food in the Chinese restaurants was abundant, according to the menus displayed outside, and we decided to sample a meal. The variety was staggering, and most settled for the usual steak, but Harry and I decided on more exotic fare and went for the shellfish. We ate prawn cutlets with bamboo shoots, together with tomato soup with shredded crab meat topped off with apple pie with thick cream. As Harry finished, he closed his eyes in bliss and remarked, 'First time I've felt full since we arrived in this country.'

Willy had a thoughtful look on his face. 'What about those poor sods out there?' he asked, nodding towards the thronging pavement. 'Come on, give me a chip apiece,' he commanded; a 'chip' was a rupee. Willy added, 'At least we can help a few of the poor sods.'

Calling the Chinese waiter over, Willy pointed to the small pile of rupee notes and uttered one word, 'Rice.' The waiter had grown used to the idiosyncrasies of the white man and swiftly arrived bearing a huge brass bowl of boiled rice.

Without a word, Willy took it outside and held it out to the nearest natives. Not one of them would touch the rice. Becoming embarrassed by the strange looks and comments he was receiving from passing troops, he put the bowl on the pavement and returned to the table. 'Silly sods, what's wrong with them?' he asked us.

The waiter who had witnessed the proceedings with interest butted in. 'Hindu religion, sir,' he advised. 'You unclean so will not eat rice.' Willy muttered and went to retrieve the rice. It was in a neat pile on the pavement, but someone had stolen the bowl. The waiter held out his hand to Willy. 'Five rupees, sir, for bowl.'

To say Willy was annoyed would be an understatement; he was absolutely livid. 'Stuff the lot of 'em,' he decreed. 'When you try to help 'em, they shit on you. Balls to the lot of 'em! They deserve to starve if they're so stupid.'

Sitting quietly as Willy ranted on, Harry eventually patted him on the shoulder sympathetically and offered, 'Religious convictions can be very powerful, Willy. What you did was a decent act, and I'm sure it will not have gone unnoticed up there. Might stand you in good stead when you get the chop.'

'Piss off!' barked Willy. 'I'm not getting the chop. No slant-eyed son of Nippon is going to shoot us down. I've been told the Japs can't see well in the dark, and if I see a fighter before he sees me, my Brownings will shoot the shit out of him!'

Harry smiled enigmatically. 'I just hope you're right, Willy.'

The remainder of the afternoon was spent in the Metro cinema, not because it was a particularly good film, but rather because the cinema was air conditioned and had a bar that was opened during the intervals. Here we were introduced to John Collins, not a person but a long drink based on gin, so much so that by the time we arrived back at the hotel for the evening meal, all were in that gentle state between intoxication and sobriety. Consequently, we had an early night ready for the next foray.

The following day was spent in the *bazaar* area and was more like the India we had imagined when at school. Metal and leather workers, wood carvers, and

Right: Willy Kirby was killed in the rear turret of Bill's Liberator on 1 April 1944. (*W. Kirkness*)

Below: On the left of this wartime map can be seen Salbani and Digri, two of 159 Squadron's three Indian bases during Bill's tenure on the squadron. Dhubalia, the third, is off the map north of Calcutta. (*M. Poole*)

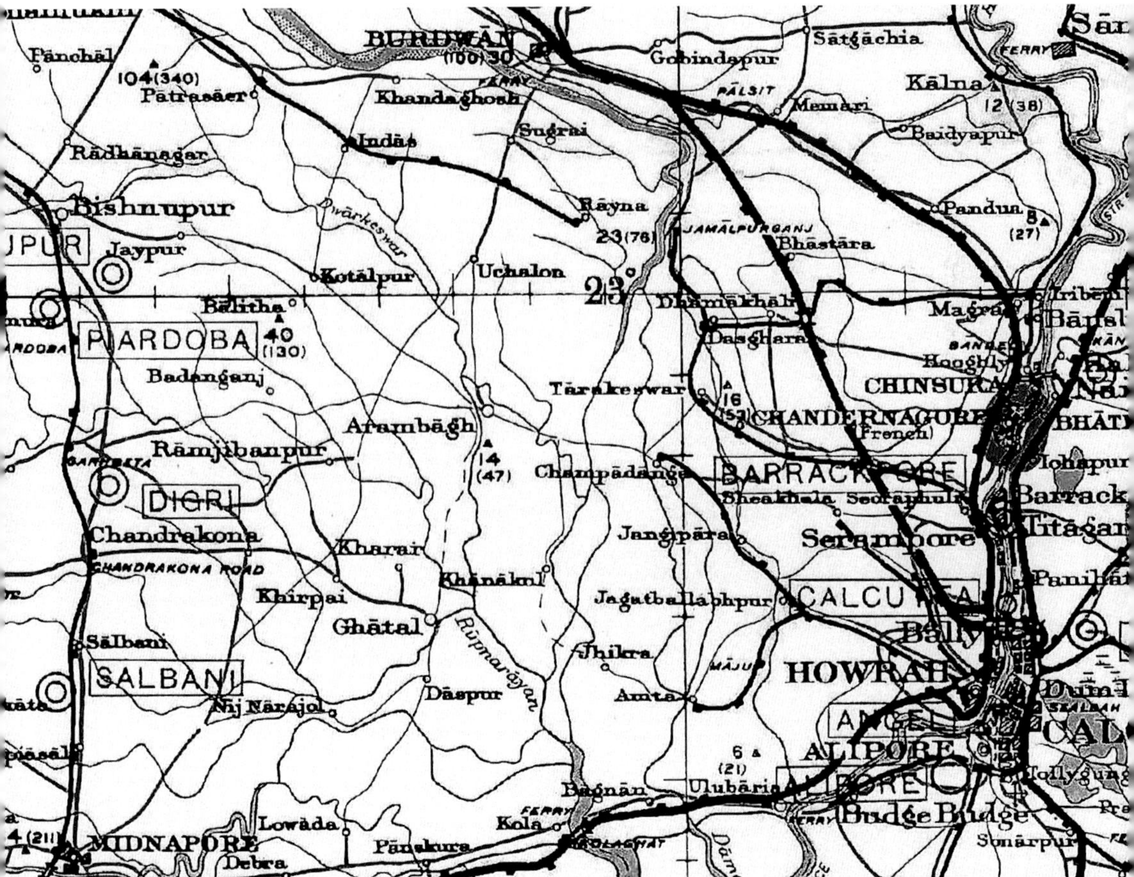

On 15 April 1943—the day after Bill and his crew arrived on 159 Squadron—Mk II Liberator AL564, wearing Donald Duck nose art, pranged at their base at Salbani when the starboard tyre blew out upon landing. The Liberator was a write-off. (*A. Lyons*)

By the evening of 27 April 1943, 159 Squadron was down to only two flying bombers after Mk II Liberator AL550 crashed into an aircraft shelter with no brake pressure. AL550 did not fly again with the squadron until 12 May. (*A. Lyons*)

Bill's *basha* (living quarters) at Salbani. (*W. Kirkness*)

At Salbani in 1943, 159 Squadron ground crew toil on a Mk II Liberator's No. 1 engine. (*A. Lyons*)

At Salbani, 159 Squadron ground crew service a Mk II Liberator in this view from atop the port wing. (*M. Poole*)

An air gunner sits to the right of his twin .303-inch Brownings, which protrude through a closed Mk II Liberator beam hatch. He sights his target through a small window immediately in front of him. Note that this air gunner wears earphones and no helmet; on the Mk II—but not later models—Bill and each of his crewmates wore an uncomfortable helmet containing earphones. (*R. Livingstone*)

Aircrew at Salbani pose with an Indian *char wallah* selling bananas (front centre). Bill's crewmates Fred Rozee (standing, third from left) and Arnie Bridgman (standing, far right) are among them. (*W. Kirkness*)

Bill and his mate, Ben Blue, perform their 'sand dance' at Salbani. Ben wears his pilot's wings, and Bill wears a half-wing brevet. (*W. Kirkness*)

Above: Unidentified members of 159 Squadron in front of Mk III Liberator BZ897's No. 2 engine. (*M. Poole*)

Below: No. 159 Squadron Gunnery Leader Bob Ustick (left) instructs ground crewman Norman Chambers (centre) and air gunner Billy Clegg at the port beam hatch opening of an unidentified 159 Squadron Liberator. A single .5-inch Browning machine gun protrudes through the opening. (*R. Ustick*)

Above: The forward fuselage and No. 2 engine of 159 Squadron Mk III Liberator BZ897. (*M. Poole*)

Below: Armourers prepare to winch high explosive bombs from a trolley into a 159 Squadron Liberator. Tail fins have not yet been added. (*W. Kirkness*)

Above: On 25 September 1943, Mk III Liberator BZ838 of 159 Squadron pranged in a spectacular heap during an attempted night landing at Salbani. There was no fire, and only skipper Freddie Stokes was seriously injured. (*M. Poole*)

Opposite above: Bill pauses during the painting of my 'DUMBO DELIVERS!' nose art design onto the forward fuselage of BZ839, a Mk III Liberator at Salbani in 1943. (*W. Kirkness*)

Opposite below: Front row, second from left: Bill poses on 9 October 1943 with members of the Massey crew in front of Mk III Liberator BZ839, which wears Bill's 'DUMBO DELIVERS!' nose art. A few hours later, the Massey crew was shot down and killed aboard BZ841, also of 159 Squadron. Back row, second from right: Bill's mate Ben Blue, formerly second pilot on the Gauntlett crew. To Ben's right is his current skipper, Sqn Ldr Louis Massey. (*W. Kirkness*)

DUMBO

DELIVERS!

The original Imperial War Graves Commission grave marker for Ben Blue and his crewmates, who were shot down and killed on 9 October 1943 aboard 159 Squadron Mk III Liberator BZ841 near Mingaladon aerodrome, Burma. Today, each crewman is commemorated with his own bronze grave marker in Collective Grave 4.J.1–8 in Rangoon War Cemetery. (*M. Poole*)

Bill's handiwork, the nose art on 159 Squadron Mk III Liberator BZ906. Not seen is the word 'Algy' to the left of the caricature. (*W. Kirkness*)

Algy, 159 Squadron Mk III Liberator BZ906, was Bill's crew's first personal Liberator. Here *Algy*, wearing his nose art, is seen heading off on ops at an unknown date. (*W. Kirkness*)

Above: Men in front of 159 Squadron Mk III Liberator BZ906, christened *Algy*. *Identified aircrew standing, left to right*: Willy Kirby, unknown, Fred Rozee, Bill, Frank Ellis (the skipper), Bill Etherington, Chris Hedley, Arnie Bridgman, and A. Forson. Note the full nose art, including the name Algy. The likely date is 27 November 1943, prior to Bill's twelfth op, to Rangoon. (*M. Poole*)

Below: Aircrew pile onto a truck during 159 Squadron's short move from Salbani to Digri on 23 October 1943. Seen are Bill's crewmates Willy Kirby (far right, with his left elbow protruding) and Fred Rozee (smiling at top centre, and holding a stick in one hand). Bill's former crewmate, Chalky White, standing at right, beams broadly. (*W. Kirkness*)

Bill and crewmates at Digri in late October or early November 1943. *Left to right:* Willy Kirby, John Gauntlett, Bill, unknown, unknown, and Rex 'Pop' Simmons. (*W. Kirkness*)

Cheel Chakkar ('Eagles Circling'), a landmark multiple-turn climb on the narrow, hair-raising motor road from Kathgodam to Naini Tal, India, where Bill spent two leaves—in December 1943 and the spring of 1944. (*N. Goodisson*)

Above: Naini Tal was a wondrous escape from the oppressive weather, insects, repulsive soya links, and responsibilities back at Digri. (*N. Goodisson*)

Below: On leave in December 1943, Bill and Arnie Bridgman were rendered speechless by the grandeur of distant snow-capped Himalayan peaks after they rode horses to this vista above Naini Tal. (*N. Goodisson*)

Above: 'GOOFY', Mk VI Liberator BZ980 of 159 Squadron, takes off from Digri in 1944. Although Bill did not fly ops in this aircraft, it is identical to the Gauntlett crew's regular Mk VI Liberator, EV843, named *Erotic Edna*. Both aircraft arrived on the squadron in January 1944. (*M. Poole*)

Below: Aircrew in front of 159 Squadron Mk VI Liberator BZ980, named 'GOOFY', at Digri in 1944. Bill's crewmate on sixteen ops, air gunner Jack O'Brien, is front row, right. (*M. Poole*)

Above: No. 159 Squadron engine mechanics work on '*GOOFY*', Mk VI Liberator BZ980, at Digri in 1944. (*M. Poole*)

Opposite above: 'B' Flight aircrew, 159 Squadron, Digri, in early February 1944. Identified as No. 1, Bill is standing top row left. Originally a member of the Gauntlett crew, Chalky White (3) transferred to another crew before flying his first op on 159 Squadron. Those who flew at least one op with Bill on 159 Squadron are: 2. Jack O'Brien (sixteen ops); 4. Fred Collins (one); 5. Ernie Richards (nine); 6. Willy Kirby (seventeen); 7. P. J. J. O'Keefe (one); 8. Arnie Bridgman (seventeen); 9. A. H. Allanach (one); 10. Bill Etherington (three); 11. Chris Hedley (four); 12. Pete Bailey (one); 13. Norman Bingham (three); 14. Ken Brailsford (one); 15. C. J. Nicholls (twenty); 16. Rex 'Pop' Simmons (nine); 17. John Gauntlett (twenty-four); 18. Jack Evans (four); 19. John 'Hoppy' Hopkins (one); and 20. Harry Hartshorn (twenty-nine). (*M. Poole*)

Opposite below: On 29 February 1944, Bill photographed ground crew (front row) and aircrew (standing) in front of Mk III Liberator BZ926 'P' for *Pegasus*, wearing his nose art. Hours later, it was shot down over Rangoon. The nine-man aircrew included Don Lomas (far left, Rangoon Jail PoW survivor), Tom O'Donohue (standing beneath the horse's front legs, died that night), Edward Stanley (to O'Donohue's left, beneath the horse's belly, died that night), and Jack King (fifth from right, died in Lomas's arms in Rangoon Jail on 31 March 1945). (*W. Kirkness*)

1
2
3
4
5
6
7
8
9
10
11
12
13
14
15
16
17
18
19
20

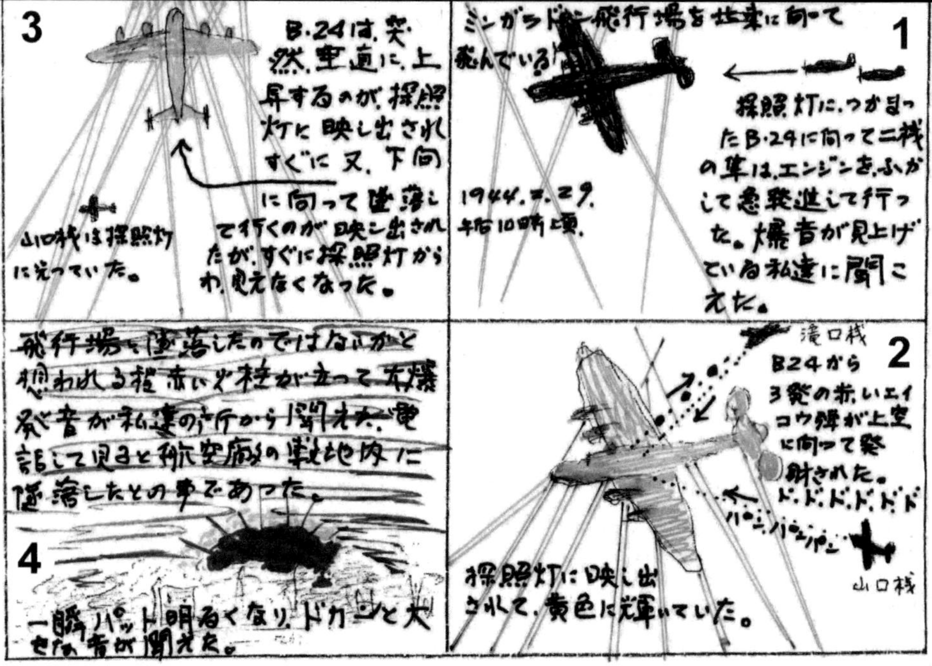

Above: Japanese eyewitness Norikazu Ohba drew sequential illustrations depicting the loss of BZ962, *Daring Diana,* one of two Liberators from 159 Squadron shot down on 29 February 1944 by 204th *Sentai* Oscar fighter aces Bunichi Yamaguchi and Hiroshi Takiguchi. Bill flew on this op. All nine of BZ962's crew died. Frame No. 1: Two Oscars trail the Liberator illuminated by searchlights. Frame No. 2: The fighters attack from the rear. Glowing tracer fire to and from the Liberator is visible. Frame No. 3: The Liberator stalls out, nose up. One fighter flies through the searchlight beams. Frame No. 4: A massive explosion lights up the night sky as the Liberator crashes. (*M. Poole*)

Below: Bill's nose art rendering of *Erotic Edna*, painted onto the port forward fuselage of EV843, his Mk VI Liberator on fourteen ops in 1944. Following battle damage and Willy Kirby's death, EV843 crash landed at Chittagong on 2 April 1944. (*W. Kirkness*)

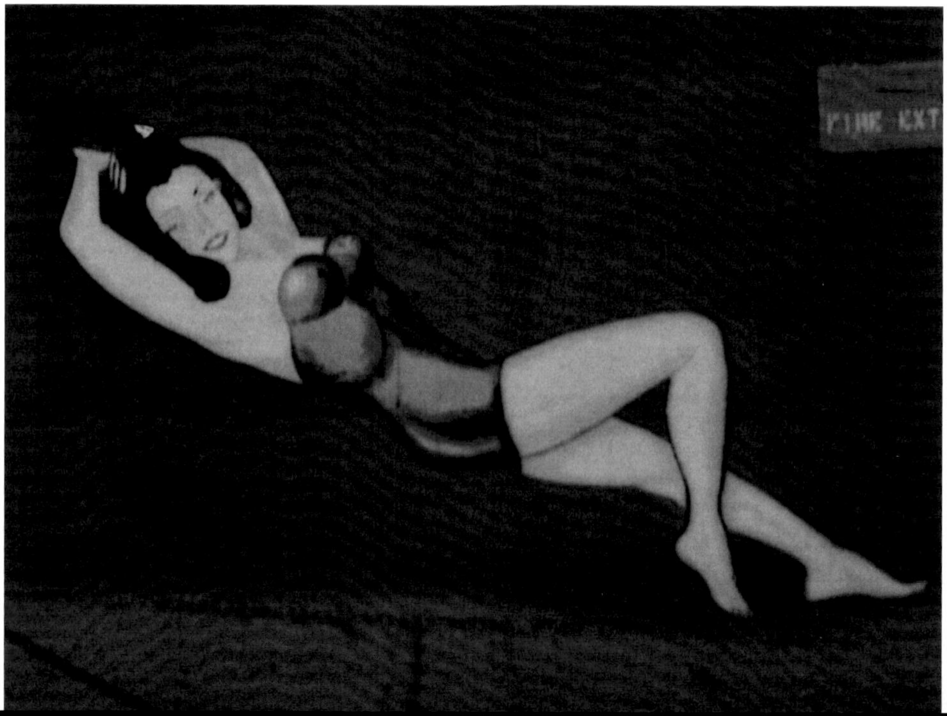

Above: On 1–2 April 1944, 159 Squadron Mk VI Liberator EV870, like Bill's EV843 and the squadron's BZ960, was attacked by a fighter over Rangoon. Despite EV870's violent crash landing at RAF Alipore in Calcutta, short of 159 Squadron's base at Dhubalia, there was no fire. All nine crewmen survived the fighter attack and prang. (*M. Poole*)

Below: RAF Salbani, 26 February 1944, four months after 159 Squadron moved to nearby Digri. The white arrow at lower left points north. The 2,000-yard-long main runway, aligned at headings of 65° and 245°, is the darker-toned of the two landing surfaces. On a narrower marshalling strip at lower left, 355 Squadron Liberators are being prepped for that evening's op to bomb Zayatkwin aerodrome in Burma. (*M. Poole*)

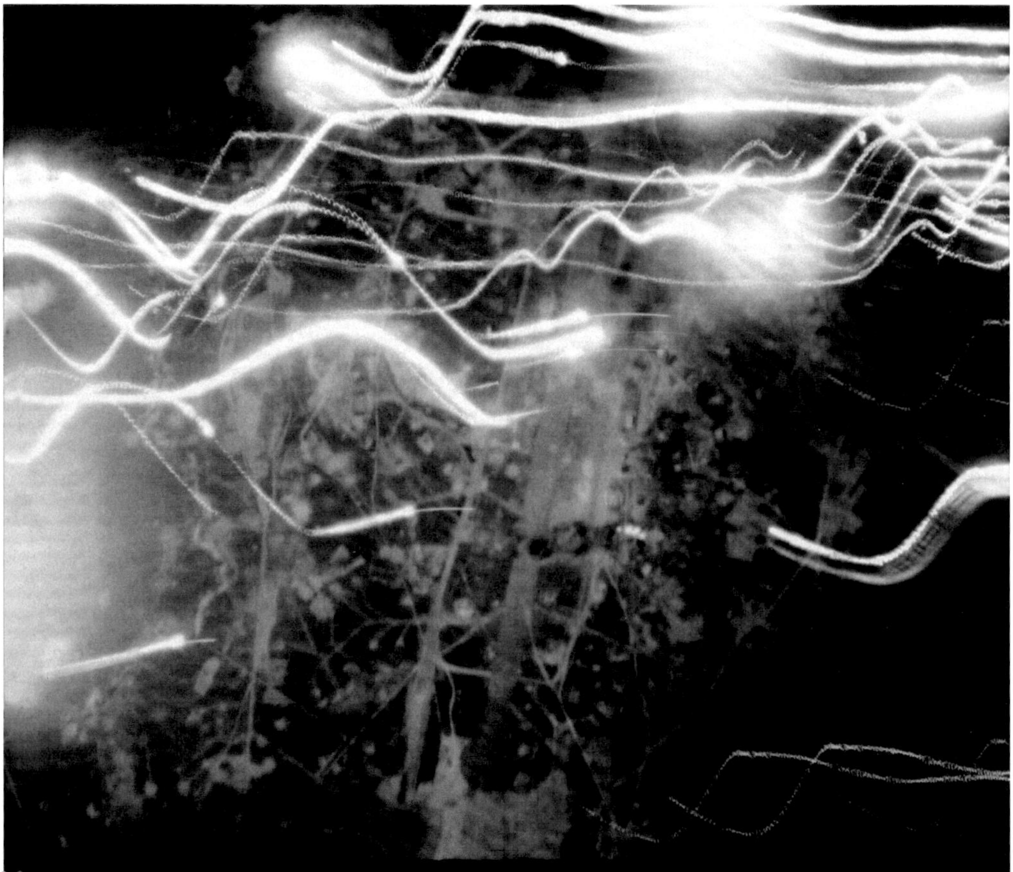

Opposite above: RAF Digri, 26 February 1944. The northern end of the darker-toned 2,000-yard-long main runway, aligned at headings of 156° and 336°, intersects a marshalling strip, upon which can be seen eleven parked Liberators being prepped for that evening's op to bomb Mingaladon aerodrome in Burma. Bill's crew did not participate on this sortie. (*M. Poole*)

Opposite below: This strike photo was taken from 159 Squadron Mk III Liberator BZ897 on 5–6 February 1944, the second successive night the squadron bombed this target, Heho aerodrome in Burma. The aircraft's bombs are seen exploding across the main runway below the centre of the image. Bill's crew successfully attacked Heho the night before, but their Liberator, EV843, was scrubbed from the second night's op. He flew on ops to Heho three times on 159 Squadron, including once when clouds obscured the target; on that op, his crew bombed an alternate target. (*M. Poole*)

Above: Rangoon's central railway station on 12 December 1944. Bill twice flew on 159 Squadron ops to attack this target. (*M. Poole*)

Above: Botataung Wharves, Rangoon, on 12 December 1944. Warehouse roof damage from Allied bombing raids is evident. (*M. Poole*)

Opposite: On the night of 31 January–1 February 1944, 159 Squadron Mk III Liberator BZ898 bombed Rangoon's Mahlwagon marshalling yards due to cloud cover obscuring Mingaladon aerodrome, the primary target. Annotated on BZ898's bomb strike photo is its stick of bombs exploding in a line across the tracks, just missing the roundhouse. Bill twice flew on ops to Mahlwagon. (*M. Poole*)

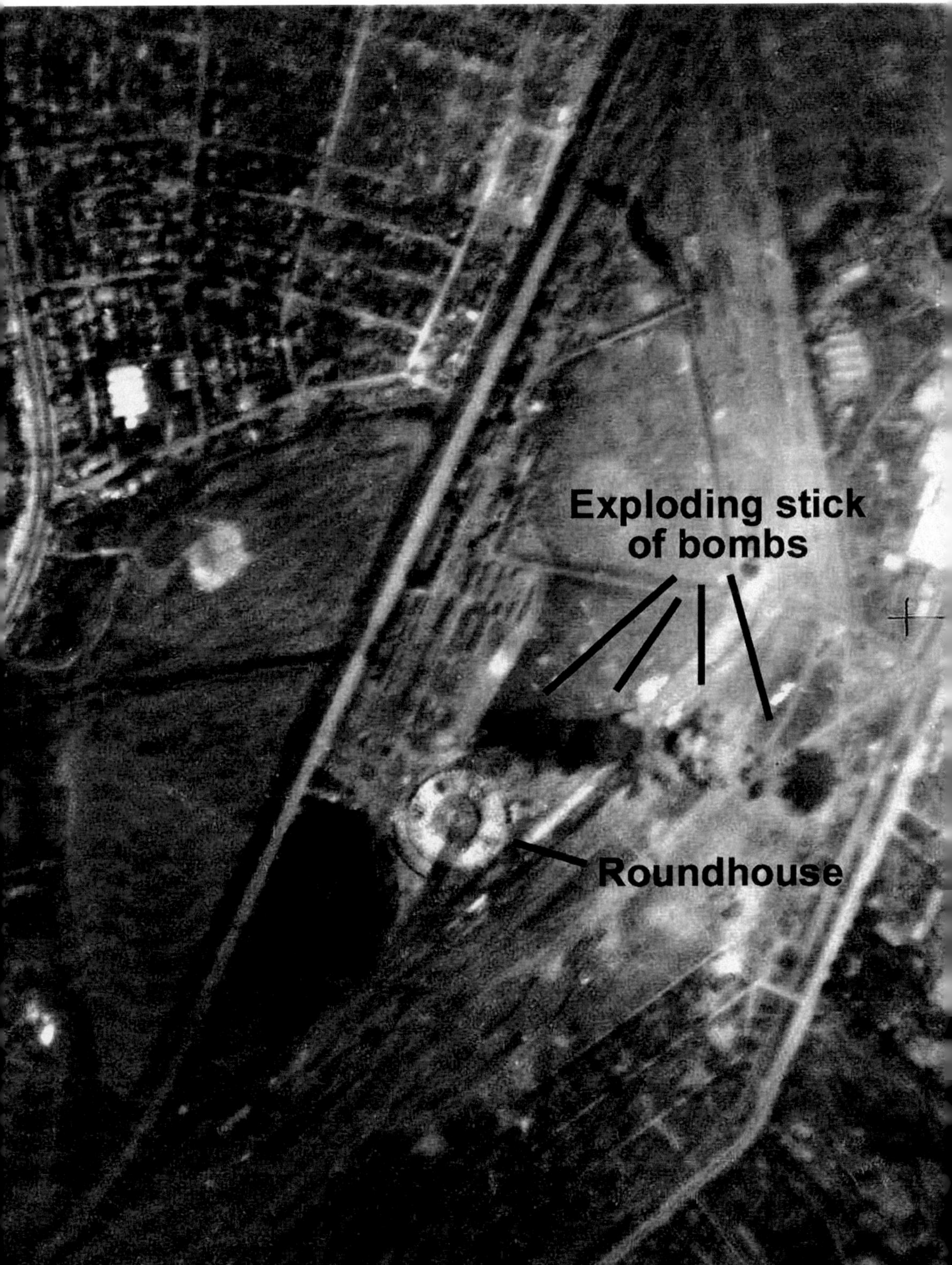
Exploding stick
of bombs
Roundhouse

Opposite: Mahlwagon marshalling yards following a daylight raid by American B-29 Superfortresses on 3 November 1944. (*M. Poole*)

Above: Mingaladon aerodrome, just north of Rangoon, on 12 December 1944. Twice Bill flew on ops to Mingaladon, but clouds were encountered each time. On the first visit, Harry Hartshorn was able to sight the target through a hole in the clouds and release bombs, but on the second sortie, Bill's crew abandoned Mingaladon and bombed the secondary target instead. (*M. Poole*)

A photo recon image looking northward away from the northern environs of Rangoon on 11 April 1944; central Rangoon is to the south. The runways of Mingaladon aerodrome appear as the bright scars below the propeller of the Lockheed F-5's port engine. (*M. Poole*)

A photo recon image looking south across Rangoon on 5 May 1944. The port engine of the Lockheed F-4 is visible in this oblique view. (*US National Archives and Records Administration*)

Arnie Bridgman's grave marker in Madras War Cemetery, Chennai, India. He died with thirteen others in a mid-air collision over India on 26 July 1945. (*J. Pillarisetti*)

sundry other tradecrafts provided more entertainment than the cinema, and some of the work we saw was outstanding. Harry paid one craftsman to send a carved coffee table home to Canada and was highly delighted months later to receive a letter from home stating that it had arrived undamaged.

On a second-hand stall, I spotted a portable gramophone at a reasonable price and bought it, together with some records of popular music. Later, we discovered that HMV records were manufactured in Calcutta, and over a period, we accumulated quite an impressive collection with which to entertain in the Sergeants' Mess.

Returning to camp was not something we relished, but we did so the next day and settled down once again to the boring routine of camp life. A subtle change was palpable; we now felt a little less depressed than previously, knowing that there was another side to life in India, where entertainment was available even if it was expensive.

11

The 1943 Monsoon Season Continues

My Fifth Op: Mandalay Marshalling Yards, 12–13 June 1943

Finding that we were on the battle order for the night of 12–13 June, we flew a one-hour air test with Fg Off. Evans in the morning of the 12th to gauge the preparedness of Liberator AL597. Another Liberator was airborne on a training flight, as well.

Looking at the other aircraft from the beam hatch, I remarked on how elegant it appeared in the air, totally different from the ugly duckling look it had on the ground. Perhaps the large twin fin and rudder units were the only discordant notes, their shapes more functional than elegant, but otherwise the bomber looked right in the air from its glazed nose to the rear turret.

On the upcoming op, John would be in the second pilot's seat. Harry would not be joining us, replaced, instead, by a sprog navigator in Plt Off. W. J. Charlton and an experienced screen navigator, Plt Off. K. P. Barton, to oversee him. I would be on the wireless and Arnie would be parked in his mid-upper turret. Fred would return to his preferred rear turret, relegating Willy back to a beam gun; only once more would Willy take the rear guns on an op when Fred manned a beam gun.

Additionally, Sgt C. J. Nicholls joined the crew as 2nd W/op/AG, meaning that he would spell me on the wireless, if need be, but primarily he would take on beam gunner duties. Nicholls proved to be a loyal, proficient and amiable crewmate on twenty-three ops, from 12–13 June 1943 through to the beginning of March 1944.

The Evans crew attended the midday briefing on 12 June with mixed feelings. Unlike our last solo op to Rangoon, this time we were to join two other 159 Squadron Liberators to attack the marshalling yards at Mandalay, Burma. We were given strict orders not to drop any bombs inside the walls of the moated Fort Dufferin, as the local bigwig, friendly to the British, lived there. This historic complex had been constructed as Mandalay Palace, the seat of government and residence of the Burmese king, but the broad site had been transformed by the British into a military fort in the 1880s, during the Third Anglo-Burmese War. Now it was in Japanese hands.

We would also be carrying a special incendiary container designed by the NCO in charge of armourers, Albert 'Chiefy' Warren. The 'Warren Coffin', as it was named, occupied one side of the bomb bay and held 474 incendiary bombs weighing four pounds each. Previously, incendiary containers, sitting on the catwalk, had to be physically kicked out of the bomb bay, but now the Warren Coffin, clipped into the bomb racks, allowed all incendiaries to be released by the bomb aimer up front in the nose.

Our Liberator, AL597, also carried six 500-lb bombs and two 250-lb bombs, and so we hoped to make quite an impression on the second largest town in Burma, used as a base by the Japanese. Photo reconnaissance had revealed more than the usual amount of traffic in the marshalling yards.

The briefing was similar to the previous two that we had attended. On our third op as a crew over Burma, we were not as apprehensive as on our earlier raids, though we still suffered from the slight gut-tightening that seemed to be an unavoidable part of every briefing. The crew would have felt much less secure had we been informed that the last aircraft to carry Chiefy Warren's coffin had failed to return.

Lacking enthusiasm at the prospects for our upcoming op, none of the crew slept that afternoon, as we were supposed to do, according to the powers that dictated these matters. Instead, the time was spent writing letters, an occupation we would all typically indulge in prior to an op. As Fred observed once, 'It's a sort of insurance. If I didn't write, I bet I'd cop it, and my mum would never forgive me.'

Entering the Mess for the evening meal, we encountered the usual half-envious, half-pitying glances from other airmen in the room who were not scheduled to fly. The envy was because we were getting one more trip in our logbooks, and the pity was in case we, still a sprog crew, did not return to fill in the aforementioned logbooks. The bacon-and-eggs ritual for a crew on ops was a welcome relief from the terrible soya links and dehydrated vegetables, but the food would have been more enjoyable had the trip been behind us instead of in the immediate future.

The waiting finally came to an end with the arrival of the gharry, which took the crew and the inevitable well-wishers to the Flights. There, Fg Off. Evans and John were already waiting. As usual, Willy fired up the APU after I had failed once again, and at 5.55 p.m., our heavily loaded AL597 climbed slowly away from Salbani on a heading towards our objective, Mandalay.

'Bet Rudyard Kipling never envisaged this way when he wrote "The Road to Mandalay",' piped Fred from the rear turret.

'He hadn't smelled your feet,' answered Willy. 'He'd have sworn you had marched there all the way in the same pair of socks.'

Willy proceeded to sing the Kipling ballad over the intercom. As the likelihood of Japanese attacks was almost nil in the early part of the trip, there was usually some acceptable banter on the part of the crewmen in the rear of the aircraft.

Unfortunately, I was stuck with my radio duties and could not participate. Having to maintain radio silence and merely listen out for any diversion was my tedious chore, and I filled the time reading novels and, every so often, obtaining radio bearings for the navigator until we passed out of range.

The hypnotic effect of the engines had lulled me into a trance, and I was startled when the navigator thumped me in the back and pointed to his earphones. I switched to the intercom in time to hear the skipper tell the navigator to go forward to the bomb aimer's compartment as the target area was approaching.

I was then told to go sit on the catwalk. 'Wireless operator,' spoke the skipper, 'let me know immediately if there are any snags with that incendiary container, and you can now remove the horseshoes.'

'Aye aye, skipper,' I replied. To Plt Off. Charlton, our young navigator, I made a request, which sounded more like a demand: 'Wait till I give you the word before you open the bloody bomb doors. I was nearly dropped out on the last trip.'

There was a slight pause before Plt Off. Charlton answered. 'Windy bugger,' he then mumbled.

I moved back to the bomb bay to perform my tasks. After removal, the horseshoes hung from the roof of the bomb bay on Bowden cables, and although the pistol in the nose of a bomb required a hefty clout to detonate, I did not like to see the dangling horseshoes bouncing against the casings of the bombs.

After I informed the navigator that I was safely seated, the bomb doors slid open. Flares that Willy had pushed out of the chute revealed the target quite noticeably, like a clear black and white photograph. Fort Dufferin, which we had been warned to avoid damaging, stood out distinctly with its great walled moat, and the target itself, the marshalling yards, was clearly visible with the railway lines reflecting the light of the flares.

The flak seemed haphazard and inaccurate. As the navigator counted off the seconds and minor course corrections were made by the skipper, we were nicely aligned to make a perfect drop at 8,500 feet. All the bombs were released in one stick, including the incendiaries. The suddenness of the bomb load's departure from the aircraft startled me.

Inquisitively, I went through the bomb bay to join Willy and C. J. Nicholls at the beam guns, where the views were both exciting and mesmerising.

As the Liberator had been equipped with a camera, Willy prepared to drop a one million-candlepower photoflash down the flare chute while the aircraft was still on the same course immediately after the bombs were released. He seemed reluctant to do this for some reason, and on being quizzed by me, he explained that he had seen an aircraft come back after a night exercise while at his Operational Training Unit with a huge hole in the side and a dead beam gunner as a result of a photoflash exploding in the flare chute.

These flashes exploded with a terrific bang that could be clearly heard inside the Liberator. It was agreed between the two of us that from this point forward I would drop them if duties allowed, as Willy, being nervous with these large pyrotechnics, was more likely to make an error.

Always wary of the big fireworks, I gave the photoflash a hefty shove down the chute. The procedure for releasing one was simple. After connecting the Bowden cable to the fuse, I removed the safety pin and pushed the flash down the chute at the appropriate moment. The flash's weight pulled it free of the cable, activating the short-delay fuse. Following a set time interval, a loud boom was heard as the photoflash detonated below us, and a resulting brilliant flash illuminated the evidence of bomb blasts and damage in the target area. The brilliance of the photoflash explosion triggered the camera, pointing downward, and an image was exposed for post-op analysis.

Our Liberator's bombs burst across the southern end of the marshalling yards. The combined ordnance of the three attacking Liberators resulted in a carpet of fire across the yards, punctuated at frequent intervals by explosions that seemed to energise the fires even more. The sight was as if some hideous living thing was devouring itself with its own fury. The return to base was quiet, and the aircraft landed at 2.55 a.m., after nine hours in the air.

One interested member of the interrogation squad at debriefing was Chiefy Warren, eager to hear how his baby had performed. He was thrilled when the Camera Section told him he could have a copy of the bomb strike photo as a souvenir. The print showed a mass of wavy white lines caused by the incendiaries, and it was obvious that his invention had been a grand success. Furthermore, the flash revealed sufficient detail to prove that the target had been well and truly clobbered.

Heard in the Sergeants' Mess, the BBC London radio service later announced, 'Long range bombers were operating in full strength over Burma last night.' There were ironic shouts of 'Three!' among the men in the Mess, by now familiar with the nuances of such announcements. Had the announcer declared only 'operating in strength over Burma,' the cry would have been 'Two!' Had he stated only 'operating over Burma,' the 159 Squadron airmen would have roared 'One!'

Although only my third combat flight with 159 Squadron, the op just completed counted as the fifth of my tour because of the two-operation credit for the April flights from the UK to Cairo. I entered a summary of this sortie in my logbook as such: 'OP #5. MANDALAY. WARREN "COFFIN" CARRIED—GOOD RESULTS. D. C. O.' 'D. C. O.' stood for duty carried out.

I would not fly another op until October.

June Continues and More Liberators Arrive at Salbani

The month of June saw the delivery of AL541, another Mk II Liberator, increasing the squadron's inventory of functioning bombers to four. AL541 was immediately used for flying activities.

With the arrival of the prolonged monsoon season, 159 Squadron attempted only five additional ops—two more in June (employing just three Libs, in total) and three in July (utilising only five aircraft, in total)—until flights commenced with regularity again with improved flying weather in early October. In fact, no ops whatsoever were attempted by the squadron in August and September.

Only three more sorties involved any of my crew, but not me, during this frustrating period. The first was on the night of 16–17 June, when John, Arnie, Fred, and C. J. Nicholls flew with Fg Off. Jack Evans and three other airmen—Plt Off. W. J. Charlton once again (navigator), FS R. J. Irving (wireless operator), and Sgt A. Webb (on a beam gun)—on their final June op. Aboard AL550, the crew set off from Salbani at 9 p.m. to bomb Toungoo aerodrome in Burma, but heavy cloud over the target spoiled the effort. Instead, they reluctantly opted for a secondary target, Myanaung railway station, which was bombed with some visible success.

Then, in the minute after midnight on 22 July, John, Arnie, Fred, Willy, and C. J. Nicholls were airborne on another op with Fg Off. Evans as captain, plus two other airmen (Plt Off. W. J. Charlton a third and final time as the crew's navigator and Flt Lt F. E. Ashworth as an air gunner), this time to Sedan, Burma. A greenish white fire was observed in the target area. What made this op most unusual was the fact that Arnie flew as the wireless operator, not as an air gunner.

Finally, in the last week of July, John was tapped to fly as second pilot to FS M. R. Davison on a raid to Sagaing, Burma, on the banks of the mighty Irrawaddy River and close to Mandalay, but again, bad weather was a formidable foe. Severe icing conditions affected two engines, one of which cut completely for twenty minutes. Given circumstances not in their favour, they opted to bomb a secondary target, Monywa, also in Burma. That was the extent of operational flying for any of my crewmates until October.

A New Mk III Liberator Arrives on the Squadron

As aircrews were sitting outside the Flight Office one dull morning, 20 July, the noise of aircraft engines alerted us. The sound did not seem like that of a Liberator, but the lone aircraft that descended through the clouds was, in fact, a Liberator. It sported the same colours as the American bombers that had landed at Salbani a month earlier—olive drab, except for grey undersides.

Our spirits were lifted when the aircraft was directed to a dispersal pen, and, closer now, RAF roundels were observed on the fuselage. It was a Mk III Liberator, an improvement over our workhorse Mk IIs. To our great surprise, we were told that this bomber was to be taken on strength on 159 Squadron, adding a brand-new Liberator to our arsenal.

In the Sergeants' Mess that evening, the newcomers aboard the Liberator, BZ833, were pumped for information on things back in Blighty.When informed of the shortages and hardships our loved ones back home were enduring, we began seeing our soya links in a different, somewhat less vile hue. The recent arrivals, however, took one taste of the soya links and rejected them outright.

One of the new airmen asked the same question John had posed upon our arrival at Salbani: 'Where are all the Libs?' With malicious glee, Willy explained the scarcity of aircraft and then repeated what we had heard on our first day here: 'Welcome to the Forgotten Air Force.'

In truth, there were finally signs that we would be a forgotten force no longer. By the end of July, the squadron's strength was up to nine flyable aircraft, including AL560, which had been swanning around the Middle East with mechanical problems since April. Now we had our first Mk III.

The Continuing Monsoon

Salbani in the 1943 monsoon season was still a trial for the men of 159 Squadron. With a paucity of entertainment options available, no white or Anglo-Indian women to even gawk at, precious little flying possible, continued gut-wrenching food options, and mildew and critters everywhere, it was no surprise that our morale took a tumble during the monsoon season. Most of the flying was of the less-exhilarating training variety, but we still accepted any flying as a monotony-busting opportunity.

In the battle against complacency and boredom, activities such as lectures and a debating society were initiated on the squadron. Every little bit helped to ease our tedium and to stimulate minds. Sports proved to be beneficial, especially football and darts. The Canadians, keen on baseball, worked to organise games played with a softball, and the groundwork for cricket and hockey competitions was established.

Football, not surprisingly, was the most invigorating of the sporting activities. The eight-team 'Monsoon League' was formed from the various sections: Maintenance, Armoury, Headquarters, Motor Transport, 'A' Flight aircrew, 'A' Flight ground crew, 'B' Flight aircrew, and 'B' Flight ground crew. One match was played every three days.

Fred was considered an excellent back and Arnie a clever halfback. They were chosen to play for 'B' Flight aircrew, along with Willy, but the team was beaten by 'A' Flight ground crew in the league final in a match that aroused all of the excitement of a Wembley FA Cup final.

A selection of the best players comprised a unified 159 Squadron squad, which competed against seven other units, winning all but one game. A charity match was even played versus the combined Kharagpur RAF team; we won four goals to one.

For cricket matches, a concrete strip had been laid at Salbani and matting wicket obtained for a covering, and it was hoped that play would commence at the end of the monsoon. My prowess as a slow left-hand bowler had to wait.

Ben was turning out to be better than average at darts. The CO, Wg Cdr Boffee, kindly presented a cup and medals for the inter-section darts competition. In the first competition, the cup was won by the Motor Transport 'A' team. So, despite the impact of the monsoon season upon efforts to bomb a much-hated enemy, the squadron was not allowed to roll over into dormancy during this period.

The most intriguing events during the monsoon were the evening thunderstorms, which often occurred at about the same time every day, around 6 p.m., just as the members of the Sergeants' Mess were preparing for the repulsive evening meal.

The outriders of the storm appeared as black banks of cloud intermittently lit up from within by vivid sheet lightning. As they rapidly approached, we heard the thunder's deep, steady rumble increasing in volume, until, when right overhead, it was impossible to comprehend speech. One could even read by the lightning.

The extremely heavy rain had one beneficial result. The insects disappeared for a time, but as the storms only lasted for an hour on average, the respite was short but welcome, nevertheless.

It was amusing to see the state of the pith helmets, better known as topees, with which most of us were equipped. They generally were valued in both brilliant sunshine and torrential downpours. Some, however, had no brims and others no tops, while yet others appeared to be shrinking, having been eaten by the termites.

The issue of Australian-type bush hats was welcomed by all as an alternative to topees. At first, all bush hats were more or less regulation pattern. Fred, pleased with his hat, got the *dhobi wallah* to press the brim, but Willy, true to form, soon was seen wearing something which resembled a limp Yorkshire pudding.

Less well-received, another piece of equipment issued to the aircrew disappeared quietly soon after its introduction. Known as a survival suit, it resembled a bright green boiler overall with a peaked cap similar to ones worn by the Japanese and a flap to protect the neck from the sun. This flap was of the same green material but was lined with a brilliant red cloth for some unknown reason. The suit had many pockets and also loops to which objects could be fastened, and the entire ensemble was completed by a vicious-looking bladed *panga*, presumably to hack through the jungle should we be fortunate enough to survive being shot down. The suits soon proved unpopular, as the loops caught on any projection inside the bomber, and we sweated terribly in them while awaiting take-off.

Ben and I enlivened the afternoons during the monsoon season by doing a double act as sand dancers, wearing shorts, a towel as a turban and little else. Some of our act would never have passed the censor in Britain, but our antics raised a laugh thousands of miles away among men stuck in rural West Bengal, India.

Occasionally, when pretending to be two American Wild West desperados having a shootout, we would each wear our Irvin trousers woolly side out, a towel as a neckerchief, an Aussie bush hat, and a low-slung .38-inch Smith and Wesson revolver. Ben used to die most realistically, but the game came to an abrupt end one day when Ben fired off a round inadvertently left in his revolver and almost blasted me to an early grave.

The laughter which had been filling the *basha* was replaced instantly by a hush as all realised what might have happened. Ben had a look of dismay on his face which did not fit in at all well with his pseudo-Western apparel, so much so that I burst out laughing at the now-woebegone appearance of the tough gunslinger of a moment ago.

'Best of three, Ben?' I chuckled, but Ben was rattled and proceeded to remove his gun and carefully lock it away in his tin trunk. Divesting himself of his comical garb, he left the hut without a word and wandered off for a walk in the scrub which surrounded the camp.

I made as if to follow, but Arnie stopped me. 'Leave him,' he advised. 'Let him calm down in his own way.' I paused, nodded and lay down on my charpoy.

In time, Ben returned, looked straight at me and quietly spoke. 'Sorry,' he said, 'it's just as well I'm a lousy shot.' The episode was closed.

The Crash of AL560: 12 August 1943

On the morning of 12 August, Liberator AL560 was scheduled to be flown on a bombing practice exercise skippered by an experienced Canadian pilot, Fg Off. Stan Pettingale. Aboard were six other airmen plus one passenger, ground crewman LAC David Cooper, who regarded AL560 as his baby and wanted to display his confidence by flying in her.

Almost immediately after take-off the port inner engine was shut down and the propeller feathered. No smoke was visible. Having made a circuit in order to get down quickly on three engines, Fg Off. Pettingale, approaching the runway much too fast, misjudged the landing and had to overshoot. Gaining a little height, he went around again on a more sedate circuit and seemed to be setting up for a good landing.

Something terribly wrong was evident. The Liberator gradually sank in a nose-up attitude, stalled far short of the runway, impacted a tree and came to rest in a paddy field about a mile and a half from the aerodrome.

The drama sickened all who witnessed the tragedy. The forward fuselage was shattered, and six bodies were strewn on the ground. It seemed that there could be no survivors, but the rear gunner, FS Gristwood, though injured in his turret, was the miraculous exception. He was even removed from the dangerously ill list at the Station Sick Quarters the following day. The funeral for the six victims was held at noon on the 13th at Midnapore Cemetery, south of Salbani.

Stan Pettingale had been a popular member of the squadron and was particularly well-known to our crew, having been the pilot who converted John to flying the Halifax the previous December back at Lyneham.

AL560 had been with 159 Squadron since 1942 in the Middle East, and one experienced pilot, John Musgrave, then a flying officer, considered it a 'wretched machine' with gremlins that confounded the best attempts by the ground crews to eliminate them. The circumstances leading to the engine malfunction on 12 August, sadly, went undiscovered.

Apart from the horror of the crash, many of the aircrew were disgusted for another practical reason. The addition of one more aircraft would have enabled us to get our ops in that little bit quicker. At the rate we were going, the length of the tour seemed eternal. Within a short time, though, things changed rapidly for the better.

More Mk III Liberators Arrive at Salbani: Late August 1943

Between 20 and 28 August, seven more Mk III Liberators were delivered to Salbani, joining BZ833, which had arrived a month earlier. America's industrial juggernaut was producing new Liberator bombers at a record pace now. Finally, 'The Forgotten Air Force' was expanding and slowly, but surely, ramping up its efforts at taking the war to the Japanese with an air armada long in the planning stages. Two more of the older Mk IIs also joined the squadron in August.

Not all the reinforcement crews and aircraft stayed with 159 Squadron; some went to form the nucleus of 1584 Conversion Unit also at Salbani, which later evolved into 1673 Heavy Conversion Unit. The unit's role—essential in supporting ever-expanding RAF Liberator ops—was to transition newly arrived airmen from other aircraft, even four-engined bombers like the Halifax, onto the Liberator and to acclimatise them to Far East flying conditions, protocol and tactics.

The Mk IIIs were different in many ways from their predecessor Mk IIs. Outwardly, they were similar in general appearance and dimensions with the thin Davis wing shoulder-mounted high on the fuselage, the graceful greenhouse nose, the boxy and roomy fuselage, and the twin oval fin and rudder units.

Three dramatic changes, however, were readily apparent. First, there was a major turret upgrade. The Mk II's Boulton Paul mid-upper turret, with its four .303-inch pop-guns, poked out of the fuselage at a point closely in-line with the trailing edge of the wings. The Mk III's Martin mid-upper turret, on the other hand, held twin .5-inch machine guns, providing far more punch than the .303-inch Brownings. Additionally, the new mid-upper turret was moved forward, aligned more or less with the engines and just behind the flight deck, offering a superior field of fire.

The second obvious change was in the beam gun setups. On each side of the Mk II fuselage, twin .303-inch Brownings protruded through the closed beam hatch. To sight the intended target, the gunner sat or stood directly in front of a small window built into the beam hatch, but offset just to the right of the side-by-side guns; he was not directly in front of the guns. In the Mk III, however, the beam hatch, hinged at the top and opened upwards and inwards, allowed a single .5-inch Browning to be positioned at bottom centre of the hatch. Standing directly behind the 50-calibre weapon at a large open window, the gunner's visibility and aiming capabilities were vastly improved over the limiting Mk II setup. The punch of a .5-inch weapon was a powerful upgrade from the old .303-inch guns.

The third obvious change in appearance, besides paint scheme, was in the engine cowlings. To accommodate added turbo-superchargers, each redesigned cowling was now oval in its cross-section shape, not circular as on the Mk II Liberator. Each Mk III engine sported two intakes, one on either side of the engine, to supply air to the turbo-supercharger (left side, as viewed from the front) and intercooler (right side). The supercharged engines gave the Liberator the advantage of a greater service ceiling; the higher the Lib flew, the better the odds of survival over enemy territory.

With new engines came new propellers. The long-hub Curtiss Electric props were gone, replaced by short-hub Hamilton Standard hydraulic props. The rear firepower in the Mk III was still a Boulton Paul power turret with four .303-inch Brownings, but all other guns were 50-calibre weapons.

The intercom system of the Mk III was a big improvement. A throat mike replaced the microphone previously located in the oxygen mask, and headphones were now used. No longer would we need to wear confining, uncomfortable flying helmets, except in the remaining Mk IIs.

The arrival of the new aircraft resulted in a marked improvement in morale on the squadron, even though the relentless monsoon conditions had yet to abate. We also raised the tempo of our work, as the wireless operators had to familiarise themselves with the new Westinghouse transmitters and receivers which, although complicated at first sight, turned out to be reasonably simple to tune and operate. Harry remarked that this was a good thing, as his crew's first wireless operator—me, of course—was a simple sod.

Armourers instructed the air gunners in the use of the new American mid-upper turrets, to which Willy displayed a strong aversion, much preferring the Boulton Paul ones of the Lib IIs. The 50-calibre machine guns, however, were warmly welcomed by most as the limited range of the .303-inch Browning was a great handicap when countering a Japanese night fighter equipped with 12.7-mm cannon.

All aircrew were required to fire the new gun on the ground. This caused our crew's two pure air gunners, Willy and Fred, and the two wireless operator/air gunners, Arnie and me, an amount of mild amusement on seeing Harry fall flat on his backside the first time he had a go with a swivel-mounted new weapon.

The 50-calibre Browning's rate of fire was much slower than that of our previous .303-inch guns. The new .5-inch weapons fired with a steady 'chunk, chunk, chunk, chunk', whereas our previous guns made a noise similar to someone tearing a piece of calico, but there was no doubting the .5-inch Browning's greater destructive power and superior range.

The Mk III improvement I most welcomed was connected with starting the APU. Some of the new aircraft still had a cord start, but the later production Mk III models had an electric self-starter. On the older models, Willy would stand quietly near the bomb bay, and if he heard fluently uttered bad language, his face took on a beatific smile. Timing things with precision, he would duck under the flight deck and push me aside, and with one mighty pull, he would have the little two-stroke purring away like an amiable cat. If, however, the machine we were allocated had an electric self-starter, I would get it going and give Willy the old two-fingered sign of derision.

Willy never seemed to resent the gesture, but I got my comeuppance one day after the electric self-starter-equipped APU engine refused to fire for me. Then, Willy came forward and replaced the plug lead he had disconnected earlier, whereupon the machine fired instantly. Obviously pleased with himself, he returned my two-fingered greeting with interest and went to his position in the rear of the aircraft.

Flying the new Mk IIIs proceeded apace. John expressed satisfaction with these kites, from his pilot's perspective, although he thought they seemed to fly slightly tail-down and, being heavier than the previous Mk II mounts, were a bit of a handful on landing.

Air-Sea Rescue of a Wellington Crew: 8 September 1943

A flying exercise during the 1943 monsoon season turned out to be one of my most satisfying trips of the period. The flight, on 8 September aboard AL597, involved firing at a target seaward of the notorious Sundarbans, at the head of the Bay of Bengal.

During this flight, I nudged Harry in the ribs while sitting at the wireless table reading an amusing paperback by Eric Knight entitled *The Flying Yorkshireman*, about a man who discovered he could levitate. Grinning, I pointed first to myself and then to the title, before quipping to Harry, 'A flying Yorkshireman reading *The Flying Yorkshireman*!' Harry responded by holding his nose and pointing the other hand thumb-down.

As this piece of mild horseplay was playing out, I was surprised to hear our call sign being transmitted by the base. Replying, I was instructed to stand by for a message. Without turning in my seat, I reached behind and thumped Harry with urgency as the Morse Code came in fairly swiftly. Harry had already placed the code machine on his table and was waiting for the complete message before decoding. Acknowledging receipt of the lengthy message, I swung round and placed my logbook on Harry's table to enable us to work together more quickly.

As the messages came in five-figure groups, when decoded, Harry and I were confronted by what appeared to be a jumble of gibberish. Fortunately, we had aboard a highly experienced second navigator who quickly sorted the message into sense by reaching for the 'Q' codebook. Harry and I returned embarrassed grins to the more skilled man, who was very forgiving of our ignorance.

Looking thoughtful, the seasoned navigator read the message to the pilot, FS Frederick Collins. 'Navigator to skipper,' he said, 'we are instructed to go to a Dead Reckoning position over the sea and look for a Wimpy which is supposed to have gone down.'

'OK, navigator,' replied the skipper. 'We'll go back to the target we were firing at and set course from there. Let the crew know fifteen minutes before we arrive at the DR position, and we can start searching early in case the position is erroneous.' The intercom went silent as FS Collins swung the aircraft round, returned to the firing range, and then set course for the position given in the message.

The crew was also hushed as we commenced the search. We were all painfully aware that we could be in the position of the downed Wimpy one day, and the thought of the big tiger sharks we had seen on previous flights over the Bay of Bengal made us hope survivors would soon be spotted.

The weather was marginal for a search, with drizzle causing poor visibility and a cloud base of only 800 feet. A sudden shout on the intercom from Willy raised our hopes. 'Beam gunner to skipper. Seen them, about a half-mile away on the port quarter!'

FS Collins executed a steep turn and descended to the wavetops. The dinghy soon came into sight, and as the Liberator passed, Willy dropped a flame float neatly alongside. This made their next run easier as the flame was clearly visible in the grey murk.

We had been circling for about an hour with increasing amounts of frustration as there was little we could do for the two occupants in the dinghy and the one in the water alongside beyond giving them the thumbs-up as we swept past at wavetop height on each run.

Arnie then acted on a bright idea. He went forward to the flight deck and picked up the gallon thermos flask of coffee. Returning aft, he threw it out of the floor hatch on the next pass. It landed about twenty feet from the dinghy. Being half-empty, it floated, and it was hoped the survivors would be able to retrieve it to slake their thirst. As he remarked later, even their awful coffee was better than no drink at all for the three unfortunate men below.

All the time we had been circling, I had been transmitting our call sign slowly to enable anyone, except the Japanese, to home in on us. Consequently, we were all gratified to see a Wellington join us in the circuit of the dinghy. On the Wimpy's arrival, our skipper opened the taps and, still circling, went up through the clouds. This was to enable the ground stations to take an accurate fix on my transmissions.

Getting low on fuel, we took one look below the cloud to ascertain that the Wellington was still there, before returning to base, tired and hungry. The exercise that should have been completed in an hour had stretched beyond seven. Despite the length of the flight, it did not count as an op.

There was a sequel to the trip. Sometime later, on a long weekend in Calcutta, by chance some of the crew met the three rescued airmen, in Firpo's restaurant. The twin-engine 99 Squadron Wimpy, we learned, had lost its port engine one hour after take-off from Jessore aerodrome, bound for a bombing op to Akyab

Island, on the eastern coast of the Bay of Bengal. A night ditching in rough seas was inevitable, despite the best efforts of the crew to lighten the aircraft by jettisoning the bomb load and discarding guns, ammo, and anything else not needed.

Only the skipper, navigator, and wireless operator escaped from the ditched and sinking aircraft; the bomb aimer and rear gunner died. Adding to their ordeal, the three found that their dinghy was gashed and could, at best, only hold two at a time, while the third floated alongside, fearing sharks. Ultimately, on the following day, they were rescued by a launch from No. 226 Air-Sea Rescue Unit after first being spotted by Willy.

The three rescued airmen showed their appreciation at Firpo's by getting us well and truly plastered. Arnie, perhaps seeking some recognition for dropping the thermos to the men, asked if they had managed to retrieve it before it drifted away. The Wellington crewmates exchanged glances with each other. 'Yes,' one of them replied, 'we got it out of the sea, and it was bloody awful!'

Arnie, somewhat deflated, said he thought that they may have been thirsty but felt even more foolish when the three laughed uproariously. 'You silly sod,' teased one of them, 'it was raining all the time!' We gave sheepish smiles. In our eagerness to help, we had forgotten the heavy showers of the monsoon season.

The Prang of BZ838: 25 September 1943

Just after midnight on 25 September an experienced senior pilot, Flt Lt Freddie Stokes, pranged Mk III Liberator BZ838 off the runway on a fourth attempt to land during a night training exercise. Ejected from the cockpit, he suffered a compound fracture of the left lower leg, requiring multiple surgeries. The second pilot, Sgt Tony Johnstone, suffered a punctured eardrum that ended his RAF flying career, while Sgt Denis Stokoe, a beam gunner, received a minor fracture of his left wrist. Given the violence of the crash, it is a wonder that there was no fire and that anyone survived at all; the four other crewmen escaped with only slight cuts and bruises.

Except for the injured pilots, the survivors took a much-appreciated leave to Darjeeling, a glorious hill station in the lower Himalayas, which I had previously visited when seeking a respite from prickly heat.

12

October 1943: Operations Resume

BZ841, with Ben Aboard, Fails to Return: 9–10 October 1943

With the close of September, the long monsoon ordeal came to an end, though storms still occasionally blew through Salbani. Flying was ramped up to take advantage of the return of decent, and ever-dryer, flying weather.

The build-up of Allied forces was becoming more obvious by the day, our own new Libs being just one small example. At the beginning of October, ops were resumed on 159 Squadron exclusively with the new Mk III aircraft; the last Mk II op was 24 July. Ben was still flying as second pilot—a 'second dickie', in RAF parlance—to the well-liked and highly respected Flight Commander on 'B' Flight, Sqn Ldr Louis Massey, but with the arrival of new bombers and new crews, he hoped shortly to have command of his own crew. He had been putting feelers out to Harry and me, and we had greeted his overtures with favourable assents should he be made a skipper. It was not that we were dissatisfied with John, but he was somewhat remote, being in the Officers' Mess.

Also, Ben was proving to be an exceptionally good pilot, yet we knew that he still lacked even our level of combat experience; the op on the night of 9–10 October would be his very first on 159 Squadron.

In early October, I completed a popular nose art commission on the forward fuselage of BZ839: the Walt Disney cartoon elephant Dumbo, wearing a flying helmet with goggles, carrying a bomb in its trunk and accompanied by the words 'DUMBO DELIVERS!' On 9 October, as a memento of my handicraft, I joined Sqn Ldr Massey and crew, including Ben, in a group photo taken with my own Box Brownie camera in front of the artwork. I figured that a few of the men would want a copy of that print to send home to loved ones, and I could hardly wait to send one to my own parents and to Gran, too.

The Massey crew did not fly that night aboard *DUMBO DELIVERS!*; instead, they were assigned BZ841, another Mk III Liberator. It was one of three aircraft sent out by 159 Squadron to attack Mingaladon aerodrome, near Rangoon, Burma.

It had become a ritual for the three-tonner to pull up outside the Sergeants' Mess to take non-flying aircrew up to the strip to watch aircraft departing on ops. The evening of 9 October was no exception. The sight of three Liberators waddling round the perimeter track was reminiscent of so many frumpy ladies out for an evening stroll; we enjoyed finding entertainment in this mundane taxiing. Not lost on us was the fact that Ben and the other lads on the three bombers were engaged in deadly serious business.

With Ben heading out on his first bombing op, John and the crew stood beside the runway to give him a send-off. Looking out of the starboard window, Ben responded to our waves by making the motions of pulling a toilet chain and giving a sweep of his arm as if to indicate what an ill-kempt lot we were. At 6 p.m., with a last wave, he was off with his crew down the runway in a great roar of sound.

When the ground was parched, as was the norm later in the dry season, a Liberator's Twin Wasp engines would make terrific clouds of iron oxide-rich dust. The audience cheering-on the departures of Libs on ops would be coated in a rusty-looking film. On 9 October, however, the soil had not yet dried to such an extreme, and dust was inconsequential.

A former RAF base lost to the Japanese in the early months of the war, Mingaladon was not a popular target. The enemy used it primarily for the protection of Rangoon and also as a staging post for forwarding aircraft to landing grounds and airfields nearer the front. It was well-defended, and recent reports seemed to indicate the use of radar to direct searchlights. Ben, with his penchant for dressing up a good story, would no doubt keep us entertained on the morrow with his description of the raid.

Returning to the Sergeants' Mess for the evening meal, which for a change was some quite palatable fish, the NCOs on our crew shared a few drinks at the bar. After some small talk, we turned in for an early night. The Mess was a quiet place when a raid was on, due to some of its members being away on other business. In this instance, despite the target being relatively hot, no one was unduly apprehensive about the enemy opposition, but the weather always seemed to be at the backs of our minds. Given what we had each witnessed of the fury of the monsoon conditions, this was of no surprise. A Liberator, seemingly a behemoth machine on the ground, was like a tiny feather in the wind if caught in a storm.

To be awakened in the morning by the *char wallah* with a muttered, '*Garum chai, Sahib*,' offering hot tea, was one of the simple luxuries all appreciated. As I swung my legs out of the charpoy and onto the already-warm concrete floor, I was only mildly surprised to see that Ben's mosquito net was still thrown over the top and his sheets unruffled. It was not uncommon for an aircraft to divert to another aerodrome on the way back from an op, for a variety of reasons.

Entering the Mess for breakfast, the unusual hush made me aware that something was wrong. Typically, the dining room was a lively place at breakfast, with members of one crew taking the mickey out of members of another, or the members of one Flight insulting their opposite numbers in the other one. This morning banter was absent, and in its place, there was an uncomfortable quiet, broken only by the tap of a knife or fork on a plate.

Arnie, as confused as the rest of the crew, asked a ground crew sergeant fitter sitting next to him, 'What's up with everybody this morning? Is the grub even worse than usual?'

Without raising his head, the sergeant answered, 'The griff is, Sqn Ldr Massey bought it last night.' The statement, made so baldly, took a moment or two to register with us all, but when it began to sink in we all spoke at once, of diversions to airfields here, there and everywhere, with our minds refusing to accept the awful truth.

Shaking his head, the sergeant held up his hand and immediately the chatter stopped. He spoke again. 'One of the other kites reported seeing a huge explosion in the sky right over the target. Looks like they received a direct hit. At least they wouldn't know anything about it.' Now we knew. Ben, our mate for the past fifteen months, was gone and would not be back.

We joined the rest of the subdued members of the Mess in seeing latecomers for breakfast go through the same awful realisation. An ensuing depression engulfed the squadron; the combat disappearance of one of our crews was the first such loss in six long months.

Although it was obvious that the worst had happened, many eyes kept looking towards the south-east throughout the day, hoping for a miracle which could never happen.

While scrounging through my steel trunk late that morning, I noticed my Box Brownie camera and remembered that its film held an eerie image: the last photo of Ben, with his crew, now dead, and I was also in the image. I knew that the print would forever have special significance to me, not so much as a reminder of my 'DUMBO DELIVERS!' nose art on Liberator BZ939, but more so as a remembrance of a kindred spirit and friend, gone forever with other unfortunate blokes also in the image.

'There, but for the grace of God, go I,' I thought. It struck me that there would now be fewer requests for a print of that image to send home.

Further realisation that Ben was really gone came later in the day when the 'Goon Squad' came to clear his bed space. They were quiet and discreet in their work of removing all of his service kit and placing it in kit bags that they had brought along for the purpose. His personal belongings were listed and dropped into a much smaller bag, which was then tied at the neck, with his name written on a label.

The two RAF service policemen were watched in silence by the members of the hut, who knew that our own belongings could one day be treated in a similar manner. Willy asked, 'What happens to the personal gear?

Without embarrassment, the SP answered, 'Things his family may like are sent to his next of kin. The rest will be auctioned off, and the money raised will be included with any returned belongings.' An uneasy silence again descended upon us. Again, Willy spoke up. 'Will the gear of the other members of the crew…' He lapsed into silence without completing the sentence.

Not unkindly, the SP answered the unfinished question. 'All the personal belongings not deemed fit to return to their families will be auctioned tomorrow night.' He added, 'Officers' gear is auctioned in the Officers' Mess.'

Looking around the hut, he spoke quickly and quietly. 'I hate this bloody job, but if I didn't do it quickly and clinically I'd go round the twist.' Turning to carry the bags and bedding to the 15-cwt gharry outside, he paused at the door. Without looking at us, he observed, 'It's customary to bid generously. Some of their parents may find the money useful.' With these words, he went quietly out to his truck, and we heard it going towards the administration block some distance away.

None of us spoke for some time, as if afraid to say the first word. Fred broke the spell. '*Punkah wallah*,' he shouted. 'Pull that sodding rope. I'll come out there and kick your bloody arse in a minute!' The remark broke the morbid mood of the hut, and normal conversations soon prevailed once again in the room.

Willy caught my eye and indicated to me to follow him outside. Putting on my bush hat, I joined Willy on the veranda. 'Let's go for a walk,' was all Willy said. Sensing that this was Willy's way of wanting a private conversation, I followed the burly gunner into the heat of the afternoon. We walked for some time without speaking, but suddenly Willy pulled up dead and asked, 'How are you going to handle this, Enoch?'

I studied a long time before answering, and when I did, Willy was surprised at the calmness in my voice. 'I reckon they have all been posted to a better unit,' I said.

'You religious or something?' asked Willy in puzzlement.

'No,' I replied, 'but I don't think there's a beginning or end to anything, Willy, so I just put it in my mind that they have all been posted to a unit which is beyond our comprehension, and I leave it at that.'

Willy moved on, and as if speaking to himself, he murmured, 'All wireless ops are crackers. It's all that Morse, all dots and dashes. You all end up dotty.' Amused at his own pun, he chuckled, and with me bringing up the rear, we returned to the billet.

The auction in the Sergeants' Mess started promptly on time the following evening. Outrageous prices were bid for the most mundane objects, while the bar was under constant attack from the thirstier members of the Mess. When the auction was closed, no one was in a fit state to care, as many of the men were inebriated, determined to both give our late friends a good send off and to numb the pain in our minds.

The main tipple was a gin distilled in India under the name 'Carew's Dry Gin', which almost automatically became known as 'Mad Carew's', after the tragic character in the well-known poem 'The Green Eye of the Yellow God' by J. Milton Hayes. When Carew's spirits were available, no one usually touched the stuff as it tasted terrible, but on this evening, the demand for Mad Carew's was intense, and its desired effects were attained.

During a lull in the evening, voices could be heard elsewhere singing a particularly bawdy ballad in harmony. With a wry smile, Arnie remarked, 'I see they're giving Sqn Ldr Massey the same treatment.'

In ones and twos, we staggered off to our charpoys to collapse into oblivion and to awake with heads like buckets but hoping that we could have an easy day. For two crews, including mine, hopes were not realised, however, as ops were laid on for the following night, and the two bombers had to first be air tested.

During the thirty-minute air test aboard BZ840 that morning, I discovered a rather unique aid for a hangover. Testing the oxygen supply at my wireless operator's position, I realised after a short spell of inhaling that my headache had disappeared, and I promptly called up the other crew members to inform them of my discovery. The result, upon landing, was an instruction to the ground crew to top up the oxygen bottles.

My Sixth Op:
Pyinmana Railway Station, 12–13 October 1943

On the full-moon night of 12–13 October, the newly promoted Flt Lt Jack Evans skippered our crew's first op in nearly three months, and our first in a Mk III Lib, BZ840. John was not with us; instead, Sgt F. N. Ellis flew as the co-pilot. Harry, Arnie, Willy, Fred, C. J. Nicholls, and I were aboard in our usual crew positions, joined by Fg Off. K. P. Barton, acting again as a screen navigator; his first op in this role had been way back on 12–13 June when he oversaw sprog navigator Plt Off. W. J. Charlton. Harry had not flown on that op.

This time Harry felt insulted to again be screened by an old bod navigator. Flt Lt Bunny Moffatt had screened Harry on his first op with 159 Squadron back on 13–14 May, but then Harry, deemed competent, had been unscreened on his second op on 22–23 May. Yet it had been a long spell—nearly five months—since Harry's last op. His guess was that the skipper did not truly trust his navigation skills after the monsoon-caused interruption in ops and wanted to bring along Fg Off. Barton for insurance.

Taking off at 6.30 p.m., we all felt a little apprehensive but hoped for the best. Our target was Pyinmana railway station, Burma, which Harry hit right on the button with his precision navigating.

The inaccurate flak caused us little inconvenience, and the op turned out to be our least nerve-wracking to date. On each of two bomb runs bursts were seen in the target area, and some decent fires seemed to be growing in size as we turned away from the target and headed for home.

Liberator BZ840 touched down at 1.58 a.m., seven hours and twenty-eight minutes after take-off. At the debriefing, all agreed that it had been a 'milk run', the common term for an easy trip.

Painting the Nose Art on BZ906

On parade one morning, the crews were informed that from now on each crew was to be allocated its own Mk III aircraft, to be flown on ops whenever possible—but not always, just when maintenance and other issues allowed. With some excitement, John led the rest of us to what would be our own particular Mk III kite, BZ906. It looked elegant in its newness, and on entering the fuselage, smell was the first thing we noticed. Cellulose, leather, rubber, high octane fuel, and other subtler odours of new construction bore no resemblance to the old Mk IIs, particularly AL597, which always seemed to have a faint whiff of vomit.

Looking around and beaming, John exclaimed, 'Better than buying a new car!'

Harry added, 'You could get a lot of new cars for what this cost.' He paused, then added, 'Think I'll get me a car when I get back home.' To most of the crew, the comments held little significance as owning a car was something lads from our backgrounds did not even contemplate.

Climbing out of our new Liberator, we acted like boys with a new toy. Arnie spoke for the rest of us. 'We'll have to give it a name,' he suggested, and, looking at me, he gave an evil grin. 'Now we'll see if you're as good a signwriter as your old man,' he said. This remark was greeted with enthusiasm by the rest of our crew.

Having previously impressed my squadron mates with my popular 'DUMBO DELIVERS!' nose art on BZ839, now I was urged to add artwork to our new Liberator. 'OK, what shall we call it?' asked John.

While John and I were all for regarding the aircraft as a female, the rest of the crew preferred a masculine name, but discussion was cut short by the arrival of the wagon to take us for tiffin, our midday meal.

Going to the noticeboard out of force of habit, we were all surprised to see our names on the ops list for the following night. All thoughts of a name were forgotten for the time being but were revived next morning when we arrived at BZ906, our Lib, to observe that the ground crew had painted a large letter 'A' on the side of the fuselage. This was the unique identification letter for the aircraft; each Liberator had its own letter code.

After some discussion, we agreed that a male name beginning with 'A' should be chosen as a suitable label for our new Liberator. Names were nominated and disregarded, but none seemed to fit the bill until Arnie came up with *Algernon*. 'The bomber,' he quipped, 'does look a bit of a dandy.'

'Sounds a bit poofy,' said Fred. 'What about *Algy*?'

There were murmurs of approval all round, and I became the centre of attention as suggestions for the lettering style and where to paint the name on the fuselage were proposed. Waving a hand airily towards them, and affecting an artistic pose, I smiled faintly and remarked casually, as though given an important commission.

'You peasants can leave it in my capable hands,' I decreed. 'Oh, by the way, do you want an estimate?'

I disappeared under the lot of them, only to emerge from the friendly scrum with a look of mock indignation on my face. 'Just a query, chaps,' I protested, 'just a query.'

All this had been observed by the Liberator's ground crew, who were standing around with big grins on their faces. Besides having our own bomber, we airmen also had our own ground crew for *Algy*, and the relationship of trust formed that day was to prove a great morale booster for us all.

Nodding to Chiefy Harvey, in charge of the ground crew, John asked, 'What do you think, Chiefy?'

'I think *Algy* will be just fine,' he replied. 'Want the lads to paint it on, sir?'

'No thanks, Chiefy, we have a resident signwriter,' responded John. 'Let him earn his pay.'

It transpired that we only flew on ops four times aboard *Algy* in two months; it was not always possible for the crew to be assigned BZ906 because of servicing or other considerations. Later, in January 1944, we bid a grateful farewell to *Algy* when assigned an even more advanced Mk VI model as our next personal Lib. Still, *Algy* was ours for the time being, even if we could not always take this aircraft on ops or even air tests. With this ownership, of sorts, came renewed pride, focus, satisfaction, and loyalty.

I quickly designed the Algy-themed nose art for the port forward fuselage of BZ906, and the two crews (air and ground) just as quickly approved my work, but not without ribald comments as to my ability as an artist. What I came up with was a cartoon figure of a dapper little man in top hat, cloak, and silver-topped cane. The figure sported a monocle, an impressive moustache, and a fine goatee beard, and the design was backed by a red disk. This had to be changed to blue as it looked similar to the red meatball insignia of the Japanese Army and Naval air forces. The name 'Algy' would be added to the left of the dapper gent. For each op flown, I would paint a single playing card instead of the usual bomb symbol.

The brushes I used were not ideal, being ordinary watercolour brushes, so at my first opportunity, I scrounged a trip into Calcutta and bought real signwriting supplies. They were so good and cheap that I bought more than I needed and sent the extras home to my father.

The completed design looked quite handsome on the nose of the aircraft. I did not tell anyone, but I had obtained the idea from an advert in *The Saturday Evening Post*, an American magazine that circulated in the Mess. Copies were usually left there by Canadians who received them in comfort parcels sent by relatives or organisations back home concerned with the welfare of their servicemen.

With my artistic talents previously only displayed on BZ839, but now also on BZ906, very soon, I was in demand with other crews, and I spent occasional mornings painting my designs on their Liberators. Cartoon characters like Dumbo and Algy were the most popular themes among the flyers.

My Seventh Op: Heho Aerodrome (Thedaw Landing Ground Bombed), 21–22 October 1943

We were on ops again on the night of 21–22 October. Arriving at the Briefing Room, we found the place more crowded than we had ever seen it as the battle order listed seven aircraft and crews in all, a record number of Liberators for 159 Squadron. In the briefing, the crews learned that the night's op was scheduled as a return visit to Heho aerodrome in Burma, the first target my crew had attacked the previous May.

John, at last, would lead his boys on an op for the first time since joining 159 Squadron, having been granted his coveted captaincy through patience, dedication, and impressive displays of flying during the monsoon down time of no ops. We were pleased to have him as our skipper.

At 11.34 p.m., John lifted *Algy*, BZ906, from Salbani's runway to commence the night's op to Heho. He was joined by his five long-time crewmates (Harry, Arnie, Willy, Fred, and me) in our normal crew positions, the newer 2nd W/op/AG (Sgt C. J. Nicholls) and Sgt Chris Hedley as second pilot. This was already Nicholls's fifth op with the crew. Harry was proud to be the sole navigator again; no screen navigator would be breathing down his neck on this flight.

Remembering the attack by the night fighter on our last visit, Willy refrained from singing his variation on the *Snow White and the Seven Dwarfs* theme, 'Heho, Heho, it's off to work I go'. There was no need to tempt the fates this night, he decided.

Unable to locate the cloud-obscured Heho aerodrome, John opted for the secondary target, one of the airfields in the Meiktila area nearly 60 miles to the west. Meiktila Lake was a welcome landmark, still recognisable in the last-quarter moonlight despite patchy clouds. Searchlights illuminated the clouds, which, in turn, revealed Liberators above quite remarkably. In all, four aircraft had given up on Heho due to clouds and were now endeavouring to find a Meiktila airfield target to bomb.

A sizeable hole briefly appeared in the clouds above Thedaw landing ground. Harry gave swift corrections to John for the run-up to the target, and from his bomb aimer's position in the nose of the Liberator, Harry toggled the bombs in one salvo. To his disappointment, the load impacted slightly to one side of the main Thedaw runway, with the separate incendiary load seen to fall on the opposite side. Although the runway was missed, small fires were observed, and we knew that we had dished out some damage down below. Becoming increasingly impatient with all the hanging around we had been doing, John dropped the nose down and headed for home.

Once we cleared the enemy coast, I went to the rear of the aircraft with my coffee and sat beside Willy at the beam hatches. 'Well, that's number eight in the logbook for me,' grinned Willy. 'Only another twenty-two and I will have finished the tour.' I smiled back and nodded, though I knew that I trailed Willy by one op. The end seemed an awfully long way off to each of us.

Observing the rising daylight, I stood up and looked out of the beam hatch. There was only the sea below, but as the sun lifted and touched the clouds just above the Liberator, the sight became incredible. I nudged Willy with my foot and pointed outside.

On standing up, Willy witnessed what had impressed me. The whole sky was irradiated with mother of pearl colours which were reflected in the sea below. The whole effect only lasted a short time, but the glorious scene took our breaths away. Willy broke the magic by commenting on the intercom, 'Now I know what it feels like to be a pearl in an oyster.'

The two pilots, having admired the sunrise from the cockpit, also remarked about its stunning beauty, but Fred in the rear turret was less enthusiastic. 'Yes, smashing, but now I can't see a bloody thing for the sun. Now it has risen, it's burning off the cloud and I'm dazzled back here.'

Willy raised his shoulders and spread his arms. With his palms uppermost, he put his head close to mine and shouted, 'These Londoners, got no soul,' whereupon he once again resumed his seat on the floor of the aircraft with his back against the fuselage side.

I stuck my head out of the beam hatch to see what Fred was grumbling about. I promptly shut my eyes. The sun was intensely bright, and so I was not surprised to see the turret doors open and Fred climb out to join the two of us, protected from the dazzle. The likelihood of an attack was remote, and as Fred explained later, had there been an attack, he could not have seen any sons of the rising sun—the Japanese airmen—because of the rising sun.

The rest of the trip home was uneventful. John eased BZ906 down for a perfect landing back at Salbani at 8.10 a.m., eight hours and thirty-six minutes after take-off. We were met by the relieved, yet still anxious ground crew. As we climbed out, Chiefy Harvey did a quick walk around the aircraft and then greeted us with words that were to become familiar: 'Have you bent it?'

'Think everything is as good as new, Chiefy,' John answered, confidently.

'Oh, aye, and what's that, then?' Chiefy Harvey asked, pointing to the tailplane.

Four holes about the size of cigarette packets were visible near the rear turret. Fred eyed them with obvious displeasure, and it did not require a lot of imagination to guess his thoughts on his own mortality.

'Well, I reckon *Algy* has been blooded,' said Arnie.

Chiefy Harvey looked as if he was more concerned about the Liberator than for its crew, but he revealed a human side by adding, 'Glad we don't have to patch you lot up. I don't think you could stand the rivets.' Following debriefing and breakfast, we returned to our billets for some richly deserved shut-eye.

A Move to Dudhkundi Becomes a Move to Digri

Starting in September, rumours had been circulating that the squadron was going to up and relocate, but no one knew where. One rumour even suggested that we were to return to England to help make up for the heavy losses Bomber Command was suffering. Then, on 3 October, an advance party led by John moved to Dudhkundi, 23 miles to the south-west of Salbani, in preparation for a squadron relocation at an undisclosed later date.

Dudhkundi, however, was not to be our new home. Originally planned as a Liberator airfield, it was instead earmarked for use by a new American B-29 Superfortress unit. This eventually became a reality, months later in July 1944, after the completion of a runway extension to accommodate the B-29s.

On 21 October, instructions were received that 159 Squadron would move to Digri, instead of Dudhkundi. Situated only 13 miles to the north of Salbani, Digri's existing facilities were allegedly superior to Salbani's. The news, however, did not appeal to most on the squadron.

Willy summed up the thoughts of the dissenters. 'Typical bloody RAF,' he sneered. 'Just as you have made a place something like home, they move you somewhere else!'

An advance party travelled to Digri the following day, followed on the 23rd by the main party from 159 Squadron. By 6 p.m. that evening, with all same-day arrangements carried out according to plan, the squadron was installed in its new home.

The place was better than Salbani in many respects, but as Willy had hinted, it initially lacked the comforts and idiosyncrasies of an established home-away-from-home. At first, we particularly missed Salbani's Sergeants' Mess, which had been decorated to resemble an English pub, but with time, our new Mess became equally popular. It already boasted of a piano, which was put to good use by a talented W/op/AG from 'A' Flight, Sgt Don Lomas.

The consensus was that 159 Squadron was better off at Digri. Each Liberator even had its own dispersal bay at Digri, and the runway was in better condition than Salbani's. At 2,000 yards, the Digri runway was the same length as Salbani's, too.

My Eighth Op: Rangoon Central Railway Station, 24–25 October 1943

A grand effort by all personnel in transferring the entire squadron from Salbani initiated 159 Squadron's tenure at Digri. Perhaps equally impressive was the serviceability success of our first op flown from Digri on the night of 24–25 October, only one day after arriving. All seven available Liberators were deemed ready to go; others, like BZ906—*Algy*—were down for servicing.

In its place, John was set to take BZ855, better known as *Butch*, on the night's op. The 11 a.m. air test in readiness for the evening's op was completed, and all systems were in apple pie order, which was hardly surprising as the aircraft was brand new.

Accompanying John on the operation as his second pilot would be FS Rex H. 'Pop' Simmons, a dry-witted, much-admired American character two months shy of his fortieth birthday. He would fly a total of nine ops with our crew over the next several months. A farmer and bush pilot from North Dakota, Pop had lied about his age when joining the Royal Canadian Air Force prior to the American entry in the war. Also aboard were the old core of Harry, Arnie, Willy, Fred, and me, plus C. J. Nicholls as 2nd W/op/AG.

At the briefing, the target was concealed behind the curtained blackboard at one end of the room. We stood up on the arrival of the CO, Wg Cdr Max Boffee, who took his place beside the blackboard and drew the curtains aside. The length of red string went directly from Digri to Rangoon, Burma. A low murmur went around the room for a moment and was hushed as the CO gave details of general interest on the reasons for the raid on Rangoon central railway station.

He was followed by the navigation officer, signals officer, armaments officer, and finally the meteorological officer—the widely mocked 'met man'. At this time of the year, his predictions were sometimes wildly inaccurate, not that he could be blamed. Violent electrical storms, for example, were still possible despite the monsoon's waning. The vagaries in the weather and the limitations inherent in forecasting conditions far away over enemy territory made his job almost impossible.

Aerial imagery collected during reconnaissance flights over Rangoon indicated that Rangoon central railway station would be full of equipment awaiting shipment up to the front. Clearly, there was apprehension in the room as Rangoon carried an unenviable reputation as something of a hotspot. As the main port of entry into Burma and the largest and most modern town in the country, it was inevitable that the Japanese would concentrate defences in Rangoon. The general

Japanese opposition in our theatre of war was not as fearsome as the German punch in Axis-held Europe, but with so few strategic targets, the Japanese tended to pack their defences around them.

Rangoon, with numerous targets, was the most fiercely defended of 159 Squadron's destinations. Among the defenders were night fighters, some of which seemed to be positively suicidal in carrying out attacks on bombers already under assault by anti-aircraft fire. After all, an exploding shell fired from below could not discriminate between friend or foe.

BZ855 was airborne at 10.03 p.m., the second of the six Liberators to take off. Unfortunately, one aircraft was forced to bow out of the op due to minor engine trouble prior to take-off. It was better to abort now than to die taking off fully laden with bombs, petrol, and crew. For the six other Liberators, each flying and bombing independently, the cloud base in the Digri vicinity was low, and it was raining with thunder rumbling around the field. Almost poetic at times with his observations, Harry remarked, 'If Wagner had seen this, he'd have written it into *The Ring*.'

Progress after leaving base was dreary and miserable, and John was not at all pleased to discover that the windscreen was leaking. The aircraft bored steadily through the night, avoiding the cumulonimbus clouds highlighted by the flickering illuminations of lightning.

Eventually Harry told the pilots to keep their eyes open for the enemy coast. A visual of the coast would enable him to obtain a pinpoint to correct any deviation in his navigating, which, he guessed, must be somewhat off-the-mark due to all the action taken to avoid the dangerous thunderheads.

Suddenly, the second pilot, Pop Simmons, drawled over the intercom, 'OK, wise guy, how'd ya do it?' and with a slow chuckle added, 'Elephant Point, right on the nose.'

Sure enough, dead ahead was the distinctive shape of Elephant Point, at the mouth of the Rangoon River. Our target was 25 miles upstream. Although there was still a lot of cloud around, breaks revealed Rangoon in fleeting glimpses.

I did my usual bit in removing the horseshoes, and then I sat on the catwalk to await developments. Over the intercom, I heard Harry start the bomb run countdown. A sudden burst of flak, uncomfortably close, was followed by two more in quick succession, each close enough to be heard as dull thuds in the Liberator.

Harry stopped counting. I thought he had been rattled by the flak, but then I heard him tell the skipper to go around again as the target had become obscured by cloud halfway through the run. Around we went again, with the same result and similar bursts of flak on the bombing run. A third attempt was necessary.

By this time, everyone's nerves were becoming stretched. We were surprised by the lack of activity. No one else had bombed yet, and with six of the squadron's Liberators operating, we expected to see some fires in the target area. As we swung onto the third run, a stick of bombs from another aircraft burst right across the station, starting a fairly large fire.

'OK, bomb aimer,' commanded John, 'drop on those fires, and let's get the hell out of here.'

'Roger, skipper,' Harry meekly replied. 'Go in on a heading of 310, and then we are on course in the general direction of home.'

I was aware of the doors sliding up the fuselage sides for the third time. With relief, I saw the bombs fall away. Harry left the doors open long enough for me to observe the explosions.

The squadron's results were dramatic. The fires erupted into one huge conflagration with masses of white smoke boiling up through the clouds, which had now again obscured the ground. This seemed to irritate the Japanese, and flak was intense.

When John emerged briefly below the clouds we witnessed large numbers of searchlights playing on the cloud base. It seemed rather a pointless exercise as all other bombers were above the clouds, but then we realised the Japanese tactic, revealed earlier at Heho, of trying to silhouette the bombers by illuminating the clouds for the benefit of night fighters. It did no good this night; Japanese fighters were not seen.

As BZ855 headed for home, Fred, in the rear turret, could be heard from time to time commenting that he could see the fire, and it was still a faint glow when almost 100 miles behind us.

The rest of the trip was unremarkable. With the coming of the dawn the CuNims were easily avoided, and we touched down at 6.58 a.m. after being airborne for eight hours and fifty-five minutes.

13

November 1943

My Ninth Op: Akyab, 5 November 1943

Aboard BZ906, *Algy*, once again, we were scheduled for our next op on the evening of 5 November, twelve nights after our last sortie. Four other squadron Liberators were to join us, as per the battle order. My crew would remain intact from our last op: John as skipper, Pop Simmons as his second pilot, the old core of Harry, Arnie, Willy, Fred, and me, and then C. J. Nicholls as 2nd W/op/AG.

At briefing, I endured a persistent stomach knot until the CO pulled back the curtains covering the blackboard to reveal the relatively easy target on the eastern Bay of Bengal coast: Akyab town on Akyab Island in Burma. It was expected to be a quick run in over the island to release a first stick of bombs, a circling back to toggle a second stick, and a return back out to sea again, towards home. The relief of the crews in seeing Akyab as the target was obvious from the way many of us exhaled in long, steady sighs. Another relief was the length of the trip, short at approximately five and a half hours when compared with the average of nine, to which we were becoming accustomed.

Airborne at 6.27 p.m., the Gauntlett crew's flight aboard *Algy* was routine, with a clear sky, poorly aimed flak, no fighter opposition, and two straightforward bomb runs and releases over the town. No spectacular fires were started, and as Harry stated on the way home, 'It was all rather a bore.' He said it in what he considered his pukka English accent, but he still sounded like a Canadian.

Algy landed back at Digri at 11.59 p.m., after five hours and thirty-two minutes aloft. Following a standard debriefing, the crew took advantage of the quick trip and called it a night.

With the leathery skin of a cowboy, second pilot Pop Simmons was a law unto himself as far as discipline was concerned. To the members of our crew, he seemed as old as the hills. Hearing Harry on the intercom at one point *en route* to Akyab, Pop had responded, 'You Canucks can't speak decent American, and you sure as hell can't speak English. Pipe down.' There was a snort from Harry, and something like a long, loud raspberry filled everyone's earphones.

We were to discover later that Pop had one fatal weakness: women. On forays into Calcutta, Pop proved to have a way with the ladies despite his age, his weather-beaten skin, his generally dishevelled appearance, and the small fact that he was married. Age or social standing held no terrors for Pop. Some of the *memsahibs*—the married white or upper-class women—were like glaciers to non-commissioned troops. When Pop got talking to the *memsahibs*, however, they melted like snow in a furnace.

Sitting outside the Flight Office one morning, Harry asked Pop a question in all innocence. 'Say, Pop, what are you, an American, doing out here in the RAF putting your arse at risk for England—the nation your own country has defeated twice, once to gain independence and then again thirty-something years later? And you joined up before it was even your own country's war.'

Pop startled us all with his vehement reply. 'Coming from a Canuck, I find that rich. You're out here fighting, you from the dominion of Canada. You are only one stage removed from colonialism yourself. I made my living in your country flying an old Stinson Reliant on floats and came to love the wild country, not to mention the way of life in the backwoods. When Britain stood alone against Hitler I thought it was time I gave the Limeys a hand against the Nazis. Hoped to fly a fighter but ended up here on a Yankee-built airplane.' Looking round at the assembled men, he added, with his twisted grin, 'With a nondescript crew.'

As Pop finished speaking, Grp Capt. N. C. Singer, in charge of 184 Wing, to which 159 Squadron belonged, went slowly past in his jeep. Everyone jumped up and saluted, except Pop. Lounging in the chair he had pulled out of the Crew Room, he watched the rest of us as the Group Captain acknowledged the salute. Lazily, Pop waved to Grp Capt. Singer. 'Hiya, Groupie,' he called. We expected the wrath of Heaven to descend on Pop's head and were stunned when the group captain merely returned Pop's wave and laughingly called over, 'Hi, Pop,' as he proceeded on his way.

All eyes were turned in Pop's direction as we regarded him with awe. 'How do you do it and get away with it?' someone asked.

'Aw, shit, it ain't nothing. Besides, I'm almost old enough to be his daddy,' he retorted, and as if to close the conversation, he pulled his battered old topee over his eyes and pretended to sleep. From under the topee, a muffled voice was heard to say, as an afterthought, 'Those yellow bastards are now our joint enemy, anyway, since Pearl Harbour.' This was said with such bitterness that it surprised us all and made us aware that underneath Pop was a hard man, indeed, although his appearance belied the truth.

He always wore his old topee and issue khaki drill, now almost white from constant washing. His favourite pants, a pair of baggy shorts, revealed his bony legs, which were typically encased in high white stockings. His feet were shod with suede chukka boots, commonly referred to as 'brothel creepers'. In Pop's case, the term was probably appropriate.

My Tenth Op: Insein (Rangoon) Locomotive Sheds, 11–12 November 1943

Six nights later in BZ900, known as *Crusader*, we operated against the locomotive sheds at Insein on the west side of our most difficult destination, Rangoon. Simply because it was pronounced 'insane', said Willy, it deserved to be bombed. The Gauntlett crew included all of the regulars: John, Harry, Willy, Arnie, Fred, C. J. Nicholls, and me. John's second pilot this time was FS Frederick Collins, who had been captain back on 8 September when a simple air firing exercise had turned into a successful air-sea rescue flight. An air gunner under training, Sgt Woods, also came along. Taking off at 5.58 p.m., BZ900 beelined for Rangoon 700 miles away. We flew under a full moon that night.

A new British bombsight had been fitted in the aircraft, and Harry had been given a short course on its use; it was not training enough. The weather presented no difficulties, but Harry's inexperience with the equipment forced John to abort the first two bomb runs. On the third, still having trouble at 16,500 feet, Harry put the 5,000 pounds of bombs beyond the desired aiming point. His error proved to be extremely lucky for us, however, as the last bomb in the stick caused a tremendous white flash followed immediately by a red fire of rapidly increasing intensity. Like moths attracted to a candle, the five other Liberators honed in upon the illumination of the fires started by Harry and added to the conflagration below.

When bursts of tracer were seen criss-crossing the sky, discretion seemed the better part of valour, and John set course for base. From the rear turret, Fred's laconic voice came over the intercom intermittently to notify us of the glow far behind in the target area. His last sight of the conflagration was when we were over 90 miles away. The raid had felt much more worthwhile than some ops, where a few *bashas* left burning were all we could discern of the damage wrought.

Tuning into All India Radio on the radio compass, I informed the crew and was rewarded by Willy singing the popular song 'I'll Be Around' in a mock crooner's voice. He was terrible.

When well on the way home, John told me to call up base for permission to land. Though bewildered, I did so. After a slight hesitation, this was granted, followed by an odd declaration: 'You're number one.'

Instantly, I realised what John was up to. When aircraft returned from a raid, they called up for permission to land, which was granted. Additionally, each Liberator was given a number that governed the height at which it would circle the aerodrome. A larger number meant a higher altitude in the stack of bombers circling the field. As each aircraft landed, the stack would descend 500 feet, until all aircraft were on the ground.

By calling up so early, John had obtained clearance to land first, even if other aircraft reached Digri before his own. In the event of a bomber returning damaged, the whole column of aircraft had to wait until it was down before normal landings could resume.

Listening to the rest of the returning Liberators calling base, I checked them off, one by one, and was relieved that no one was missing.

Our landing was accomplished without incident at 3 a.m., after a flight duration of nine hours and two minutes. The waiting ground crew heard a brief description of the success caused by Harry having set up the bombsight incorrectly. We wisely kept these details to ourselves, though, when debriefed.

At debriefing, John received a rocket from the CO for his clever practice with the landing. After this affair, no one could ask for permission to land until within 25 miles of base.

Girl Trouble Back Home

As we had now been on the squadron for seven months, the initial homesickness that had even contributed to physical discomfort for some was now slowly becoming a thing of the past. This was generally the natural progression experienced by other crews, too.

On the squadron, some men's strong ties to wives and girlfriends left behind remained intact or even intensified. For quite a few, however, girlfriends and sometimes wives had either stopped communicating or had written to say that they were attached to someone else or they wanted to split. Most men, not all, took such news philosophically enough, and whenever a man received one of these letters, known as a 'messpot', he would pin it on the noticeboard. This was an invitation to a big binge to help him forget the girl. A majority had lost interest in the girl by the time the letter arrived anyway.

The odd one or two were badly hit, though, on receipt of such letters. One airman, in particular, changed dramatically from being a quiet, non-smoking and non-drinking introvert. Hitting the bottle in a big way, he became the complete extrovert, being the first to join in any of the madcap schemes we thought up to kill the endless boredom when not flying. After a month, he simmered down but never reverted to his former quiet self.

In many ways, he became an easier chap to get along with. It was Harry's brutally frank statement that brought him down to earth when he was in the depths of misery. 'Can't see why you are so steamed up about the bitch,' Harry said. 'After all, you may not live to see her again.'

The remark was true, but it shocked those listening as none of us liked to be reminded that our monastic lives could be terminated in uniform at any time—because of flying accident, air combat, pye-dog attack, snake bite, heatstroke, alcohol poisoning, or even murder by a pro-independence Indian.

The lack of feminine company got to us at times, but, for some, not unduly so. We each had a mosquito net fastened permanently to four bamboo poles nailed to the legs of the charpoy on which we slept or just lay. Most had pictures of women in various stages of undress lying face down on the top of the nets, and visible from below. Many an idle moment was passed by studying respective art galleries.

An Air Test and a Close Call: 13 November 1943

In mid-afternoon on 13 November, during an air firing exercise, John decided to do an altitude test in BZ900. He took me along as his W/op. Being inattentive on the intercom, I missed John's command to go onto oxygen at 10,000 feet. All I remembered about the test was reviving from unconsciousness while lying on the cabin floor. John, by chance, had turned around to find me passed out from oxygen starvation. I was saved from death by an oxygen mask slapped onto my face.

Apart from feeling a bit drowsy for a while, I was no worse for the incident, although I later chastised John on the quiet for wrongly assuming that I had heard his command.

My Eleventh Op: Pegu Railway Station, 15–16 November 1943

Frustratingly, our Liberator, *Algy*, was again unavailable to us on the night of 15–16 November as it had been assigned to another crew. Instead, John once more piloted *Crusader*, BZ900, on 159 Squadron's six-aircraft attack upon a relatively safe target, Pegu railway station in Burma. Second pilot Sgt Chris Hedley joined John on the flight deck. Of John's regular crewmates, Harry, Arnie, Fred and I were aboard for the op. Filling out the crew, Sgt W. Etherington replaced C. J. Nicholls as the 2nd W/op/AG, and Sgt P. J. J. O'Keefe, an AG, manned a beam gun. Take-off was at 10.50 p.m.

Our main bugbear came in the form of scattered clouds obscuring the target on our independent bomb run; the winding Pegu River was Harry's only landmark, and his release of bombs from 14,500 feet was based upon an estimated, not visible, location. He hoped, this time, that he had correctly set the bomb sight before dropping BZ900's load.

The other Liberators met with varying conditions, but serious smoke and flames were witnessed in the vicinity of the rail station. On the trip home, when over the Bay of Bengal well clear of the enemy coast, John dropped down to about a thousand feet to be more comfortable. On the intercom, he announced, 'I'm going lower. I'll call you up if I see any sharks, and you can practise on them, beam gunners.'

I immediately went aft and, pulling seniority, commandeered the port beam gun from Sgt Etherington. He begrudgingly moved forward to take over wireless duties until my target practice had completed.

The beam gun hatches had been closed and the .5-inch Browning guns swung in and stowed to dramatically reduce drag once the threat from enemy fighters had passed. Now, in preparation for our expected shark target shoot, each hinged hatch was again lifted open and then fastened to the roof of the fuselage. The 50-calibre Brownings were swung into firing position, and the wind deflector on each hatch's leading edge was extended.

John spotted about half a dozen sharks and warned us to be ready. He took the big Liberator down until we were almost swishing through the wavetops.

The sharks came up rapidly on my side and I opened fire. Despite the amount of deflection I had allowed, my bullets hit the water well ahead of the sharks. Sgt O'Keefe, looking over my shoulder from his starboard beam gun position, roared with laughter.

John's voice on the intercom was crisp. 'Coming up on the starboard side this time, and do try to hit the bastards. That last effort was pathetic.'

Suitably mortified, I looked over O'Keefe's shoulder and saw him blow one of the big tiger sharks to bits. As the target had to be fired upon as soon as it appeared, I was impressed, but I had seen how O'Keefe started firing well behind the shark and let the forward progress of the aircraft advance his bullets through the spot where the shark swam. On my next pass, I did the same, but my results, although improved, were not a patch on what O'Keefe had achieved.

Calling the exercise off, John climbed to a safer altitude and resumed course for base. I again took over wireless duties, and Etherington returned to his beam gun position.

All the time the firing had been going on, Harry had been grumbling about how his navigation log was going to be out, so when we resumed course he asked me for some assistance. I promptly called up three widely scattered ground stations and received a QDM, or course to steer, from each of them, in turn. Plotting them gave Harry a neat triangle on his chart—their position. Harry was over the moon, as the triangle was right on the track he had been working on prior to our fun and games with the sharks.

John landed at 7.50 a.m. to complete a nine-hour round-trip sortie. When entering the raid details into his flight logbook the next morning, Harry remarked with some satisfaction that having reached the ten-op mark, he was one third of the way through his tour. Arnie, already at thirteen ops flown, killed Harry's pleasure by stating that all it meant was that he had to fly exactly twice as many ops as had already been flown.

This sortie also marked the thirteenth for Fred and John, and it was my eleventh op. There was a finish line, but it was a fuzzy one in our minds, and still far off.

On the night of 18–19 November, Arnie flew an op, his fourteenth, as a fill-in mid-upper gunner aboard FS J. C. Stuart's BZ840. They successfully bombed Heho aerodrome in Burma. Arnie, however, remained the regular mid-upper gunner on the Gauntlett crew.

Harry Hatches a Scheme

Shooting the breeze one afternoon, we realised that many familiar faces on the squadron had gone to pastures new as they had become 'tour-expired'; each had finished his tour of operational flying with 159 Squadron and had reported to a new non-combat assignment elsewhere. Although we were pleased that they had survived their tours, we were sorry to see almost all of them go, including some we would not want our sisters to marry. Our squadron was a focused unit whose members shared a common purpose. Being stuck in the boondocks tended to breed a bolshie attitude to authority, perhaps, but we looked at ourselves as brothers sent to do a nasty job, and to do it well.

The recent stretch of frequent combat ops was welcome in the sense that it stirred up excitement and gave us a chance to feel that we were contributing to eventual victory over the Japanese. Not to be overlooked, it advanced us towards our own tour completions.

Since Ben's death the previous month, the squadron had not lost an aircraft, although there had been one odd casualty. At 12,000 feet, a kitehawk had crashed through a Liberator's windscreen and embedded itself in the chest of the second pilot. The casualty was whisked away, and his fate was a mystery to all but his crew and the squadron's senior staff, most likely.

The mornings were now becoming cooler, much to the satisfaction of all concerned. The ground crew, in particular, had long suffered from prickly heat, some so severely that their bodies were a sorry sight with large septic areas on backs and chests. To give them slight relief, whenever possible, a Liberator going up on an air test or exercise would take along the suffering ground crew to benefit from the temporary access to the cooler air at altitude.

Once back on the ground, though, many again had to toil in stifling conditions, such as within the confines of a broiling Liberator fuselage, so the prickly heat's discomforts continued. With the coming of the cooler weather late in the year, at least those with heat rash could expect some temporary freedom from the eternal itching.

From a flute Willy had fashioned out of a piece of bamboo, Harry hatched an idea and put it into motion. Taking Arnie and me to a clump of bamboo growing just outside our billet, he proceeded to cut some lengths, all approximately two inches in diameter. Arnie and I also cut some pieces. We ended up with about ten lengths approved by Harry.

Back on the veranda of the billet, Harry sat down to explain what it was all about. 'I think the Japs are still using old-fashioned sound locators for their flak,' he surmised. 'If we make some whistling bombs, they might throw off the locators and let us get in and out a damned sight more safely than we can at present.'

As the defences at Rangoon were already beefy, and potentially lethal, Harry's suggestion met with our approval. We were soon joined by Willy and Fred, who did not need any persuading to assist in the 'bomb factory'. Harry cleanly trimmed each bamboo segment above and below a ring in the tree. Cutting a slot at one end, he carefully inserted a piece of leaf into the cut to act as a fin, and having borrowed a tool from the workshops, he drilled a hole through the undamaged section.

Showing it around, he asked for comments. Willy was all for putting a point on the opposite end to the leaf, but on realising that a point could not be fashioned onto a hollow tube, he agreed to follow Harry's pattern. After about six had been completed, Fred asked, 'Think these things will work?'

'Tell you what we'll do,' Harry schemed. 'When we go up on an air test tomorrow, you gunners listen as we go over the airfield. Tell us if you hear anything.' The gunners did not have to fly on air tests and agreed to listen for the whistle of the bamboo bombs. Taking off the next day with John at the controls, Harry and I were like two schoolboys sharing a secret. John had not been told of the experiment.

After a quick check of the radio, I nudged Harry in the ribs and motioned with my head towards the rear of the aircraft. Harry grinned, and the two of us went through the bomb bay to the closed beam hatches. We only opened the port one, as the air had a distinct nip in it, indicative of the approach of the cool season. Sticking his head out into the slipstream, Harry surveyed the ground below and pronounced, 'All clear!' In a swift movement he reached down, scooped up the bamboo bombs, and hurled them out of the beam hatch. I closed it and we went forward again to our normal duty stations in the warmer end of the aircraft. John landed shortly afterwards.

On arrival at our dispersal pen, we were surprised to be greeted, not by the gunners but by the CO, Wg Cdr Boffee, who without any preamble asked John if the Liberator was OK. Somewhat mystified, John answered in the affirmative.

'Well,' said the CO, 'something fell off when you were over the field, and it made a hell of a screech as it fell. Let's have a look at the kite.'

Harry coughed, and the CO regarded him quizzically. 'Have you something on your mind, warrant officer?' he asked.

With a sheepish smile, Harry told the CO of our experiment, its purpose and his deliberate action in dropping the missiles over a safe area. The hard look disappeared from the officer's face and he stood in silence for a moment. 'Might be a good idea, but in the future drop them on the Japs. You caused the emergency services to be called to readiness.'

With a nod, the CO climbed into his jeep and disappeared in a cloud of red dust. Harry and I breathed sighs of relief, only to face an irate John. 'Next time you two silly sods have any bright ideas,' he admonished, 'put me in the picture. You don't have to eat in the same Mess as the Commanding Officer!'

After an awkward pause he asked, 'How many more of these contraptions have you?' Uneasily, I answered, 'About thirty.' A slow smile crossed John's face. 'OK,' he said, 'put 'em aboard. Try 'em on the next op. They might just spoil the Jap's aim.'

My Twelfth Op: Rangoon, Botataung Wharves and Railway Depot, 27–28 November 1943

My last sortie in November, my twelfth op, was once again aboard *Algy*, BZ906, on the night of 27–28 November, but this time John was not commanding the aircraft. Instead, Sgt F. N. Ellis flew as captain, with Sgt Chris Hedley as second pilot. Harry, Arnie, Willy, Fred, and myself, plus Sgt W. Etherington, the 2nd W/op/AG from our last trip, rounded out the crew. *Algy* was one of seven Liberators from the squadron earmarked to participate.

At the 11.30 a.m. briefing on the morning of the 27th, the target was revealed as our least popular destination, Rangoon, and specifically the Botataung Wharves and railway depot. The resulting silence in the room hinted at the dread among us. Because the flak over Rangoon was expected to be as intense as we would face, our bombing height for the raid was set at 17,000 feet. It would be bloody cold in the rear of the Liberator over the target.

An op to the Botataung Wharves and the associated rail depot was usually laid on after a photo reconnaissance aircraft had returned with pictures of ships tied up to unload stores for the Japanese Army in Burma.

In the seven and a half months since our crew had arrived on 159 Squadron, the defences had been improved dramatically, and a healthy respect for Rangoon had been engendered in all crews. It had become an increasingly hot target; it was not that any bombers were guaranteed to be damaged or knocked out of the sky or that crewmen would be injured or killed, but the negative odds were on the rise.

At the end of the briefing, Wg Cdr Boffee added that the squadron intelligence officer, Fg Off. George Betteley, would be riding in *Algy*, aircraft 'A', to try and pinpoint the flak batteries. This caused mild consternation in our crew aboard

Algy as we were becoming increasingly superstitious and tended to regard with deep suspicion anything that differed from our normal routine.

Discussing our passenger-to-be, Willy summed up how the man would be treated. 'If he's back on the beam hatches for his observation of the flak batteries and the shit starts flying, I'll kick his arse out the hatch if he gets in the way.'

None of the crew disliked the intelligence officer; in fact, he was popular, as he was keen on his job and didn't ask daft questions when debriefing us after a raid. Still, the chance to grouch gave us an opportunity to release some of the tension that we all felt before a sticky raid.

Seven Liberators from 159 Squadron departed for Rangoon that evening. Take-off in *Algy* was at 7.01 p.m. On the way to the enemy coast Sgt Ellis kept *Algy* well below 10,000 feet, above which the aircrew must plug into the oxygen system or risk inevitably passing out. The air below 10,000 feet was a pleasant temperature. Willy instructed the intelligence officer on the oxygen plug-in points and where to sit to be out of the way should we be attacked.

Eventually, over the intercom, Sgt Ellis gave the order to don oxygen masks, as a climb to bombing height had begun, and he instructed me to go aft and remove the horseshoes from the pistols on the bombs. I no longer had to sit on the catwalk to observe the bomb explosions, as the camera now did it for me, but I still had to remove the horseshoes, a task I never enjoyed. After completing this necessary chore, I went farther aft to join Sgt Etherington and Willy at the beam guns, where Fg Off. Betteley, the IO, was also parked.

Approaching the target, we were startled by the amount of flak being put up by the enemy. Also, there were more searchlights than we had ever seen before. Harry came up on the intercom, 'Navigator to wireless op. Don't forget the bamboo bombs. Let's see if the Japs are using sound detectors or radar.'

Starting at twenty, Harry counted out the seconds in reverse order while giving the skipper corrections left, right or steady. Having previously briefed the IO on the 'whistling bombs', I threw the bamboo out through a beam opening when Harry was at ten on the bomb run countdown. Both the IO and I peered eagerly downwards, hoping to see some wavering by the defences.

We were disappointed. As if in answer, a brilliant mauve-coloured radar-directed searchlight locked straight onto us. This, in turn, attracted the hand-controlled white searchlights and *Algy* was 'coned', as we called it, in the converged beams of multiple searchlights.

The resulting blinding dazzle caused most of us slight panic for a moment or two, but Harry seemed to be unaffected by the light show and continued the countdown in his usual clipped Canadian accent. Upon hearing 'Bombs gone,' Ellis immediately stuffed the nose down.

I pushed the photoflash out of the flare chute, and although the flak was booming around us, we clearly heard the resultant sharp crack of the exploding photoflash.

Although the aircraft was being thrown about by the pilots in an attempt to shake off the searchlights, their efforts were without immediate success. Trapped and illuminated as we were in a cone of lights, we fully expected a fighter attack at any moment. Partly through frustration, but mainly to relieve the tension, Willy fired down the beam of the mauve-coloured master light, thinking for an instant that if he could knock it out, then the manually directed searchlights might lose us. It was a futile exercise; bullets fired from such a height would have struck the ground nowhere near their intended target.

As we had been diving away from the target steadily since the bombs were released, the angles of the searchlight beams became more acute. Suddenly, as if a giant was blowing out candles on a cake, all the searchlights were extinguished, only to reappear moments later when the master searchlight locked onto another Liberator.

Fred reported tracer fire coming from this newly coned aircraft. It seemed likely that the unfortunate occupants were being subjected to a night fighter attack, but there was nothing we could do to help but mentally wish our boys luck. We later learned that two fighters were seen, but thankfully no Liberators were damaged, after all; the outgoing tracer fire we witnessed must have fought off, or just plain scared off, the bomber's attackers.

Now clear of the target area and at a lower altitude, Sgt Ellis commanded the crew to dispense with oxygen. I was surprised to find that my shirt was soaked with sweat, although it had been cold over Rangoon.

Fg Off. Betteley grinned with relief at Willy, Sgt Etherington, and me. When I asked whether he had managed to plot any of the defences, he held up one finger. 'The mauve one,' he replied. 'It's near the marshalling yards.'

Willy made a movement with his hand like an undulating snake. 'Mobile, yes, I suppose it would be,' shouted the IO. Looking at the three of us in turn, he added, 'Perhaps you can see if it's in the same position when you come again.'

Willy, with a grim smile, replied, 'Let's get home from this trip first.' I went forward to focus on my wireless operator duties for the return trip to Digri.

Algy set down unscathed at Digri at 3.45 a.m. following a sortie of eight hours and forty-four minutes. It was soon learned that one Liberator had turned back for home early in its flight with a petrol leak. The six other Liberators bombed Rangoon, although the searchlight dazzle interfered with the best efforts to accurately bomb.

The debriefing for *Algy*'s crew was short due to the presence of our passenger, the IO, who expedited matters with efficiency.

As we prepared to leave the debriefing, Wg Cdr Boffee said casually, 'You chaps on *Algy*'s regular crew, go on a fortnight's leave starting next week. Have a good time, and come back fighting fit.'

The news was received with mixed feelings. Although we would be safe from the myriad elements which made our profession so risky, we also knew that two weeks away from Digri would prolong the time it would take to reach the magic goal of 300 operational hours or thirty trips. Luck seemed to be on the side of the squadron at the moment. When we returned from leave, the pendulum might have swung the other way. With conflicting emotions, then, we went to bed. For me, sleep was a long time coming after the stress of the previous hours.

John, as the only officer among the crew, decided on taking his leave separately. Officers' accomodations would be superior to anything we could secure, and he also preferred the company of fellow officers. We understood, and there were no hard feelings.

Much improved the following morning were the moods of the six NCOs on the crew chosen for a needed break: Harry, Arnie, Fred, Willy, C. J. Nicholls, and me. Over at Accounts, where we collected our pay for the ensuing leave, we were nonplussed when asked where we wanted our travel warrants made out to. We had not even thought about a leave venue. With the whole Indian subcontinent to choose from, we had little idea where to go; such was our ignorance of the country in which we were living. I had enjoyed my leave in Darjeeling earlier in the year, but there were other top prospects to consider. Asking around in the Sergeants' Mess of men who had already taken a leave produced conflicting answers, but the favourite venue seemed to be a hill station named Naini Tal.

Before the date of departure, however, Harry and Willy were each called upon to fly another op, on separate nights—and safely, to the relief of their non-participating crewmates. On the night of 1–2 December, Harry navigated for FS J. H. Jones aboard *Algy* on a conventional sortie to Zayatkwin aerodrome in Burma, north-east of Rangoon, for his twelfth op. Willy bagged his thirteenth op on the night of 3–4 December as a beam gunner for Sgt Cecil Cox aboard *Crusader*, BZ900, on an easy trip to Heho aerodrome in Burma.

14

Leave to Naini Tal

A Tedious Journey

Having decided upon a venue, we six NCOs in the regular crew set about getting our leave passes and travel warrants, and we arranged with the adjutant's office to reserve our compartments on the train from Calcutta. We seemed to have a great deal of money since we had drawn our credits and pay, yet we were to discover towards the end of the leave that we were all scratching a little to make ends meet.

The great day dawned, and with some excitement, we boarded the gharry for the short ride south from Digri to Kharagpur railway station. From Kharagpur, we blissfully rolled by train into Howrah station in Calcutta, where, after some disagreement between ourselves and the guard in reference to our booked compartment, we finally settled down to savour the delights of Indian travel.

We had been informed that we would be two nights on the train, but this had not registered. We passed the time waiting for the train to move off by watching the nearly indescribable bedlam of the platforms. Beggars were everywhere, but we were so used to them by this time that the abject poverty did not touch us. Or so I thought. Horribly mutilated bodies reached out scrawny hands for *baksheesh*, but we had been taught that these Indians were deliberately disfigured at birth to gain sympathy in their profession, which was begging. The ones who looked the most pitiful were mothers, with one or two chicos at their heels. These women merely stood gazing at us with lacklustre eyes while making timid hand gestures.

After a while, I could stand it no longer and placed a one rupee note in the hand of the nearest. It was the worst thing I could have done. Within seconds, our compartment was the centre of a wild scrimmage as beggars from near and far converged, thinking they were on to a soft touch. Fortunately, the train set off with a jerk, and my mates and I were on our way.

Examining the coach led to some surprising discoveries. For a start, it was self-contained, with its own washroom, which was adequate. The toilet, however, caused some hilarity as it merely consisted of two large footprints and a hole in the floor, through which the track could be seen racing away below. This brought forth ribald comments about keeping one's piles well clear of the axles. The top bunks were normally stowed but could be let down on chains to form passable beds. As each compartment slept four, the six of us split into two compartments. Communication between compartments was done by leaning out of the window and shouting, something at which we became adept.

The train did not seem to be going very fast, but this was deceptive, as the larger gauge of the rails did not produce the clickety-clack with which we were familiar back home. At one point, the train pulled up, and a nondescript meal was produced, which we consumed in silence.

Darkness fell swiftly in this latitude. The top bunks were let down, and all turned in to await the morn. During the night, I got up to visit the toilet and stayed for some time gazing out the window. There was nothing to see but blackness. Here and there, a few little lights would betray the presence of a village, but apart from these small features the world outside might as well not have existed, so I turned in and slept until morning.

Waking, I became aware of the dull, monotonous rumble of the train and a distinct hollow feeling in my stomach—hunger. 'Anyone know when we eat?' I asked.

'Haven't a clue, but I'm sure it won't be long. I could eat a horse,' said Harry, and as if in response, the train started to slow down, and it eventually stopped.

A bearer in the customary uniform of belted white coat and turban came to the compartment. 'You want breakfast, *Sahib*?' he asked.

'Too bloody true. Wheel it on, bearer. What you got?' asked Willy. The breakfast was surprisingly good. Bacon, eggs, tea, and bread with the equivalent of butter, called *ghee*. There was also marmalade to finish. We were content. Soon, the train was off again.

Looking out of the window, the overall impression was of a slightly red landscape. Even the air had a reddish tinge about it, probably due to the dust. Despite our efforts, we were all covered in a fine red coating, which came in through the open windows.

Towards midday we were becoming bored with the apparently interminable journey and lack of exercise, but the thing which really got to us was the absolutely flat nature of the landscape.

This land, however, gave us our only piece of excitement. The train had stopped, probably to take on water, and the track on either side was bounded by elephant grass. Willy, who was idly looking out of the window, suddenly let out a strangled cry and pointed with his arm towards the grass. Glad of anything to break the monotony, we glanced towards where he was pointing and sat bolt upright. There, for us to see, was the forefront of a tiger gazing at the train with a look of complete indifference. It was a magnificent creature and seemed to peer right through us. The train gave a tiny toot, and immediately, the animal leapt back into the grass and was lost to view.

'Whew, I thought they were shy creatures,' breathed Harry. 'What a beautiful animal it was. Glad nobody shot it.'

'All the same, I'm glad we were in here and it was out there,' said Willy, and all agreed with him.

Shortly afterwards, when the train had halted for the midday meal, Arnie asked an official when we would arrive at Bareilly, the place where we had to change. 'Tomorrow morning, *Sahib*, very early,' replied the man, and with another little toot the train was off again.

By now, the journey had become tedious in the extreme, and we sat about attempting to read or lethargically watching the unceasing plains going by. Talk was unfocused and lacking in enthusiasm. Even the evening meal failed to rouse us to any great extent. Upon turning in for the night, and bored stiff with the train excursion, we looked forward with some anticipation to the morning and the last leg of our journey—and finally leave at Naini Tal.

Roused from our sleep by much shouting, we discovered that the train had at long last reached Bareilly. With much cursing, we got our bedrolls together, organised our kit, and staggered out onto the platform. Bearers in attendance soon whisked us onto a narrow-gauge train for the 65-mile trip to Kathgodam, nearly 1,000 feet higher than Bareilly but still only at the base of the Kumaon Himalayas mountains.

Alighting at Kathgodam, we once again transferred, this time to road transport for the climb upwards into the lower mountains to Naini Tal. Only 9 miles in straight-line distance separated Kathgodam from Naini Tal, but the road journey, gaining nearly a mile in altitude, more than doubled that.

In places, the road appeared perilously narrow, forcing Harry, sitting on the outward side of the wagon, to clamp his eyes closed, grit his teeth and shudder. I leaned over to have a look. The mountain descended sharply for 2,000 feet. We, who thought nothing of flying at 20,000 feet, were squeamish on this mode of transport.

Along the route, we were awestruck at the sight of muscled mountain men bearing incredible loads on their backs while traversing the same track we negotiated by vehicle. A broad webbing band, wrapped around the forehead and the article being hauled, supported each man's Herculean efforts. We even saw one man carrying a piano—on his back. These natives, from Nepal, were a different breed than the scrawny little Bengalis we were more accustomed to seeing.

Suddenly, our driver turned a corner and cut the engine. Slightly stunned, we were about to berate him when Arnie pointed and said in a hushed voice, 'Look!'

We followed his outstretched arm and were awed into speechlessness. In front of us was a large kidney-shaped lake surrounded by thickly wooded mountains.

Glorious Naini Tal

At last, we had reached the hill station at Naini Tal. Booked into a hotel without knowing its amenities, we were pleasantly surprised to find it was not far from where the wagon halted. Slowly, we removed our gear from the gharry, and bearers appeared as if by magic to convey it to the hotel. We followed closely behind. The place was incredibly beautiful and the proprietress of the hotel charming. She took quite a shine to us, in a motherly sort of way.

The first thing that we noticed was the cool. At an altitude of nearly 7,000 feet, and it being December, there was a distinct nip in the air, so after showering, we quickly changed into our blue tunics and slacks. The proprietress gave us the geography of the place, and we noted where the bars and dance hall were. This looked like it had the makings of a great leave.

After a meal, we all sat on the veranda looking out across the lake. The place had an air of utter peace and tranquillity, which was only interrupted by the faint notes of a bell coming from across the lake.

Seeing our confusion, the proprietress smiled. 'Don't be alarmed,' she said. 'It's only the holy man. The lake is sacred to the Hindus, and he rings the bell to remind them of their devotions. Because it is holy, no fishing is allowed.'

With a chuckle, she told us the story of an old Scottish doctor who, many years previously, had stocked the lake with trout and proceeded to fish for them. On being told of the lake's sanctity, he apologised profusely and stated that he would spend the rest of his life trying to rid the lake of them. She gave a wink and grinned. 'A canny Scot, eh?' she teased. Judging by the rings that were dimpling the lake's surface, he had not been too successful.

Evening found us set for our first foray into the town. We found a quiet bar and proceeded to drink in moderation until Willy let out a whoop. 'Hey,' cried Willy, 'they've got beer on!'

This caused a mild excitement, which was quickly and pleasantly reinforced by the arrival of a foaming tankard before each one of us. It tasted slightly of onions but was regarded with reverence. Back at Digri, beer was seldom made available.

Next on the list was the dance hall, which was surprisingly luxurious inside, but with about ten men to every female, we chose to prop up the bar. We had been there some time when Fred nudged me in the ribs, saying, 'Hey, that Chinese bird fancies you.'

Already slightly muzzy-headed from beer, I snuck a peek. Sure enough, a petite Chinese girl was looking in my direction, but when she saw me staring back, she averted her eyes demurely to the floor. With drink making me brave, I walked across and asked her to dance. Without a word, she got up and with a shy smile joined me on the dance floor. As we waltzed past the assembled crew, I gave my mates an exaggerated nod. She could not speak much English, but we managed to converse in a halting fashion. When the dance finished, I took her back to her seat and with a bow excused myself to rejoin my pals.

'Well, I'll be buggered!' said Willy. 'The ugliest sod here and he scores!' I grinned and replied, 'She's not going anywhere. I'll dance with her again tomorrow and ensure her continued interest.' The others looked doubtful but decided to let matters take their course. Shortly afterwards, we opted to retire to the hotel, as it had been a long day.

The next morning dawned clear and fresh as we set forth in search of adventure. There was plenty to investigate and sample in limited time. Rowboats and sailboats, for example, could be hired for pleasant excursions out on the lake, even in the cool December air. One establishment in particular, a milk bar, caught our attention, and the clean taste of the chilled milk, unheard of since our arrival in India, was refreshing in the extreme.

Arnie and I hired two horses and set off on a tour of discovery. The track we were following wound steadily upwards, and, looking back, the lake seemed tiny. We rounded a bend and reined in to wonder at the sight which met our eyes: snow-capped peaks as far as we could see.

For some time neither of us spoke, both overwhelmed by the sheer grandeur spread before us in the clear air. Eventually, Arnie turned to me and pondered, 'Reckon I could get to like this part of India without too much difficulty.'

I merely nodded. The magnificence was overpowering, but at last I spoke. 'Yes, and it will still be here thousands of years from now. Makes you realise that we are less than the dust, and shortly we'll be back trying to impose our puny little wills on the Japs.' Shaking my head, I uttered one word with great emphasis. 'Barmy!' Yet I firmly believed in giving my all to defeat the Japanese.

Slowly, we retraced our steps back to our starting point and paid for the nags, which had been docile and well-behaved. The little man in charge was most helpful and tried to get us to book the horses for the next day, but we declined and told him that we would book them if and when required.

A good meal was the next priority, and this we accomplished at a neat little café beside the lake. The rest of the crew were nowhere in sight, but Arnie and I were not bothered, as we knew we would meet up for the evening meal in the hotel.

Ambling round the lake, we discovered a diving platform on the far side and made a mental note to later try basking here in the sun. Continuing our walk, we encountered the Chinese girl of the previous evening and convinced her to stroll with us. She was full of surprises, we discovered. She had been engaged to a British soldier in Shanghai, but he had been killed, and she had escaped to Hong Kong, then India. Now she lived in a camp for refugees in Naini Tal.

By the time she had told us her story in her limited English, we had arrived back at our hotel. We made arrangements to meet that evening at the dance hall, and she wandered off, presumably back to the refugee camp. She had a difficult name to pronounce, so I nicknamed her 'Cherry Blossom'. I found myself oddly attracted to her.

Meeting the rest of the crew produced one useful piece of information. There was a girls' finishing school at Naini Tal, and the girls would be at a tea dance the following afternoon.

The evening followed the usual routine: a few drinks in one of the many bars, then a visit to the dance hall. I spent considerably more time with Cherry Blossom, and she seemed to have been well accepted by the crew as she sat at our table. She even offered to buy a round of drinks, but at the end, she would not allow any of us, not even me, to escort her back to her camp. The crew meandered back to the hotel, and after some desultory conversation, we all fell asleep.

The days developed into a pattern for me. I passed most mornings by lazing around the pleasantly sunny diving platform with Harry, and my afternoons were spent on the lake, usually in the company of Cherry Blossom. The evenings were devoted to dance hall fun.

The tea dance had been a bit of a fiasco, as although the girls were there in plenty, they were so closely chaperoned that it was impossible to engage them in intimate conversation. Only Arnie seemed to have any success, but as he was a married man, we dismissed his relative popularity with the girls as being of no importance.

Harry's behaviour was causing us some puzzlement. He would disappear shortly after breakfast, and no one would see him until the following day when the process would be repeated. Finally, the mystery was solved when he admitted to spending time at the home of the wife of an Indian Army major. We were allowed to see the lady eventually. Considerably older than Harry and attractive in a blowsy sort of way, she seemed to find Harry irresistible, and he made the most of his opportunities.

Shortly before we were due to return to 159 Squadron, and following an afternoon together on the lake, I escorted Cherry Blossom to the evening's dance. Taking me by the arm after a slow waltz, she led me outside. The air was quite cool as we looked out on the lake, and without a word, she put her arms around me. I replied with ardour, and, in silence, we tenderly made love.

It was obvious that the girl had taken a big shine to me, and that I was enamoured of her. Gently, I pulled her to her feet, almost as if afraid of breaking something fragile, and we went back into the ballroom. Now, there was a subtle difference in our relationship. I was more considerate towards Cherry Blossom, and almost all of my remaining time on leave was spent with her.

On the morning of our departure, she was at the terminus in tears. I knew there could be no future for us. The RAF severely looked down upon any relationship that had the slightest trace of colour about it. I quietly took her to one side and promised that I would come and see her on my next leave. There was no point in writing as she could not read English, but I told her that I would send word with the other aircrews coming up on leave behind us.

Somewhat mollified, she nodded agreement, but contact between us evaporated. I never saw Cherry Blossom again; she was gone when I returned to Naini Tal with Fred and Harry at the end of April 1944 after my 159 Squadron tour of ops had concluded.

We Return to Digri

The three-tonner set off back towards the railway station at Kathgodam to begin the first leg of our lengthy return journey to Digri. The driver succeeded in frightening us all to death as he swung the wagon this way and that on the hairpin turns of the road back to the rail head, but finally we arrived and boarded the train to begin our rail adventure homeward. We caught our connection at Bareilly, and after a long and boring slog, we finally returned to camp.

On the train back from Bareilly to Calcutta, Arnie had complained of a pain in his foot. Back at our *basha* at Digri, seated on his charpoy, he asked us to examine it. The side of his foot was noticeably swollen, and an ominous red streak was creeping up the leg. Down at the Station Sick Quarters, Doc Kelly took one look, cleansed the swollen area, chose a sharp surgical instrument, and lanced the foot. An evil-smelling mixture shot out and Arnie passed out.

'Leave him here,' ordered Doc Kelly. 'He'll be alright in the morning,' he said as he tucked Arnie into a bed.

15

December 1943: A Return to Operations

A New CO on 159 Squadron

No. 159 Squadron had flown five ops during our absence. While we were gone, Wg Cdr Max Boffee DFC, the CO since February, informed the squadron that he was leaving us for a new posting. He thanked everyone for working tirelessly and in cooperation with him during his tenure. Taking over as the new CO on 13 December was Wg Cdr John 'Hoppy' Hopkins DFC, who, like Wg Cdr Boffee, was a veteran of aerial combat over Europe with Bomber Command.

My Thirteenth Op: Bangkok, Bansuk Marshalling Yards, 23–24 December 1943

A thirty-minute air test aboard *Algy* on the morning of 21 December reintroduced me to flying, and I felt not the least bit rusty in my wireless operator's responsibilities. Although I instinctively knew the inherent dangers of flight, even those pertaining to a short test hop, I equally sensed a natural affinity with my chosen airborne duties. Ops complicated the picture by deepening the anxiety, discomfort and in some instances intense fear, but I could not deny the satisfaction and thrill that came from flying, and surviving.

With Christmas almost upon us, we hoped to avoid ops until after the holiday, but we were disappointed to find our names on the battle order for the night of 23–24 December. Immediately upon hearing this, a tight, sinking feeling, absent since my last op, gripped my gut.

At the 8 a.m. briefing on the 23rd, we wished for a milk run to be handed to us as a sort of holiday gift, but when the new CO, Hoppy Hopkins, drew back the curtains over the blackboard whistles of dismay echoed through the space. Seven Liberators—matching 159 Squadron's highest total for a single op—were to fly to the Advanced Landing Ground at Dohazari, across the Bay of Bengal near Chittagong, India. After refuelling, the force would proceed to Bangkok, Siam, before returning to Dohazari. The round trip from the ALG to Bangkok and back would be at the limit of a Liberator's range. The squadron had successfully made its first trip ever to Bangkok four nights earlier, staging out of Dohazari, and a return attack so soon would most certainly shock the Japanese.

On this op, two Liberators, including *Algy*, would target Bansuk marshalling yards, two would bomb the Bangkok Military Arsenal, and three would single out Bangkok terminus railway station. Attacking three separate targets would add to the enemy's confusion.

This was my first op since my recent promotion to flight sergeant. Flying aboard *Algy*, I was joined by regular crewmates Harry, Willy, Fred, and C. J. Nicholls. Sgt F. N. Ellis was our skipper for a second and final time, assisted by an Australian second pilot, Sgt W. J. Garrity. One other airman completed the crew: FS Ernie Richards, manning the mid-upper gun as a replacement for Arnie, who was excused from ops while his foot mended.

With apprehension all round, we dutifully climbed aboard *Algy* and set off at 9.55 a.m. for the two-hour-and-fifteen-minute daylight flight to the ALG at Dohazari. Arriving without much difficulty, we sat around under the wings awaiting the signal to go.

As Dohazari was predominantly a fighter and dive bomber strip, the visiting four-engine Liberators were the objects of much curiosity that afternoon. Willy could not resist ribbing one of the onlookers, a navigator on one of the plentiful Vultee A-31 Vengeance dive bombers on the field. Considered a good aircraft, the Vengeance was the Allied equivalent of the German Stuka, characterised by hair-raising dives to deliver bombs on the target.

'Do you go far in one of those things?' Willy asked his victim. Innocently, the navigator replied that no, the Vengeance was a close-support aircraft for the infantry. When informed that the Liberators were going all the way to Bangkok, the navigator looked impressed. Willy grinned. 'Yes, we carry a couple of those for lifeboats,' he said, nodding towards the Vengeances.

The navigator took the humour good-naturedly. 'Hope you don't need them tonight,' he replied.

Eventually, we boarded our precious *Algy* and set off after sunset at 5.38 p.m. With only a crescent moon, the ground was but a sensation of endless jungle, stretching below us for mile after mile. It was hopeless country for a crash landing.

With the flight settled down to its usual boring drill, I tuned the radio compass for some dance music and found a good station broadcasting Glen Miller, Tommy Dorsey, and other big band orchestra sounds, interspersed with Japanese propaganda, which the crew ignored. Instead, hearing the music, I was flooded with memories of our late pal Ben, good ol' Ben, pre-war clarinettist supreme with Teddy Joyce and His Orchestra. Only sixteen months ago, on leave with me,

Ben had spontaneously displayed his talent before a dance hall crowd back in Leeds; it seemed like yesterday to me.

We had passed Rangoon and were on the final leg to Bangkok when I glanced at the radio compass needle. It was straight up, meaning that we were headed directly for the station, broadcasting from Bangkok.

Willy had been singing into the microphone until told by the skipper to shut up, whereupon a sulky silence pervaded the aircraft. The music from Bangkok, however, continued in our headphones until the preparation for bombing demanded our undivided attention.

While *Algy* was still on approach to Bansuk marshalling yards, our assigned target, the attack by other Liberators began. Evidence of bomb bursts and growing conflagrations dotted the ground below. With both inaccurate flak and searchlights being of no grave issue, *Algy* made two separate runs over its target, releasing bombs each time.

Sgt Ellis set course for home with a crew well pleased with our night's work, with one exception. In time, over the intercom, came Willy's plaintive voice, 'Hey, Enoch, how 'bout some music for the ride home?'

'We blasted 'em off the air, Willy,' I said, quite satisfied.

There was a grunt heard over the intercom. 'Hummph! Rotten sods!' exclaimed Willy. He had failed to take the lack of music as a probable sign of attack success.

The rest of the flight back to Dohazari was accomplished without incident, and Sgt Ellis landed at 4.30 a.m. after being airborne for ten hours and fifty-two minutes. Following a quick petrol drink, *Algy* took off again at 4.55 a.m. for a two-hour flight back to Digri. All told, from start to finish and including the legs to and from Dohazari, our flight time for the Bangkok op amounted to fifteen hours and seven minutes.

I was pleased to learn that the initial two-hour-and-fifteen-minute jaunt from Digri to Dohazari, fully bombed up, counted towards my total hours for ops flown on my tour. The return two-hour hop back to Digri from Dohazari, minus bombs, did not. Two aircraft, but not *Algy*, were found to have minor damage.

Christmas 1943 is Celebrated on 159 Squadron

Christmas for men stationed in isolation so far from their loved ones could be a difficult season. In the best of RAF traditions, on 159 Squadron the effort was made to bring cheer by temporarily dispensing with the strict privileges of rank. A mixed football match, all in good fun and with participants dressed in silly outfits, was a great opportunity to forget about the war.

Later, the officers served the NCOs our Christmas dinner, and a good sing-song was had. For a change, the food was delicious and plentiful: asparagus soup, chicken broth, *hors d'oeuvres*, roast turkey and savoury stuffing, roast goose, roast pork with apple sauce, baked potatoes, cabbage, cauliflower, carrots, green peas, Christmas pudding, brandy sauce, fresh cream, cheese and biscuits, coffee, and dessert—heavenly. Plus, soya links were nowhere to be found. The flow of alcohol did a world of good, too.

We enjoyed a much-welcomed chance to renew mutual friendships with John, now a busy flight lieutenant given additional duties beyond just a pilot's work. John had not been our skipper since mid-November, but late in January of the new year, that would change.

The good cheer continued on the 26th with an evening performance of the 159 Squadron Concert Party's riotously entertaining farcical revue, entitled 'Jankers Away.' A repeat performance was also grandly received the following night.

My Fourteenth Op: Rangoon, Mahlwagon Marshalling Yards, 30–31 December 1943

Before the year concluded, however, it was back to the business of waging war. On the night of 30–31 December, we were off to a hotspot, Rangoon's Mahlwagon marshalling yards in an eastern district of the town. Again, 159 Squadron set a new record in the number of Liberators deployed, with eight aircraft scheduled for the operation—four from 'A' Flight and four from 'B' Flight.

Aboard *Butch*, BZ855, regular crewmates Harry, Arnie (healed now), Willy, Fred, C. J. Nicholls, and I were led by a skipper with whom only Harry had previously flown on ops, the recently promoted WO J. H. Jones. FS M. B. Murphy, also new to us, was the second pilot, and Sgt Herbert Allanach on beam gun completed the crew roster.

For the crew of BZ855, the flight was memorable for the cigarette drop organised by Willy. No one had thought much about his absence from the billet during mid-afternoon, but the reason for his disappearance became readily apparent when we arrived at the aircraft in the evening and climbed aboard. The rear end of the bomber was like the inside of a tobacconist's warehouse with quantities of 'V' for Victory cigarettes. Manufactured in India, these were issued free to the troops and were so awful that even the natives tended to avoid them.

It was all Willy's doing as he proudly explained. 'I thought that as we're going to Rangoon, we could lob these out, and maybe they'd drop into the jail area. Well, at least some of them. Those poor sods might be glad for them. To a smoker a bad smoke is better than no smoke, you know.'

He referred to the Allied Prisoners of War held by the Japanese in Rangoon Jail, an easy-to-spot landmark in the heart of the town. No doubt as captives of the notoriously brutal Japanese, the prisoners were having a grim time of it and might appreciate smokes—even the god-awful 'V' for Victory cigarettes.

The skipper shrugged and commented, 'Can't do any harm, I guess, as long as you prioritise your crew responsibilities.' With our heads nodding in affirmation, not another word was necessary.

Take-offs went smoothly, except for aircraft 'P', BZ842, which suffered from a balky engine. While the seven other Liberators departed Digri between 5.07 p.m. and 5.19 p.m., including our BZ855 at 5.17 p.m., BZ842's engine gremlin persisted until a successful 5.50 p.m. take-off was made.

The trip aboard BZ855 was uncomplicated until over the target, when the usual pandemonium broke out, with formidable searchlight and anti-aircraft defences endeavouring to conspire against us, and with at least one night fighter spotted. My preoccupation with tossing cigs out the beam hatches with Willy helped to distract me from my fears.

On the way back, silence reigned in the bomber until suddenly broken by Harry. 'Navigator to crew,' he said. 'Say, you guys, it's after midnight. Happy New Year's Eve!' We had completely forgotten in the excitement. It was the last day of 1943.

Like the other seven Liberators on the sortie, BZ855 made it home unharmed. For my crew, a landing at Digri at 3.26 a.m. closed the book on both a ten-hour-and-nine-minute Rangoon operation and our 1943 flying.

16

January 1944

My Fifteenth Op: Moulmein Minelaying, 10–11 January 1944

Two sorties in January 1944 by squadron Liberators—including one on the 2nd–3rd when Fred flew as WO J. C. Stuart's rear gunner—were successfully flown before our full crew was called upon for our next op on 10–11 January. That night aboard BZ840, known as *Eagle*, Harry, C. J. Nicholls, Arnie, Willy, Fred and I were skippered by Fg Off. Ken Brailsford, a veteran of bomber ops in the UK, the Middle East and the Far East. Pop Simmons came along for the ride, but also joining us was a third pilot, 159 Squadron's new CO, Wg Cdr Hoppy Hopkins.

Again, eight Liberators from 159 Squadron participated, as did six Liberators from 355 Squadron. It was a special op—minelaying by six of the 159 Squadron Libs, including us in BZ840, plus five Libs from 355 Squadron, in the Moulmein, Burma area. One of the 159 Squadron Liberators made a diversionary bombing attack upon gun emplacements at Battery Point in Moulmein town, while another 159 Squadron aircraft targeted Martaban railway station in the vicinity. One Liberator from 355 Squadron bombed Moulmein shore defences. Each of these three attacks was coordinated with the minelaying part of the op.

Earlier, on the morning of the 10th, the six bombers from 159 Squadron assigned to minelaying took off from Digri for a thirty-minute flight to the American B-24 base at Panagarh, 48 miles to the north. With an empty bomb bay, our BZ840 departed Digri at 8.45 a.m. for this short hop. Three other Liberators each carried one American-made 1,000-lb aerial-dropped magnetic sea mine, nicknamed a 'vegetable', in its bomb rack; 159 Squadron had no more. From the stockpile at Panagarh, sea mines were loaded into each bomb bay, so that, when bombed up, each of the six Liberators carried four 1,000-lb vegetables for the night's assignment. We were fed by the Americans prior to the op.

At 5.01 p.m., BZ840 set out from Panagarh, bound for Moulmein. For me, the thought of four 1,000-lb mines in the bomb bay did nothing to soothe my nerves.

In bright moonlight, Harry successfully released BZ840's mines into the channel at Moulmein from the twitchy height of 230 feet. The action was fairly quiet, with only sporadic machine gunfire and light flak blindly stabbing out at us from the aroused enemy ashore, but no damage was inflicted upon *Eagle*.

Aboard *Algy*, manned by another crew that night, Aussie FS W. J. Garrety flew as second pilot. He had joined our crew for an op only eighteen nights earlier. This time, however, he was not so fortunate. During the release of vegetables in the Moulmein—Martaban Ferry stretch of water at 11 p.m., FS Garrety suffered a serious gunshot wound. Nobody else was injured, but the minelaying run was abandoned with two mines still aboard. BZ906 immediately headed for Alipore, in the Calcutta area, to allow optimal medical attention to be rendered to FS Garrety at the earliest opportunity.

Though the bullet did not enter FS Garrety's abdominal cavity, the resulting compression fracture to ribs lacerated his liver. Initially placed on the 'seriously ill' list, he recovered from his wounds and eventually returned to flying to complete a full tour with 99 Squadron on Liberators. There were no other casualties among the airmen from 159 and 355 Squadrons.

BZ840 returned to Digri, landing at 4.52 a.m., after a flight time of eleven hours and fifty-two minutes. Harry and I had each completed a fifteenth op—halfway to the magic thirty.

My Sixteenth Op: Rangoon Central Railway Station, 16–17 January 1944

The core members of my crew were by this time classed as experienced airmen. We handled our equipment with confidence, and long gone were the fears of men new to the realities of operational flying. Yet a dodgy target or challenging weather still put us on edge and rattled our bones.

In an environment of constant change, our strict crew makeup had evolved since we arrived in India the previous May. Chalky White asked for a reassignment before our first op last May, to distance himself from Ben. Ben died on ops. John had not been our skipper since mid-November. Now, Willy—such an enriching character on the ground and in the air, and a valued air gunner—was seconded as rear gunner to WO J. C. Stuart. To the RAF brass, Willy seemed just another interchangeable part, as if the bond forged between crewmates really did not hold much value, but to Willy's long-serving crewmates, losing him, for an undefined period, spilled some of the wind out of our sails.

However, we forged on, strongly, as we knew we would. Willy was still our mate back at Digri; it's just that we worried about him like brothers and wanted him with us, on our aircraft, over Rangoon, or Heho, or Bangkok, or any of the other faraway places we only viewed from altitude. Little did we realise at the time that he would not rejoin us until mid-March.

On the night of 16–17 January, our dwindling core crew was sent on another op to hot Rangoon, this time to the heart of the town: Rangoon central railway station. Aboard the familiar BZ900, *Crusader*, but not *Algy* as we had hoped, Harry, C. J. Nicholls, Arnie, Fred, and I flew with FS Chris Hedley as our skipper. This was our fourth op with FS Hedley, but the first with him in the captain's seat. It was fine, however, because we liked him, and we trusted his skills and instincts.

Flying as second pilot was the ever-intriguing Pop Simmons. A new crew position, flight engineer, was being introduced on some Liberators, and Sgt Pete Bailey filled the role for us. Finally, in Willy's place on a beam gun, Australian FS Norman Bingham joined us.

After the 12 p.m. briefing, a record nine 159 Squadron Liberators, each carrying 4,000 pounds of bombs, including incendiaries, were airborne between 3.50 p.m. and 4.05 p.m. for the long trip to Rangoon. We took off in BZ900 at 4 p.m. Putting up only nine Liberators would have been enough to make Bomber Command boys back in the UK double-over with laughter, but the scale of aerial warfare in the Far East could not be rightly compared with that over Europe.

Regardless of the numbers comparisons, the work by 159 Squadron aircraft and men was inherently dangerous for a variety of reasons. Yes, enemy defences, including night fighters, were not nearly as deadly as over Europe, but we knew that in other ways the threats we faced were worse than in Bomber Command. For example, we realised that the odds were not in our favour here should we go down over the unforgiving jungle or the Bay of Bengal, or worse, should we fall into Japanese hands.

Anti-aircraft fire and searchlights, as always, made for some anxious minutes over Rangoon for each Liberator that night. Ground haze added to the challenge for the bomb aimers. Successfully avoiding night fighters, as well, all nine aircraft bombed the target and returned with uninjured airmen to Digri.

Our BZ900 landed at 1.45 a.m. after nine hours and forty-five minutes of flying. Following a customary post-op debriefing, and feeling exhausted, my crewmates and I sought sleep.

Mk VI Liberators Arrive on 159 Squadron

Deliveries of the latest Mk VI model Liberators swelled the inventory of war-ready aircraft on 159 Squadron during the month of January 1944. Six were delivered to Digri in January: BZ960, BZ962, BZ973, BZ980, BZ982, and EV843. The most striking visual change over the Mk III Liberator was the addition of an American-built Consolidated A-6 turret, in the nose, offering further defensive firepower against frontal fighter attacks. The new turret's twin .5-inch Brownings replaced a single hand-aimed .5-inch machine gun.

The senior RAF technical honchos, however, did not deem the new turret essential for our ops, all flown under cover of darkness. Additionally, a functioning nose turret would have required another dedicated crewman. The turret, however, was left unoccupied, and no ammunition was carried for its dual .5-inch Brownings.

Even though unmanned on ops and lacking ammo, this aerodynamically disruptive turret, plus its two Brownings, added drag and weight which degraded the flight characteristics of the Mk VI versus the Mk III model. More petrol was required for an op compared with the same flight aboard a Mk III, and fewer bombs were carried.

A reduced bomb total seemed a steep price to pay for retaining an unmanned front turret devoid of ammunition. To my contemptuous fellow airmen and myself, the whole point of risking our lives was to pound the enemy with as much firepower as possible, so the lower bomb load of the Mk VI angered us.

Harry, like other navigator/bomb aimers, took an instant dislike to the Mk VI because the nose was more cramped with much-reduced visibility. No longer was there a sweeping view out of a roomy greenhouse nose.

The Mk VI's tail still held the Boulton Paul power turret, with four .303-inch Brownings. It was still seen as a wise precaution to carry considerably more ammo for the rear turret, given that most night fighter attacks were from the rear. Each Liberator's rear turret was always stocked with 6,000 rounds of .303-inch ammo, while the most any other manned gun—all of 50 calibre—carried on ops were 820 rounds in the mid-upper turret.

At some point after I'd finished flying with 159 Squadron, the Boulton Paul tail turret, with its four .303-inch peashooters, was replaced with a Consolidated A-6 turret and its robust twin .5-inch guns.

The new Mk VIs, overall, baffled us on 159 Squadron, but change was inevitable. Technological progress was sometimes two steps forward and one step back, and we were told to have faith in our newest Liberators. There were other improvements in the Mk VI, resulting from the combat trials-by-fire of the earlier Liberator versions and the remarkable wartime innovations of science and industry.

The Mk VI carried all the hardware needed for the installation of a ball turret in the fuselage's belly, with twin .5-inch Brownings, but 159 Squadron chose to eschew this turret until late July 1944, after my departure. Even then, the ball turret was only used on a scant few ops before its removal as a weight-saving measure.

My Seventeenth Op: Meiktila Railway Station, 22–23 January 1944

On 22–23 January, Mk VI Liberators made their 159 Squadron operational debut when BZ962, BZ973, and BZ980 joined seven Mk III Libs on a bombing raid on Meiktila railway station in Burma. The total of ten aircraft aloft was yet another personal record for the squadron. Indicative of the differences between the Mk III and the Mk VI, each Mk III carried 5,500 pounds of bombs, while each of the Mk VIs carried only 4,000 pounds.

After having flown no ops with his old crewmates for over two months, finally John was our skipper again, aboard one of the new Libs, BZ962. Joining John aboard BZ962 were four of his boys dating back to 1942 in the UK: Harry, Arnie, Fred, and me. No flight engineer was added this night. C. J. Nicholls, on the crew since the previous June, was flying with John as his skipper for the fifth time; twice more John had been his second pilot on ops in 1943. Pop Simmons was John's second pilot for a third time on a sortie.

With Willy seconded to WO J. C. Stuart's crew, a replacement beam gunner was needed, and Sgt Jack O'Brien was the man. Jack, who blended in with the others from the start, was destined for a long stay with our crew.

Having been christened *Daring Diana* by another crew, BZ962 had already been anointed with appropriate nose art of a leggy, busty, and scantily clad woman with a 'come hither' look about her. This was not one of my artistic creations, however, but already the bomber had personality and a name. Our general disapproval of the Mk VI as an aircraft was offset somewhat by our collective satisfaction in flying aboard a Liberator already dubbed *Daring Diana*. John took off at 4.58 p.m. as the fourth Liberator to depart from Digri.

The squadron expected the Meiktila raid to be a relatively easy do—not exactly a milk run, but nothing like the fury anticipated when attacking just about any Rangoon target.

For our crew on *Daring Diana*, the flight did not go quite as smoothly as planned. The trip out to the target had been without incident. Meiktila railway station was clearly visible, and Harry toggled the bombs in two sticks, one on each of two runs over the target. No flak seemed to burst close to us, nor were there night fighters about, but coming off the target suddenly engine No. 2, the port inner engine, slowly windmilled to a stop. John feathered the prop without difficulty, rotating the blades so that they presented the least drag against the onrushing air.

Daring Diana maintained height reasonably well on the remaining three engines, and John set down at Digri at 12.20 a.m., after seven hours and twenty-two minutes in the air.

For eight of the Liberators, the op was unremarkable, as expected, with no Japanese defences worth worrying about. WO J. C. Stuart's BZ980, however, another of the new Mk VIs, suffered an engine malfunction and then a brief fire on the outward leg but landed temporarily at Double Moorings, near Chittagong, to address the problem. Airborne again, BZ980 successfully reached and bombed the target. On its way home, but struggling to maintain height, BZ980 put down at Chittagong. Willy was the rear gunner on this Liberator, and his delay in returning to Digri caused a spot of bother for us, his overprotective mates on the Gauntlett crew. It was Willy's seventeenth op.

The faulty engine on *Daring Diana*, of a type—the Pratt & Whitney Twin Wasp—with legendary reliability, was a complete mystery to the 159 Squadron engine mechanics. Their first job after John landed BZ962 was to examine the offending engine. Four neat holes were immediately found in the cowling, tell-tale evidence, it seemed, of small arms fire, but this just added to the mystery. We had bombed from a height of 10,500 feet, too high over enemy territory—and at too fast a speed—to have been vulnerable to small arms fire resulting in a closely-grouped spread of hits.

The priority of the bewildered engine mechanics, however, was to make the engine right, not to determine how and when the cowling holes had appeared. Had the Liberator been shot at in Indian airspace? That was the general conclusion, and of course, we hoped there would be no repeat of this action.

My Eighteenth Op: Mingaladon Aerodrome, 31 January–1 February 1944

Nine days elapsed until the squadron's next op on the night of 31 January–1 February. This time, at the 2.30 p.m. briefing, eleven crews learned that the target was Mingaladon aerodrome, a hornet's nest of activity just 9 miles due north of Rangoon's docks. Mingaladon was also the target where Ben had bought it the previous October, so it was with a healthy respect for our adversary that we approached upcoming duties.

After the last op, we claimed one of the new Mk VI Liberators, EV843, as our personal upgrade from *Algy*. Henceforth, we would fly all but one of our remaining ops aboard 'our' aircraft. Even more so than *Algy*, then, this new aircraft was truly ours to fly.

On the nose of the bomber, designated as aircraft 'E', I had swiftly designed and painted a voluptuous wench lying back with her hands behind her head. We named our new Liberator *Erotic Edna*.

On this night, the Gauntlett crew was identical to that from the previous op to Meiktila: John as skipper, Pop Simmons as his second pilot, Harry as navigator/bomb aimer, myself as wireless operator, C. J. Nicholls as a beam gunner and 2nd W/op, Arnie as mid-upper gunner, the 'new bloke' Jack on the other beam gun, and Fred in the rear turret.

The force of Liberators departed Digri for Mingaladon in the evening, led by EV843, which took off at 4.25 p.m. One Liberator, BZ922, ran into trouble at the end of the runway when a main wheel bogged down in soft ground off the concrete. Unable to rectify the embarrassing problem, the aircraft was reluctantly scrubbed from the op. *Algy* and its crew were also dropped from the sortie because of mechanical issues. In total, then, nine aircraft took off for Rangoon.

John approached the greater Rangoon area without difficulty, but then the curse of clouds began to obscure the target. Forced to cancel the first bomb run, Harry called for John to go around again. On the second run-up, a hole in the clouds revealed the aerodrome, giving Harry a good sighting to set up the toggling of bombs.

Having removed the horseshoes from the bombs, I felt the sudden urge to face my fears by sitting on the catwalk as Harry opened the bomb doors and began the countdown to the release point. This had not been required of me since the previous October, but on this occasion, feeling invincible, or foolhardy, I simply sought a thrill. Coned in searchlights now, we all knew that we were vulnerable to anti-aircraft fire on the straight-and-level bomb run.

Peering downward through the open bomb bay doors, my heart did a somersault when, almost directly below us and only about 100 yards away, I spied a Japanese night fighter. Illuminated by its own searchlights and vulnerable to its own flak, it was flying parallel to our heading.

'Wireless op to skipper,' I warned, 'there's a fighter stalking us, immediately below! Let's bombard him with incendiaries, and then you, rear gunner, stand by to blast him when he reacts!'

Receiving affirmative replies, I gave the signal, 'Prepare to release incendiaries ... Go!' Selectively toggled by Harry up front, the Warren Coffin incendiary containers dropped from their bomb bay clips, and the incendiaries began to scatter, as designed. They missed the fighter below, but the Japanese pilot responded violently to avoid potential disaster and was picked up by Fred in the rear turret.

A brief rattle from Fred's guns followed.

'Rear gunner, give a report!' barked John.

'Rear gunner to pilot, I don't think I got him, but I sure as shit frightened the little bugger to death. He's run away,' answered Fred in his usual emotionless voice.

With no more fighter sightings, John regained the bomb run. After another countdown with course corrections dictated to the skipper by Harry, at last came the words, 'Bombs gone!'

It had been an exciting few minutes.

Accuracy was less than desired, but given the circumstances we were pleased that we had been able to hit the primary target at all.

We made our escape without further hassle from fighters and arrived back at Digri for a touchdown at 1.52 a.m. EV843 had been airborne for nine hours and twenty-seven minutes.

Owing to cloud cover, only two other Liberators found and bombed an unidentified aerodrome believed to be Mingaladon. Three more aircraft jettisoned their bomb loads far from the target in order to minimise risk upon landing. One Liberator attacked an alternate target in the Rangoon area, Mahlwagon marshalling yards; one bombed Prome, on the Irrawaddy River in Burma; and one target was believed to be Akyab, bordering the Bay of Bengal. It was not one of 159 Squadron's better results, but clouds, not just the Japanese, were our bitter enemy on occasion.

17

February 1944

The Loss of BZ973 'F' on 1 February 1944 and a Suicide

One of my nose art commissions, nearly completed, never flew on ops. The crew of the new Mk VI Liberator BZ973, aircraft 'F', had asked me to paint a winged beer barrel and the name *The Flying Firkin*—a firkin being the term given to the nine-gallon beer barrel in current use back in English pubs. I had spent all morning painting my creation on the forward fuselage to the delight of the air and ground crew. When the gharry took us back to the Sergeants' Mess for tiffin, I had only the lettering left to complete.

While we were having our midday meal, a hefty explosion was heard coming from the flying field. Several of the ground crew sergeants in our Mess looked at each other in puzzlement. The explosion, they sensed, could not have been due to enemy action, as radar stations had given no advanced general warning of incoming raiders, and there were no overhead sounds of attacking aircraft. The aerodrome had never been attacked.

The initial news, soon received over the Sergeants' Mess telephone, resulted in one of the sergeants taking off on the double for the flying field. I had noticed that the sergeant was the ground crew chief of 'F'. I attached no undue importance to that fact as I thought the man might have been Duty Sergeant for the day and, thus, was required to attend to the emergency.

No one who heard the explosion was unduly worried, as the sound had been more of a whoompf than a sharp explosion. Word, however, soon went around the Mess like lightning: '"F" has gone up!' Everyone crowded outside, and the evil black column rising into the blue sky supported the gossip. A great wave of sympathy went out to the ground staff of the aircraft, especially to the sergeant, as he would likely be held responsible.

By the evening, the full story had been accurately gathered. Two men had been working on the machine—an electrician in the bomb bay and an instrument fitter on the flight deck. The bomb bay was notorious for the strong odour of lingering petrol fumes. When one of the two fired up the auxiliary power unit, a spark apparently touched off the fumes in the bomb bay, followed in turn by wing tanks igniting—up she went.

One of the two ground crew died three days later in hospital. It hit the ground crew sergeant badly. He withdrew into himself, and although the aircrew laid on an enormous binge, the drink seemed to have no positive medicinal effect on him.

The following morning, he was missing. He had been a popular member of the Sergeants' Mess, and a widespread search was conducted. The railway station was investigated and the surrounding areas searched, but all without success. There were rumours that he had been sighted around one of the many small crossroad villages nearby. It was even feared that he may have been murdered by a more militant anti-British element of the Indian community, but enquiries uncovered nothing.

He was finally found about a week later by one of the bearers taking a shortcut through the scrub jungle at the back of the Mess. He had hanged himself.

My Nineteenth Op: Heho Aerodrome, 4–5 February 1944

In the Briefing Room at 2 p.m. on 4 February, twelve crews, including ours, were notified of a daring plan by combined US and RAF bomber forces to hammer Heho aerodrome, Burma, on successive days. As planned, one RAF Wellington squadron, one US B-24 outfit and 159 Squadron's Liberators would begin the mayhem that night in independent attacks. On the following day, an American B-25 raid and another US B-24 attack would strike Heho in daylight. Finally, on that second night, Heho would be bombed separately by 99 Squadron Wellingtons and 159 Squadron Liberators. This added onslaught would further confound our already-battered foe.

In addition to suffering heavy damage, the Japanese would be left with a false and demoralising impression of enemy bomber strength. So many aircraft over one aerodrome would be interpreted as a much more substantial force than there existed, and a paranoid Japanese strategic reaction could then be anticipated by the Allies.

Most of the twelve Liberators from 159 Squadron—another record number for one sortie—would release bombs on two separate runs over the target per night, adding to the bluff that an even more superior bomber force was attacking. At least two bomb runs per aircraft was typical for 159 Squadron during many of our ops.

The effort would be taxing on the squadron's aircrew, ground crew, and machines, but Wg Cdr Hopkins emphasised to us that the maximum effort, two nights running, represented the culmination of all we had trained for. It would be a chance to prove the extraordinary capabilities of 159 Squadron to others. We knew that the CO's words rang true, even though the task at hand would be exhausting and most worrisome.

On the positive side, each also knew that every trip in the logbook put him one nearer the end of his tour, and maybe, just maybe, two ops in two nights would ultimately lead to a quicker return to Blighty, or Oz, or wherever one called home. At least, it would lead to a safer posting, still in India.

Piloting EV843 again, John lifted from the Digri runway at 9.34 p.m. and set a course for Heho. EV843 was the third of the twelve Liberators in the air. Joining John were his same seven crewmates from four nights earlier: Pop Simmons, Harry, C. J. Nicholls, Arnie, Jack, Fred, and me. In addition, a second navigator, Plt Off. Tony Sanders, was also aboard for experience.

Bombing on a clear moonlit night from 13,500 feet on our first run and 13,300 on our second, the Gauntlett crew met no substantial opposition, apart from persistent searchlights which dazzled us and caused some slight discomfort. We managed to do our business and escape back to Digri, where we landed at 6.30 a.m. after eight hours and fifty-six minutes of flying time.

One other squadron Liberator, BZ980, turned back early with mechanical difficulties and jettisoned its bomb load over the Bay of Bengal. All other 159 Squadron aircraft attacked Heho and returned to base undamaged. Nine Liberators from 355 Squadron, unable to locate their primary target, Aungban aerodrome, diverted to add to the destruction at Heho.

Back at Digri, we were both relieved and disgusted to learn that we would be pulled from the next night's action because of a minor mechanical fault in EV843. Among our squadron mates, we would have to endure the mostly good-natured ribbing for missing the second night's action, and, of course, we would not get credit for a second op. Just the same, being safe and comfortable on the ground back at base was not lost on us.

Except for the scrubbing of EV843 and BZ980, each down for repairs, the second night's attack by 159 Squadron was a carbon copy of the first night. The same Liberators participated, with identical bomb loads and similar results—including no injuries, deaths or aircraft losses.

Considered a success, the 159 Squadron attacks on successive nights boosted the morale of the squadron, even for our crew, despite our own disappointment at missing out on the second night's action. The intensely personal double-whammy assault upon the major enemy aerodrome at Heho using a record number of 159 Squadron Liberators, in conjunction with other RAF and US bomb squadrons, was a powerful indication to us that the Allied forces were destined for ever-increasing might in this no-nonsense battle against the hated Japanese.

My Twentieth Op:
Bangkok, Makasan Railway Workshops, 10–11 February 1944

At 8.30 a.m. on 10 February, aboard the gremlin-free and fully bombed-up EV843, our crew took off from Digri for a two-hour flight to Feni, another RAF advanced landing ground with refuelling capabilities. Situated 17 miles inland in the north-eastern corner of the Bay of Bengal, Feni would serve as 159 Squadron's temporary base for an eight-bomber op to Bangkok, Siam and back, this time to attack the Makasan railway workshops overnight.

From Feni, one separate Mk III Liberator was tasked with bombing a different target as a solitary raider: Moulmein, Burma.

Destined for Bangkok, our crew aboard EV843 was nearly identical to that of the Heho op six nights earlier, with two changes. For this and three more ops John's second pilot, in the cockpit alongside him, would be Sqn Ldr J. M. Hillier, replacing Pop Simmons. Also, the second navigator from the last trip, Plt Off. Tony Sanders, was absent this time. The crew, then, consisted of John, Sqn Ldr Hillier, Harry, C. J. Nicholls, Arnie, Jack, Fred, and me.

Sqn Ldr Hillier proved to be a friendly chap, but John was wary of this former tail-dragging Spitfire pilot's ability to land a Liberator in one piece. Sqn Ldr Hillier had demonstrated his competency in flying the Liberator, with its nose wheel design—after all, he was a certified pilot on a Liberator squadron. Nevertheless, on this op John insisted on handling the take-off and landing duties, tasks he sometimes relinquished to his second pilot.

This would mark a milestone twentieth op for both Harry and me. John would reach the seventeen-operation mark and C. J. Nicholls would reach sixteen. Fred (twenty-three ops) and Arnie (twenty-two ops) still led the way. Relative newcomer Jack would only be on his sixth sortie, and fourth with the Gauntlett crew. Aboard WO Stuart's BZ980, Willy would notch his eighteenth op.

Taking off at 5.45 p.m., EV843 endured a bumpy ride in dreary weather towards its destination, but though we were delayed in reaching Bangkok, the city was clear of clouds. Harry's welcome pronouncement, 'Bombs gone,' followed a straightforward run in to the target from 10,000 feet. There was no obvious fighter activity in the area, and our time over Bangkok was smooth and free of serious opposition; only weak and inaccurate flak and clueless searchlights were noted.

Harry's toggled bombs pranged the Makasan railway workshops; bursts were seen diagonally across buildings in the target area. In all, six of the seven other Libs also placed bombs on the workshops, and we witnessed many fires started by these aircraft. The seventh bomber, suffering from a faulty bombsight, was not as accurate with its bomb aiming.

Eleven hours and twenty-five minutes after take-off, John landed back at Feni at 5.10 a.m., three hours after the return of BZ906, *Algy*, which had bombed the Moulmein railway workshops. EV843 had performed perfectly for us.

On the ground at Feni, we learned that once again *Algy* sustained damage in the Moulmein area, exactly one month after its previous troubles. This time a single night fighter attacked over the Gulf of Martaban during the return trip to Feni. Fortunately, the damage was not serious and there were no injuries.

Following breakfast, 159 Squadron's visiting Liberators departed Feni for the return flights to Digri. With no bombs weighing us down in EV843, we were back home ninety minutes after our 10.30 a.m. take-off. In all, we had been airborne for an exhausting fourteen hours and fifty-five minutes over the previous 28.5 hours.

For the second time—the first being back on 23 December—I was allowed to add the time of our crew's initial hop to the advanced landing ground (carrying bombs) to the sum total of my op hours flown on my tour. All told, I had now accumulated 187 hours and thirty-five minutes of operational flying, well on the way to the magic 300-hour milestone.

On the night of 12–13 February, Willy safely completed his nineteenth op as WO J. C. Stuart's rear gunner aboard EV843, one of two Liberators sent out in an Army support role to attack Myebon village on the Bay of Bengal coast in Burma.

My Twenty-First Op: Bangkok Terminus Railway Station (Moulmein Railway Jetty Bombed), 15–16 February 1944

On 15–16 February, 159 Squadron matched its previous personal record of twelve Liberators on the same op, set on the Heho raid of 4–5 February less than two weeks earlier. The effort as planned, however, would split the Liberators between three targets: one Liberator to Myebon, Burma; seven aircraft to Bangkok, Siam yet again; and four to Prome, a village on the Irrawaddy River in Burma used by the Japanese for storage dumps. With no advanced landing ground being used, the Bangkok contingent of aircraft would be flying the longest op ever for the squadron.

Our crew was scheduled to be part of the Bangkok force. Our personal Mk VI Lib, EV843, had been assigned to a newer aircrew headed to Prome, a much shorter distance from Digri; instead, we were assigned a Mk III, BZ924. Joining me were John as skipper, Sqn Ldr J. M. Hillier as second pilot, Harry as navigator, C. J. Nicholls as a beam gunner (and second wireless operator), Jack on the other beam gun, and Fred in the rear turret.

There was one more major change: my closest mate on the squadron, Arnie, was no longer on the Gauntlett crew. Replacing him in the mid-upper turret was FS Ernie Richards, who had flown once with the crew, back on the 23–24 November 1943 op. Already with the experience of over twenty ops as an air gunner on 159 Squadron, Ernie became a permanent crewman, while Arnie soon became FS Westmorland's regular mid-upper gunner, never to return to our crew.

The solitary Mk VI aircraft destined for Myebon took off from Digri at 5.59 p.m. Having fulfilled its assignment, it arrived back at Digri at 12.46 a.m., just twenty-nine minutes after the last of the Prome raiders departed. The seven-strong Bangkok force, all Mk III Liberators, took off between 6.30 p.m. and 6.40 p.m.

Dense, obscuring ground haze at Bangkok that night proved just as detrimental to our mission as would have clouds. Despite poor visibility, one Liberator chose to bomb the target, Bangkok terminus railway station, based upon a timed run from a landmark river bend. With ground haze making target identification impossible, the six other Bangkok raiders reluctantly diverted to secondary targets in southern Burma.

Harry successfully targeted one of the three railway jetties on the Moulmein waterfront (which one, I do not know). Three Liberators bombed in the vicinity of Moulmein south railway station. One Lib targeted the south railway jetty, while one attacked Thanbyuzayat, Burma, 36 miles farther south of Moulmein.

The four Libs sent to Prome, each a Mk VI carrying 5,000 pounds of bombs, were the last to take off, between 12.05 a.m. and 12.17 a.m. on the 16th. They succeeded in bombing Japanese storage dumps. Having avoided trouble from defensive fire and fighters, the four aircraft landed at Digri interspersed with the seven Liberators returning from the Bangkok part of the op. Willy, sent to Prome aboard WO J. C. Stuart's BZ980, reached the twenty-operation mark.

We finally touched down back at Digri at 7.56 a.m. It was no surprise that we were exhausted, having just flown for thirteen hours and twenty-three minutes, which included sortie time wasted over the Bangkok haze before diverting for Moulmein.

My Twenty-Second Op: Mandalay Marshalling Yards, 18–19 February 1944

The heavy schedule of ops continued in this period of ideal flying weather. While the workload was demanding on our psyches, almost every airman on the squadron was imbued with a resolve to take on and crush the Japanese. Of course, there were the rare exceptions to this mindset, but I did not surround myself with such men.

At noon on 18 February, ten crews were notified of their target that night, the Mandalay marshalling yards in Burma. I had been there only once, way back on 12–13 June 1943, when the Warren Coffin was first deployed as a means of releasing incendiaries over a target. June, eight months earlier, seemed like yesterday to me, but here I was, on the verge of my twenty-second op. My previous visit to Mandalay was my fifth op.

Aboard EV843 again would be the crew from three nights earlier: John, Sqn Ldr Hillier, Harry, C. J. Nicholls, Ernie, Jack, Fred, and me. There would be one more crewmate added this time: Sgt C. Church, a flight engineer.

Arnie's twenty-third op would be as mid-upper gunner aboard FS Westmoreland's Liberator, BZ982, and Willy would be on his twenty-first sortie, again as rear gunner with WO Stuart as his skipper aboard BZ980.

One Liberator was scratched from the op, but nine took off for Mandalay in the early evening. Our EV843 departed at 4.58 p.m., the fifth Liberator in the air. Although Mandalay town was better defended than Bangkok, on that night the defences caused us no undue alarm. We hit the target squarely and headed back to base without difficulty, and with nothing negative to observe other than the usual sniping from fatigued aircrew.

John landed EV843 back at Digri at 12.19 a.m., after what thankfully was an uncomplicated flight of seven hours and twenty-one minutes. To the crew chief after engine shutdown, I shrugged a false apology and offered, 'Not even a dent from a mosquito collision. Sorry to be so boring!' Deep down, we all wished that each future op would be so mundane.

The Impending Move to Dhubalia

For myself and many of my fellow squadron mates who risked their lives in 'the noisemakers', as I sometimes called Liberators, the unnamed senior military planners pulling the strings were readily despised and rarely seen. Yes, sometimes high-rankers visited us, even way out at Digri, but we distrusted the generic 'them', who, we felt, toyed with our lives recklessly. Even some of 'them', no doubt, wanted to crush the Japanese, but the consequences of bafflingly bad decision making were hard to fathom on occasion.

Senselessness reared its ugly head again in mid-February 1944. Rumour mongering was an art form among my peers, and the hot air of gossip making the rounds hinted at another move by 159 Squadron. Yet it had been only four months since our jump from Salbani to Digri. Then the rumour morphed into reality with the announcement of an impending relocation of the entire squadron to Dhubalia, 60 miles north of Calcutta. In straight-line flying distance, Dhubalia was 85 miles north-east of Digri.

First, a small advance party set out on a road journey to Dhubalia on 19 February. An air contingent of the advance party left Digri for Dhubalia on the 21st.

Meanwhile, at Digri, those of us not participating in the Dhubalia scouting just prosecuted the war as usual, via bomb-laden Liberators sent out to smack the enemy by night.

My Twenty-Third Op: Sagaing Shore Railway Station, 21–22 February 1944

Another transportation target, Sagaing shore railway station in Burma, was revealed to eleven crews at a 12 p.m. briefing on 21 February. Sagaing was only 9 miles south-west of our more familiar target of three nights earlier, Mandalay marshalling yards, on the opposite bank of the Irrawaddy River. 'I expect this op to be a run of the mill job and of no particular difficulty,' confided Sqn Ldr Gordon Clegg, acting CO in the absence of Wg Cdr Hoppy Hopkins, and it was, all things considered.

The Gauntlett crew, aboard our familiar EV843, would be identical to the personnel on the previous Mandalay op: John, Sqn Ldr Hillier, Harry, C. J. Nicholls, Ernie, Jack, Fred, Sgt C. Church, and me.

The griping among our crew focused upon the bomb load discrepancy between each of the six Mk VIs, including EV843 (only 5,240 pounds on this op, including incendiaries), and each of the five Mk III Libs (6,740 pounds, including incendiaries). 'Newer is supposed to be better,' bemoaned Harry, 'but more bombs are really what's better.'

I chimed in. 'And we've had Mk VIs for over a month now, and still we're dropping fewer bombs than we should. Wish the engineering officer would get his finger out!' Experimentation with the capabilities of the new Mk VIs, affecting bomb-carrying totals, would continue.

I was not alone in feeling that the lesser bomb load of each Mk VI, compared with each older Mk III's total, was an unceasing insult. And so was hauling that confounded, empty front turret on ops. 'We're not carrying a ball turret underneath, though the Mk VI is equipped for it, so why carry a nose turret if we aren't using it? I'd remove it and fair over the hole, if you asked me,' I insisted.

Acceptance that there were growing pains in learning how best to use the upgraded Mk VIs was slow in coming.

Until this op, 159 Squadron's Mk III aircraft held one 50-calibre Browning machine gun in the nose. Two hundred rounds of ammunition had been carried on board for this gun. From the 21–22 February op onward, the bullets for this .5-inch gun, as well as the 150 rounds for a single downward-firing .5-inch belly gun, were no longer carried—in part because the need for these guns was deemed minimal, and perhaps partly due to their ineffectiveness when used in rare instances. Likewise, as the front turret was still unoccupied in the Mk VI, no ammo was carried for these twin .5-inch guns.

The eleven Liberators departed Digri between 4.52 p.m. and 5.16 p.m. on 21 February. John was the sixth to take off, at 4.54 p.m. On an almost moonless night, the eleven Liberators set course independently for Sagaing. Our sister squadron, 355, sent five Liberators to join 159 Squadron in a combined attack.

For fifteen Liberators—ten from 159 Squadron and five from 355 Squadron—Sagaing shore railway station was bombed with precision, starting a large fire. With enemy opposition being ineffective, John made two runs over the target, each from 10,600 feet. Harry's sighting on the first run put the bombs west of the Aiming Point, but on the second run bursts were seen across the target area.

The ten aircraft from 159 Squadron which bombed Sagaing landed back at Digri between 1.24 a.m. and 2.21 a.m. John touched down at 1.48 a.m., after eight hours and fifty-four minutes of flight, the sixth Liberator to return.

The eleventh 159 Squadron Liberator, FS Westmorland's BZ982, with Arnie as mid-upper gunner, missed a turn over the Irrawaddy due to clouds concealing a landmark, and then the crew could not find Sagaing. Instead, Sedaw, Burma was bombed, and Westmorland was the last to land, at 2.24 a.m. Arnie now had flown twenty-four ops.

Old mate Willy completed his twenty-second op that night, still as WO J. C. Stuart's rear gunner aboard BZ980. Again, the squadron suffered no casualties on ops. As Sqn Ldr Clegg had predicted, it was a 'run of the mill job'. The five Liberators from 355 Squadron also returned undamaged from the op.

My Twenty-Fourth Op: Moulmein Barracks (Moulmein Railway Station and South Railway Jetty Bombed), 23–24 February 1944

Only two nights after the Sagaing op, nine Liberators and crews were on for a raid to faraway Moulmein, Burma. Three different Moulmein objectives were assigned at our 12 p.m. briefing on 23 February: the Army barracks, Moulmein railway station, and the south railway jetty. Five Mk VIs and four Mk IIIs were to participate.

Our EV843 crew was comprised of ten men: John, Harry, C. J. Nicholls, Ernie, Jack, Fred, and me as the regulars, plus Pop Simmons once again as second pilot, Sgt C. Church again as flight engineer and FS F. Reed as a sprog gunner thrown into the Gauntlett crew to experience his first 159 Squadron op. We took off at 3.56 p.m., as the fourth of the nine Liberators departing from Digri.

It was considered a good showing, with all bombers attacking in two runs. Harry could not locate our primary target, the barracks, so each of the two alternate targets received his attention on successive runs. On the first run from 7,700 feet the south railway jetty was clobbered. On the second run, from 8,000 feet, bursts were seen exploding across the railway station, and one bomb triggered a large fire still visible 30 miles away.

Harry later obtained a copy of a magnificent photograph showing his bombs bursting right across the jetty. He was justifiably pleased to have this visual proof of his spot-on bomb aiming.

One more op was in the books with the return of all nine Liberators between 2.04 a.m. and 2.47 a.m. EV843 landed at Digri at 2.41 a.m., next-to-last, after a flight time of ten hours and forty-seven minutes. Willy successfully completed his twenty-third op, this time aboard BZ980 as WO Stuart's rear gunner.

Three nights later, on 26–27 February, when our crew was not called upon to participate, Willy once again flew aboard BZ980—his twenty-fourth op—as WO Stuart's rear gunner on a sortie to Mingaladon.

My Twenty-Fifth Op: Rangoon, Mahlwagon Marshalling Yards, 29 February–1 March 1944

159 Squadron had not suffered an operational Liberator loss in over nineteen weeks, since Ben and his crew were shot down on the night of 9–10 October. Indeed, on only one other op, to Moulmein on 10–11 January, had there been as much as an injury. That would change dramatically on the squadron's tenth and final op of February, the thirty-ninth group combat sortie since Ben and his crew died.

At the noon briefing on 29 February, Sqn Ldr Gordon Clegg, the acting CO, revealed yet another transportation target, Rangoon's Mahlwagon marshalling yards on the eastern side of town. I had already been to this target once, two months earlier on 30–31 December.

Although I had the experience of twenty-four ops under my belt, I still felt a rising discomfort the moment Sqn Ldr Clegg drew back the curtains obscuring the blackboard to reveal the target map. It was Rangoon, bloody Rangoon. Including Mingaladon aerodrome, it would be my eighth trip to the most heavily defended area we attacked. This was Rangoon, with at least one radar-controlled master blue searchlight to guide the numerous manually controlled searchlights. With more anti-aircraft guns than were found at any other target in the theatre. With night fighters, based at Mingaladon and elsewhere, which would fly through their own searchlights and flak to attack us. With a Prisoner of War pit, Rangoon Jail, dreaded by all airmen on the squadron because of rumoured Japanese cruelties. The Rangoon skies were also where my pal and former crewmate, Ben, was shot down and killed with his crew.

In the afternoon, having completed a nose art painting on the forward fuselage of BZ926, named *Pegasus*, I felt compelled to record my handiwork for posterity with my Box Brownie camera. I pinched the basic artwork design, a winged horse in flight, from an advert for Mobilgas found in *The Saturday Evening Post*, an American magazine. Posing for photos in front of the nose art were various air and ground crew, including four of the men who were to fly on the op that night aboard *Pegasus*. I was especially proud of my latest creation. To also photograph some of the men who were thrilled with my artwork on their Liberator added to my personal satisfaction.

The preparations for the op were typical of a well-functioning bomber squadron continuing to forge ahead with frequent sorties in the dry season. This time only nine Liberators were involved: four Mk IIIs and five Mk VIs, the latter including our crew's EV843.

The usual core of John, Harry, C. J. Nicholls, Ernie, Jack, Fred, and myself comprised the bulk of EV843's crew. We were joined by two young airmen in Plt Off. Tony Black as second pilot and Sgt J. R. Whipfler, who became our regular flight engineer.

As the fifth Liberator aloft from Digri, at 4.22 p.m., EV843 set forth on its four-and-a-half-hour journey to Rangoon in darkness, and alone; as always, formation flying was impossible at night. It was an uneventful outward-bound trip for our crew.

The Liberator skippered by FS Roy McDougall, in which Arnie was flying as a beam gunner, turned back with a petrol leak, but having reached enemy airspace, each crewman was credited with an op. It was Arnie's twenty-fifth.

The eight other aircraft, circling Rangoon counter-clockwise from the south, approached the rail yards and independently initiated their bombing runs.

This, however, was Rangoon, and I expected a fight. True to form, the defenders were riled, reactionary and terrorising. This time, our crew witnessed glowing tracer fire briefly flying backwards and forwards in the night air, an obvious sign that Japanese fighters were scrapping with one or more Liberators.

Fortunately, aboard EV843 we went unscathed amidst the light show and the cacaphony of booming anti-aircraft guns, exploding shells, and bomb bursts.

In the vicinity of the target, Harry settled down to his bomb aimer's duties while exhibiting his usual amazing ice-cool demeanour. On the straight-and-level bomb run at 13,400 feet he counted off the seconds as if he held a mundane peacetime job. The flak bursts were near enough to bounce the aircraft about, but John held true to the course refinements dictated by Harry. Upon hearing the magic words, 'Bombs gone', John swung the Liberator away from its constant heading and pointed to the north-west, still eluding the searchlights, bursting Ack-Ack, and fighters.

We had just begun our homeward leg when Fred, in the tail, announced quietly, 'Rear gunner to crew. Someone's bought it. I can see an aircraft going down in flames, to starboard.' Few words were spoken in reply, but all hoped it was one of the enemy fighters.

The journey back to Digri was accomplished painlessly, though solemnly, and John landed at 1.05 a.m. after a flight of eight hours and forty-three minutes; we were the second Liberator to land. After an early debriefing, we all turned in tired; the fatigue did not surprise us, given where we had been and knowing that something seemed amiss. There would likely be more unpleasant detail revealed in the morning.

We were met with the grim news as we went in to our midday meal. Two aircraft, 'D' for *Daring Diana* and 'P' for *Pegasus*—the latter wearing my nose art—had failed to return to Digri or any other Allied airfield, and two other 355 Squadron Liberators, from a separate force also targeting Mahlwagon marshalling yards, had survived fighter attacks. Two Liberators and their crews lost—*Pegasus* from 'A' Flight and *Daring Diana* from 'B' Flight. It was an anguishing outcome.

The second wireless operator/beam gunner aboard *Pegasus* was Don Lomas, the popular Sergeants' Mess pianist. Don was one of the *Pegasus* crewmen I photographed that previous afternoon posing in front of my recently completed nose art commission adorning their aircraft. It sickened me now to realise that I had taken the last photos of *Pegasus* and four of her crew who failed to return, and, similarly, that my camera captured an image of Ben and his crewmates just before they died the previous October. I swore that I would never take such a group crew photo prior to an op again.

Word soon came through on the grapevine that members of one unidentified crew had been captured. If true, perhaps they would end up in Rangoon Jail, where it was hoped that at least some of the 'V' for Victory cigarettes had fallen two months beforehand, when Willy and I had dumped packets by the armful out of the beam hatches.

The vague story of capture, unsubstantiated and unreliable though it was, jolted the men of 159 Squadron and added to our collective mourning. In a scale of air warfare far smaller than that over Europe, never before had we faced such a tragedy on a single op: two of our Liberators missing and eighteen of our mates lost.

Unanswered questions tormented us. Did men already die, and how did they suffer—in the air combat itself, in the plummeting of doomed bombers in flames, upon impact, with mortal wounds on the ground, or at the hands of ruthless Burmese villagers or Japanese captors? Perhaps some of our lads were really facing the hell on earth of Japanese incarceration.

The rumours filled us with a fury hard for an outsider to imagine, and also sympathy for our missing mates and their families back home. My logbook succinctly summed up the op: 'Operations—RANGOON—Mahlwagon Yards. Stiff opposition. "D" & "P" lost.'

18

March 1944

My Twenty-Sixth Op: Mingaladon Aerodrome (Zayatkwin Aerodrome Bombed), 3–4 March 1944

Eighteen empty charpoys, an absence of boogie woogie piano tunes in the Sergeants' Mess, less light-hearted humour, and noticeably edgy, curt chatter marked 159 Squadron in the immediate aftershock of the Mahlwagon marshalling yards op. Yet this off-kilter blip in emotions and sensibilities would largely, but slowly, dissipate as the demands of no-nonsense squadron duties redirected and refocused our attention.

The month of March had begun, and march we would, onward through the continuing dry season, when the flying weather was at its best and squadron changes were the norm. New bods replaced the missing men, and the production pipeline from America continued to feed us new aircraft from time to time, without fail, to replace the war-weary, the damaged, the destroyed, and the missing.

Despite our adversity, 159 Squadron headed out again on the evening of 3–4 March, three nights after the loss of two Liberators, and again the target was in the Rangoon area. Mingaladon aerodrome, once more, would be our focus, as dictated at our late 6 p.m. briefing on the 3rd. The squadron had last bombed the aerodrome only six nights before, when our crew had been given a rest from flying duties.

One Mk III Lib and six Mk VI Libs loaded with bombs and incendiaries and one Mk III carrying only incendiaries took off from Digri between 10.30 p.m. and 10.45 p.m. John, skippering EV843, departed second, at 10.33 p.m., joined by a crew consisting of Pop Simmons, Harry, C. J. Nicholls, Ernie, Jack, Fred, Sgt J. R. Whipfler, and me. Fred led us all in cumulative ops flown; this would be his twenty-ninth.

One Mk VI bomber returned early owing to engine problems, but the seven others cruised onward across the Bay of Bengal and into enemy skies.

The incoming attackers found that the aerodrome at Mingaladon was largely obscured by ground haze, not clouds. With the disorienting dazzle of an estimated eight to ten searchlights compounding the bomb aimers' dilemma, just two Liberators released bombs on Mingaladon. One, plagued by a faulty release mechanism, managed to only drop two 500-lb bombs, plus incendiaries, and it still retained most of its load. The other, suffering the hang-up of all bombs on its first run, jettisoned the full load on a second run and immediately thereafter headed homeward.

Approaching Mingaladon, from our aircraft two Liberators were seen ahead to be coned by searchlights at 15,000 to 16,000 feet and subjected to inaccurate anti-aircraft fire. Losing height and increasing speed in order to evade, each Liberator avoided battle damage and casualties, but the tenacious searchlights, directed by a master radar-controlled blue light, held each, in turn, until the aircraft was out of range.

The secondary target, Zayatkwin aerodrome, lay over 20 miles to the north-east of Mingaladon. One Liberator, having already bombed Zayatkwin after mistaking it for Mingaladon, was on its homeward leg early. Another Liberator, the one that had jettisoned only two bombs over Mingaladon, set a course for Zayatkwin to release the remainder of its load. For each of five other aircraft, having not bombed Mingaladon due to haze and searchlight dazzle, the decision was reached to abandon that target completely and instead attack Zayatkwin.

At 12,000 feet, we were the fourth Liberator to strike Zayatkwin, and Harry released EV843's bomb load in one pass. Explosions and incendiary fires were seen along the length of the Zayatkwin runway. The success of the other five Zayatkwin raiders was mixed; accuracy varied, and some results were not confirmed. Defences at Zayatkwin were minimal.

Although enemy night fighters had been seen over Mingaladon, the force of Liberators reported no fighter attacks, and all bombers returned unhindered to Digri—the one that had turned back early; the Liberator that attacked only Mingaladon; the bomber that erroneously targeted Zayatkwin, thinking it was Mingaladon; and the five that knowingly bombed Zayatkwin.

John touched down at 7.57 a.m. as the fifth of the seven returnees, after nine hours and twenty-three minutes aloft. In its first op since the tragedy of 29 February–1 March, 159 Squadron lost no aircraft and suffered no casualties, yet it was a dissatisfying effort, by and large.

159 Squadron Moves from Digri to Dhubalia

Meanwhile, the activity associated with the squadron's move from Digri to Dhubalia intensified; in the midst of the rigours of frequent bombing ops 159 Squadron personnel succeeded in pulling off a second relocation in five months. This move proved far more challenging than the Salbani-to-Digri transfer of the previous October.

Various parties left Digri by road in the early morning of 6 March and by air late in the evening on 7 March. The main party travelled primarily by rail via Calcutta, arriving on the 8th at Dhubalia. A final road party arrived in the early morning hours of the 10th.

The primitive ferry across the river at Krishnagar, just south of Dhubalia, proved totally inadequate for transporting a large number of heavy motor vehicles. A considerable delay was encountered. Much extra work was entailed in unloading motor transport before they could be ferried, transferring the offloaded materials separately across the waterway, and reloading the vehicles again on the opposite river bank. The personnel concerned tackled the heavy, thankless task with a unified curse-and-spit determination which exemplified the squadron's cooperative spirit in 'getting the job done'.

Dhubalia was far from being ready to receive a heavy bomber squadron. The cookhouses were in a gross state of unpreparedness. The washing-up facilities and even cooking arrangements were inadequate. Drainage was primitive and dangerous; for example, disposal of sullage favoured fly breeding, with consequent health dangers. The water supply was abysmal, and only two water points existed for the whole squadron—one for officers and one for all others.

Malaria in the Dhubalia area, already elevated among the native population, was predicted to be unacceptably high among RAF personnel, because of the vast reservoir of infection from the considerable number of Indians living in the camp area. There was at least one large Indian village between 159 Squadron's domestic and technical sites.

Upon arrival at our new surroundings, my crewmates and I were appalled. Our general health, and even the very lives of squadron personnel, would be menaced by malaria and other communicable diseases, as long as the native habitations remained in such close proximity to the squadron's personnel. It was a night-and-day difference from either Salbani or Digri, and it just reinforced our disgust with the powers-that-be who made the mind-boggling decision to pull up stakes and move from Digri to Dhubalia.

Worst of all, however, was the physical reality of our new aerodrome's only runway. In its present condition, it was found to be unsatisfactory for activities involving heavy bombers.

'What the bloody hell are we doing in Dhubalia?' I thought. As did Harry, Fred, Arnie, and John—and the list went on.

Thirty-Op Tours Become Thirty-Three

Fred's next op—his thirtieth—would be his last-required 159 Squadron sortie, reached before he had accumulated 300 hours of operational flying. It would be a proud air gunner who, in red ink, annotated his flight logbook with details of his thirtieth op. As a tour-expired airman, Fred would be secure in knowing that he would then be posted to non-operational duty for at least six months before rotation back to an active combat squadron.

Just one more op to reach thirty. Might it be an easy milk run? Would it be a nail-biter to Rangoon, during which Fred would expend some of his 6,000 rounds of .303-inch ammunition in warding off Japanese night fighters attacking from the rear? If he came home in one piece, or at all, then the pressure would ease and his life expectancy would surely be improved.

God willing, Harry and I would also soon attain our magic thirtieth sorties to successfully conclude our tours. The next op would be number twenty-seven for each of us.

However, then came a startling admission from John. In a crew meeting, and looking a little shamefaced, he revealed that he had volunteered for another ten percent beyond his thirty ops, adding three sorties to his tour. This applied only to himself; he could not volunteer to extend the tours of crewmates by three ops.

For the newer members of the crew, John's decision to extend his combat flying would be seen in a favourable light; if all went according to plan, they would not have to endure a replacement skipper for three ops longer than expected. Feeling that they were in great hands when he was their captain, they were thrilled to see his tour prolonged.

The departures of much-valued senior crewmates—Fred, Harry, and me—before John could complete his tour was inevitable, however, because we were ahead of him already in total ops flown; Harry and I were three ahead of John (whose next op would be his twenty-fourth), while Fred was six ahead. Should none of us extend our own tours to thirty-three, John would have to fly nine ops without Fred, and six without Harry and me. Should we also volunteer to extend our tours by ten percent—three more ops—only the last six ops of John's tour, not nine, would be without Fred. Only three ops, not six, would be without Harry and me.

John confessed that he selfishly wanted his most experienced boys aboard for as many ops as possible in the latter stages of his own tour, to increase his odds of survival. He made it clear that he was not asking his longest-serving crewmates to formally extend their dangerous tours; that, he said, would be unfair and disrespectful.

Caught off-guard, Harry, Fred, and I were initially dumbstruck. To say yes to three more combat sorties than required would add risk that was our right to refuse, we knew, but we recognised and applauded John's leadership and flying intuition. We also loved being part of a crew whose core believed in one another's abilities and loyalties. The crew entity, in essence, was bigger than our own individual lives, even though there were no guarantees of safe flying ahead.

Besides, we believed that odds would be in our favour during our three extra ops, based on the scarcity in casualties, and ignoring the anomaly of 29 February–1 March. Every member of the Gauntlett crew had been trained by the

RAF to fly and fight, and calculated risks were part of the accepted package in our brand of warfare.

Harry, Fred, and I had never before faced up to a truth we now could not deny: that our allegiance to our beloved skipper, forged through over 350 hours of flying together and dating back to the summer of 1942, was wholehearted, unbreakable, and ever-strengthening. It was inevitable, then, that each of us would say yes to extending his own tour and accepting new challenges in order to continue flying with John as long as would be granted. Our overwhelming desire, we realised, was to ensure as best we could that John survived to reach the honourable and justly deserved status of the tour-expired airman.

Not wanting to be shut out, Willy took swift action when he learned of John's tour extension, and then those of Fred, Harry, and myself. He, too, craved the chance to protect John beyond his own tour's standard conclusion. By the time of his next op on 14–15 March, Willy was once again assigned to the Gauntlett crew. Having by then flown the same number of ops as John, his eventual thirty-third and final op would coincide with John's thirty-third. The thought of being with his favourite skipper for three extra sorties, to the very end of John's scheduled tour, immensely pleased Willy.

If all proceeded smoothly, the newer members of the crew, not just John, would benefit from the experiences of Fred, Harry, Willy and myself aboard their Liberator for a bonus stretch of three sorties each beyond the normal conclusion of a thirty-operation tour.

My Twenty-Seventh Op: Kamaing–Mogaung Targets, 10–11 March 1944

We would fly one more op without Willy, on the night of 10–11 March. At the noon briefing on the 10th, Sqn Ldr Clegg, still the acting CO, laid out the logistics for our evening's flights; it would be a different kind of mission in support of the British Fourteenth Army.

On this, 159 Squadron's first op from our new home at Dhubalia, eight Liberators—three Mk IIIs and five Mk VIs—would fly staggered single-aircraft sorties. Starting at 5 p.m. and ending just after midnight, one aircraft per hour would depart Dhubalia to attack the same three targets in northern Burma: the Kamaing–Mogaung Road, a reported Japanese storage dump at Mogaung village and a hill feature east of Mogaung. In addition to plastering the reported dump, the intention would also be to destroy motor transport and to inflict casualties upon troop concentrations, even if not seen by the attackers above despite a bright night sky illuminated by a full moon.

The Gauntlett crew led the way, in EV843, taking off as planned right at 5 p.m. John's crewmates were Plt Off. Tony Black as his second pilot, and 'the regular boys'—Harry, C. J. Nicholls, Ernie, Jack, Fred, Sgt J. R. Whipfler, and me.

For Fred, this marked his thirtieth op, but it was really just another sortie to him as he knew that his tour had been extended. This would also be the twenty-third and final op for Nicholls as 2nd W/op on the crew. Henceforth, he would fly with WO M. B. Murphy as his skipper.

Navigation for Harry was a snap on such a clear, moonlit night. The key landmarks plainly visible included the 15 mile-long Indawgyi Lake, the Mogaung River, the river junction at Mogaung village and the Kamaing—Mogaung Road.

The Gauntlett crew bombed each of our three specific objectives from 9,000 feet. At 8.15 p.m., Harry released two 500-lb bombs on the intersection of the Sahmaw Road and the Kamaing–Mogaung Road. In the cloudless sky, it was seen that the second bomb touched off a fire. Five minutes later, Harry toggled 2,000 pounds of bombs plus incendiaries on the reported storage dump area in Mogaung. We witnessed bursts in the target area, followed by a white explosion. Finally, at 8.28 p.m. Harry released 1,500 pounds of bombs on the hill feature east of Mogaung. Again, we saw the bursts. We hoped that a concentration of enemy troops was on the receiving end of our gifts.

Searching from altitude for road vehicles and troops, even with the aid of moonlight, was akin to looking for needles in a haystack. Neither John nor the crew spotted any activity whatsoever at Kamaing, Mogaung, along the road joining these two towns or on the hill we bombed. This bitterly disappointed us as we were itching to avenge the loss of the two crews back on 29 February–1 March by machine gunning targets of opportunity, including road convoys.

Stooging around, then, was paying no dividends. With opportunities for target practice all but non-existent, John did not linger over the area for long. The first to take off, EV843 would be the first home. John touched down at Dhubalia at 12.31 a.m., having been airborne for seven hours and thirty-one minutes.

The other Liberators also reported a lack of activity, with only one aircraft seeing what was possibly a solitary vehicle in motion—that was it. Scattered fires were spotted and noted by these aircraft as being evidence of the attacks by the earlier-arriving Liberators, but for each of eight participating aircraft, the op was dull—thankfully dull—compared with a typical Rangoon extravaganza. All aircraft returned to Dhubalia.

For his thirtieth op, Fred really did not mind an easy trip. Arnie completed his twenty-sixth as FS F. Westmoreland's mid-upper gunner aboard BZ982.

My Twenty-Eighth Op: Rangoon, Victoria Lake Storage Dumps, 14–15 March 1944

At the noon briefing on 14 March, Sqn Ldr Clegg broke the news to the ten antsy crews listed on the battle order: on that night Rangoon, once again, would be our destination. The attack by 159 Squadron, he added, would be part of a much larger mixed heavy and medium bomber force, all targeting the major Japanese Army storage dumps at Victoria Lake in Rangoon. A total of twenty-two RAF Wellingtons were scheduled to strike first, followed by 159 Squadron's Liberators. Last on the scene would be twenty-two B-24s of the American 7th Bomb Group. The dumps would be hit hard, really hard.

Although Rangoon's reputation for fierce defences no doubt weighed on every airman's mind, learning of the concentrated force of bombers going for the same prize seemed to perk up the crews sitting in on the briefing, perhaps because we felt part of a bigger, coordinated effort.

With Harry and me nearing the ends of our tours, the time had come for us to screen new, inexperienced airmen during a challenging sortie, just as we had been mentored on our initial 159 Squadron combat ops. I would oversee Sgt G. McKay on wireless duties, while Harry would cast a watchful eye on Sgt Bruce Reed in the navigator/bomb aimer role.

John's full crew, aboard our reliable EV843, would also include Tony Black again as the second pilot, regulars Ernie (the final op of his tour), Jack, and Fred, and then good ol' Willy back on board once again. Fred, tired of being tail-end Charlie, gladly relinquished his cramped rear turret position to Willy and instead manned a beam gun opposite Jack.

Two Mk III and seven Mk VI Liberators took off between 11.21 p.m. and 11.47 p.m., loaded with a mix of incendiaries and demolition explosives. One Mk III aircraft, suffering mechanical issues, was left behind. John was the third aloft at 11.28 p.m. Arnie, still flying as mid-upper gunner with the Westmoreland crew aboard BZ982, was on his twenty-seventh op.

On a cloudless night, the first of the squadron's Liberators, arriving at 3.10 a.m., reported significant fires resulting from the earlier Wellington attacks. In Rangoon, a mere four to six searchlights were in action, and only for brief periods, while at Mingaladon to the north, up to eleven were reported. This time, 159 Squadron's force of nine Liberators avoided searchlight detection, including the much more harrowing radar-controlled blue master searchlight.

Our bombers were also spared the intensity of Ack-Ack experienced on previous ops in the Rangoon environs. At nearby Mingaladon, inaccurate light AA was seen being fired into searchlight cones, up to 12,000 feet, short of the attack height of any Liberator. Elsewhere, ground flashes from heavy AA fire were detected, and air bursts were reported, but again the aim was inaccurate, and far less concentrated than on previous attacks.

It was evident that Japanese night fighters were out and about, identified by their red and green wingtip lights. Perhaps these lights were to help ground anti-aircraft gunners to recognise them, or maybe the intent was to attract the attention of the aircrews aboard the bombers while other fighters, lights extinguished, pressed in unseen for attacks. This latter ploy, we had been forewarned, was a Japanese tactic. On this night, however, not a single fighter attack occurred.

In the belly of the beast, above our most formidable target, 159 Squadron fared exceptionally well. Harry's string of explosives and incendiaries, released from 15,500 feet at 3.32 a.m., was seen to impact across the Victoria Lake storage dumps target area. This night afforded him a perfect setup to hit his mark: a cloudless sky, good visibility below, a surprising lack of searchlight interference, a target already alight, a skipper who implemented Harry's course corrections on the bomb run, ineffective anti-aircraft fire and no immediate fighter threat. For Harry, cocky about his abilities and always intent to prove his worth, it did not get any easier than this.

The whole of the storage dumps area was covered with fires (large and small) by the time the last of the 159 Squadron Liberators departed six minutes behind our EV843. Intermittent red-glowing eruptions with sparks flying hinted at exploding ammunition stores.

On such a clear night, the intense fires were still visible over 100 miles away, as a reminder to the returning flyers that the might of the bomber force had brought forth tangible results.

At 8.23 a.m., John landed at Dhubalia as the fifth returning bomber. EV843 had completed its op in eight hours and fifty-five minutes.

The squadron received word later that day that the American bombers arriving at the target after 159's departure were hassled by searchlights and fighters, with some resulting damage, but no B-24s were lost and no casualties were suffered.

Photo reconnaissance soon confirmed widespread damage at the Victoria Lakes storage dumps. The news was most satisfying to us, but it was expected that the Japanese—or slave labour, maybe including Rangoon Jail Prisoners of War—would rapidly clear and renew the sites for the storage of fresh military supplies. In fact, 159 Squadron would be sent out again to the same target fifteen days later.

My Twenty-Ninth Op: Ywataung South Landing Ground, 17 March 1944

Not every target resonated in the minds of readers of war despatches and communiqués printed in *The Illustrated London News*, *The New York Times*, or even Calcutta's *The Statesman*. Rangoon, Bangkok, and Mandalay were recognisable destinations to the average reader, but not Meiktila, Akyab, or Mogaung. While it was pride-engendering for us on 159 Squadron to fly on a big-name raid—that is, to participate and contribute—we still knew that our bombs, toggled by resolute specialists like Harry, packed a wallop no matter where they were deposited.

Our sensations of accomplishment were heightened when the big targets were hit, but for us, a destination need not be as far away as Bangkok or as typically lively as Rangoon to be deemed worthy of our best efforts. It did not have to be a major enemy air base such as Mingaladon or Heho or an impressive-sounding transportation site such as Rangoon central railway station for us to feel satisfied.

The squadron's target in the early morning of 17 March was one such lower-tier destination, unknown to the general public: the unimproved north and south fighter landing grounds situated at Ywataung on the east bank of the Irrawaddy River near Allanmyo, Burma. At the 5 p.m. briefing on 16 March, Sqn Ldr Clegg laid out the plan for five Libs to bomb the north field and five to bomb the south. Because these landing grounds were not major flying centres, the Japanese, it was hoped, would be caught with their collective guard down, with dire consequences—for them.

One bomber destined for the south landing ground was scrubbed before take-off, but John in EV843 led the nine other 159 Squadron bombers up and away from Dhubalia, starting with his take-off at one minute after midnight on the 17th and continuing with take-offs over the next 19 minutes. Aboard EV843 were John, Tony Black, Harry, Sgt G. McKay (for a second straight trip), Willy, Jack, Fred, Sgt J. R. Whipfler, and me—nine men, one less than on our most recent sortie.

Willy was in the mid-upper turret this time, replacing Ernie Richards, and Fred was again tail-end Charlie in the rear turret. Harry was spared screening duties, which pleased him to no end; there was no second navigator along for the experience. Harry preferred to be allowed to do his job unhindered, with his usual cool focus and attention to detail.

With Jack as the only dedicated beam gunner aboard, Sgt McKay, as 2nd W/op/AG, acted primarily as the other beam gunner during the flight, although I made certain to give him a go, when possible, on the wireless equipment. McKay, after all, had been added to the crew as a permanent replacement for Sgt C. J. Nicholls, and so I felt that to give McKay wireless experience could only benefit the crew.

The bombers reached the Ywataung complex without interference from the enemy. Minimal heavy Ack-Ack was reported 1,000 feet below and ahead of one of the incoming bombers, and only one single-engine aircraft was spotted, silhouetted in the reflected light of a half-moon, but with no wingtip lights showing. There were no direct encounters between the Liberators and the Japanese aircraft.

John made two runs over the south landing ground. At 3.35 a.m., from 8,400 feet, Harry dropped the first stick of bombs, aimed at the north-south runway, and the bursts were seen but not pinpointed. From the second stick, toggled at 3.42 a.m. from 8,200 feet, the last two bombs were seen to explode across the runway.

The results, overall, were favourable. Blazes, including scattered incendiary fires and possibly a burning aircraft, were sighted in the vicinity of the north landing ground. All crews reported more fires on the south landing ground than on the northern airfield, with secondary explosions also witnessed. From 9,000 feet, one aircraft reported two bright red explosions from the target area when 20 miles away on the return flight.

The nine returning Liberators, none damaged, landed back at Dhubalia between 7.25 a.m. and 7.55 a.m. EV843 was the fifth returnee at 7.35 a.m., having been airborne for seven hours and thirty-four minutes.

In my logbook, I noted that my twenty-ninth op brought 'good results'. As this sortie was so perfunctory for its seasoned participants, like me, look-back recollections of wartime exploits shared with grandchildren one day would not likely include this one. It was so mundane, so easy—as far as ops went—that it seemed almost like a gift from the bigwigs, in gratitude for a string of higher-intensity ops flown in recent weeks. Except, gratitude from the highest levels of the military leadership was exceedingly rare. Still, none of us complained about an easy op.

My Thirtieth Op: Prome Railway Station, 20–21 March 1944

Fred's thirty-third op with 159 Squadron, completing his tour, was scheduled for the night of 20–21 March. At the 12 p.m. briefing on the 20th, we learned that while nine Liberators would be sent out around 9 p.m. to attack the Moulmein, Burma area, our crew would depart in EV843 over two and a half hours earlier on a one-bomber strike upon Prome railway station on the east bank of the Irrawaddy River in Burma. Fred, especially, liked the idea of going solo on his final op. The Prome raid would also mark the thirtieth op for Harry and me, three short of completing our extended tours.

John, as skipper of EV843, was joined for a fifth and last time by Tony Black as his second pilot. The remainder of our crew consisted of Harry, Sgt G. McKay, Willy, Jack, Fred, Sgt J. R. Whipfler, and me. On his last ride, Fred again took his rear turret position, relegating Willy to the mid-upper turret for a second straight flight.

Just like Fred's thirtieth ten nights earlier, this shaped up to be just another op, until John informed the crew that as part of an authorised experiment our take-off weight would be 67,000 pounds, exceeding the maximum all-up weight limit. Take-off, then, would be more nerve-wracking than expected.

At 6.17 p.m., like a tired old lady, the heavily laden EV843 lumbered down the runway to commence its lone-raider foray into Burma. I watched the air speed indicator with some trepidation. As the end of the runway loomed, and with minimum flying speed barely reached, John coaxed the Liberator into the air. It sank again, skipped off a dry and dusty paddy field, and slowly, ever so slowly, gained in altitude.

Fred's final-scheduled 159 Squadron flight came perilously close to being his last flight ever, as well as the final flight for John, Harry, me, and for each of five other airmen. With a full petrol load aboard, and armed to the hilt, a take-off prang would have likely ended up as a funeral pyre.

The Liberator was commonly called a heavy bomber. EV843 certainly was heavy that evening. Later, Tony Black recorded the op in his logbook with a succinct note: 'Take-off hard 67,000 lb.'

The crew's collective anxiety eased as EV843 climbed to cruising altitude. Then, at 9,000 feet, our relative sense of operational normalcy was shattered when a kitehawk flew into the propeller of No. 3 engine. The shock of the impact ruffled our feathers, so to speak, but caused no mechanical damage to the impacted prop and its engine, or to the aircraft's wing. The bird's wings, on the other hand, were pulverised, as was the entire creature.

After we regained our composure from the bird strike, the flight finally became 'just another op', to the relief of all, including John, whose demeanour still exuded confidence and fearlessness, even under stress—as always.

On a clear, dark night with no low clouds, our main issue now was visibility. Prome was easy to identify on a bulge of land jutting north-westerly into the Irrawaddy River, but to pinpoint the railway station, inland several hundred yards from the shoreline, would have been difficult even for the best bomb aimer in the RAF. Only a slight ground haze was evident, but with a waning moon, there was little natural illumination to aid Harry in picking out the railway station below. The town was blacked out completely.

Harry's assignment, given the conditions, was thankless. To improve his chances at accuracy on the first bomb run, two of our three parachute flares were dropped over the town to give him just a little more light for choosing an aiming point. Harry did his best under the trying conditions.

The first stick of bombs, dropped from 7,400 feet at 9.33 p.m., totalled 3,500 pounds of high explosives, plus incendiaries. Five minutes later, from 7,000 feet, and aided by our final flare's artificial light, Harry toggled an additional 2,500 pounds of bombs onto the target below, now obscured not only by mist, but also by smoke and dust from the first bombs. Small fires, not precisely located, were seen as EV843 headed homeward.

The Japanese reaction was inconsequential. Prome, an area of military storage dumps, seemed to be strangely low on the priority list for Japanese defences. The scarce few anti-aircraft guns in action on this night were ineffective, as if manned by inexperienced soldiers firing at random. We felt that the challenge of taking off in an overloaded, fuelled-up flying bomb was far more dangerous than of occupying airspace above Prome.

After an ordinary return flight, John landed back at Dhubalia at 1.11 a.m. EV843 had performed perfectly on ops for 90 straight hours. The last six hours and fifty-four minutes of Fred's tour concluded quietly when Tony Black, on John's command, shut down the aircraft's four Pratt & Whitney engines.

Following the usual ops debriefing with the intelligence officer, Fg Off. George Betteley, we chose to make an early night of it. Except for crewmates shaking Fred's hand warmly in congratulations, the celebration of his tour-expired status would wait for another time. Besides, Fred preferred no fanfare for doing what he felt was expected of every one of us. The base was quiet because the other Libs were still out on their op to Moulmein; it was an opportune time to turn in early.

Between 8.57 p.m. and 9.20 p.m., only seven of the squadron's nine Liberators scheduled for targets in the Moulmein area that evening had taken off; two aircraft were left behind. Despite thick ground haze, six aircraft dropped bombs and returned safely to Dhubalia between 7 a.m. and 7.35 a.m.

The exception was EV864, a Mk VI Liberator skippered by Pop Simmons, formerly John's American second pilot on eight previous ops. Finding conditions at Moulmein too poor for bombing, even after thirty minutes of searching for improvement, he opted for Prome, the secondary target, and approached the darkened town at 3.15 a.m.

As with our crew nearly six hours earlier, even with minimal moonlight the tell-tale bulge in the Irrawaddy River's course, signifying the town's location, was recognisable to Pop and his crew upon approach. On arrival, however, clouds obscured the town. The Japanese, perhaps cunningly, kept their heads down and put up no Ack-Ack, and the fires from our attack, having been extinguished, could be of no help now.

Ultimately, after forty-five minutes of stooging around and waiting in vain for improved visibility, bombing with any semblance of precision was determined to be improbable. Pop left the Prome area at 4 a.m., still carrying a full bomb load.

His crew was not concerned until well on the way back, when he came on the intercom to tell the wireless operator to replace the horseshoes in the bombs. With reluctance, the task was accomplished.

'OK, that's fine,' announced Pop when informed by the wireless operator. 'Now we can take these babies home.'

'But skipper, why risk it? Why not leave 'em in the Bay of Bengal?' queried his second pilot, Sgt Ron Clift.

' 'Cos I'm a goddamn taxpayer, and I hate waste!' was Pop's reply.

There were some anxious faces aboard EV864 as Pop came in to land. They need not have worried. Pop put the aircraft down with a gentle touch at 7.35 a.m. Proud of himself after exiting the bomber, he strutted like a schoolboy with everything going right. Nodding to the bomb bay, he grinned, 'Reckon they'll be put to better use next time.' Without a backward glance, he vaulted into the gharry taking his crew to debriefing.

My Thirty-First Op: Rangoon, Victoria Lake Storage Dumps, 29–30 March 1944

Feeling as though we old bods on the Gauntlett crew were being dragged through filth, we learned that our next op, on the night of 29–30 March, would again be to our *bête noire*, the formidable town of Rangoon. Specifically, Wg Cdr Hopkins, standing at the blackboard at the 1 p.m. briefing on 29 March, drew open the curtains to reveal to eight Liberator crews that our destination that night would be the same Victoria Lake storage dumps in the heart of Rangoon that 159 Squadron had bombed only fifteen nights earlier. This would be a smaller do than last time, however. Seven Liberators from 355 Squadron were also assigned the same target.

From 159 Squadron, three Mk III Libs and five Mk VI bombers were on for the op. John, piloting our trusty EV843, was the fourth to take off from Dhubalia, at 5.39 p.m. For his twenty-eighth op, he was joined up front by a Canadian second pilot, Flt Lt Johnny West. Harry and I were each flying op number thirty-one, while Willy in the rear turret was on his twenty-eighth and Jack on a beam gun his fifteenth. Rounding out the crew were Sgt G. McKay as 2nd W/op/beam gunner, WO Norman Bingham as mid-upper gunner, and Sgt J. R. Whipfler as flight engineer.

The regular crew, at first, felt a bit ill at ease without our level-headed mate Fred aboard, but we had been well aware that this day would come. We quickly settled down for the outward-bound flight and hoped for a safe and successful trip overall, without Fred.

Arriving at the target, there was the usual chaos of flak, searchlights and the occasional burst of tracer from an active night fighter presence, but though sweating mightily, we emerged unharmed after bombs were released. EV843 beat a hasty retreat from the Rangoon vicinity. In fact, the eight Liberators of 159 Squadron and all seven from 355 Squadron departed the area without loss.

On the trip home, and feeling much relieved to have left Rangoon behind, Willy and I shook hands. I then went forward to man the radio.

After landing back at Dhubalia at 2.38 a.m. as the seventh of eight returnees, following a flight of eight hours and fifty-nine minutes, we gave our report to Fg Off. Betteley, the intelligence officer. The newer members of the crew, excited by the raid and naïve about how to finish the debriefing efficiently, slowed down the proceedings. All I wanted to do was go to sleep.

While shaving the next morning, Fred ribbed Willy and me, his now-former crewmates. Grinning, he asked, 'How are our two intrepid volunteers this morning?'

'Aw, go shit in it,' answered Willy in disgust, and I silently echoed his sentiments.

19

Early to Mid-April 1944

My Thirty-Second Op: Rangoon, Kemmendine Railway Station, 1–2 April 1944

The sortie of 1–2 April did not go as planned for our crew. Harry and I each flew our thirty-second op on that night—a swansong flight with 159 Squadron for each of us; there would be no thirty-third op required to conclude my tour or Harry's tour with 159 due to unforeseen circumstances. Nor would John or Willy reach thirty-three. John's first tour officially ended with this, his twenty-ninth op. Willy's twenty-ninth ended in tragedy.

With resignation, our crew assembled on 1 April for the standard pre-op meeting in the Briefing Room, where Wg Cdr Hoppy Hopkins revealed our target for that night: Kemmendine railway station on the western fringe of Rangoon.

'Jeez,' spat Harry, 'ain't there no other target in Burma except bloody Rangoon?' Of course Harry knew, but his outburst reflected the frustration of most of the men in the room in learning that the Rangoon defences must be faced yet again.

The usual mission preliminaries were reviewed as the briefing progressed, although I could have repeated most of them blindfolded, so familiar was I with the routine.

That evening, 159 Squadron would send three Mk III Libs and seven Mk VI bombers to Rangoon, while 355 Squadron would put up six Liberators in its attack upon the same target.

Aboard our trusted EV843, laden with 8,500 pounds of bombs plus incendiaries, the Gauntlett crew took off at 5.32 p.m. as the third bomber airborne from Dhubalia. Harry, myself, Willy in the rear turret and Jack on a beam gun were the other experienced stalwarts in EV843 under John's command. On the flight deck John was accompanied for a second straight op by Flt Lt Johnny West, the Canadian second pilot. For a fifth time Sgt G. McKay flew as John's 2nd W/op/AG. WO Norman Bingham (mid-upper gunner), Sgt J. R. Whipfler (flight engineer) and Fg Off. Dave Bruce (navigator) filled out the crew.

Harry really did not mind screening Bruce; it was a pleasure to connect with a fellow Canuck from Ontario, and Bruce readily impressed Harry with his intuitive navigation skills and willingness to be mentored.

The crew settled down after take-off as EV843 set out across the Bay of Bengal for Rangoon; that is, everyone except for me. I was still perturbed by Willy's behaviour that day. Earlier in the afternoon, having written and sealed two letters, Willy asked me to post them the following morning. 'Post them yourself, you lazy sod,' I snapped.

Quietly, Willy answered, 'Don't think I'll be around to post them.' This shook me to such an extent that I chewed Willy up a bit with a sharp-tongued assault. Willy merely smiled and said nothing, but the memory was still upsetting me on the outward-bound leg of our flight.

The Rangoon night sky was bright. A half-moon's illumination filtered through a thin, patchy layer of altostratus clouds above the bombers bearing down on the target from the north. A slight ground haze was evident, but it was insignificant.

Being Rangoon, it was acknowledged that a slog through its airspace for the attacking Liberators could prove challenging. Searchlights were already active when the bombers reached Rangoon. Approximately eight lights were operating at Mingaladon, 7 miles north of Kemmendine railway station, but up to twenty searchlights were on the prowl in Rangoon town.

The Japanese anti-aircraft and night fighter defences were also very active as we would quickly learn.

EV843 made a first bomb run, which, on approach to the target, seemed ideal. No searchlights had locked on to us yet, Ack-Ack was inaccurate, and fighters had failed to single us out. Harry, acting as bomb aimer, toggled the load.

Suddenly, Harry came on the intercom. 'Enoch,' he directed, 'go down in the bomb bay and see if we have any hang-ups.'

Complying, I found three 500-lb bombs still in the racks. I reported this to John, who promptly decided to go round again for a second bomb run. A rising sense of dread was palpable among the crew.

At 12,600 feet, John initiated the straight-and-level bomb run. We were halfway through this vulnerable stretch and beginning to think that we would escape unscathed when a vivid blue radar-controlled master searchlight locked straight onto us. Seconds later, numerous standard white hand-controlled searchlights converged on the blue master light, one by one.

Aided by the searchlights, the flak gunners modified their aim. The bursts became uncomfortably close. We cringed at nearby explosions and recognised the unnerving rattle of exploded shell fragments striking the skin of the aircraft, somewhat like pebbles being thrown against a tin roof. The din, combined with the blinding light, was terrifying. We were now in the bullseye as a result of one bloody radar-controlled searchlight.

Without hesitation, Harry released the remaining bombs.

Then came a scream over the intercom. No one knew who it was, but having commandeered the port beam gun from Sgt McKay, I had a sinking feeling that it was Willy in the tail turret not far to my left.

Suddenly, from my gun position, I caught a glimpse of the propeller and spinner of a single-engine Japanese Oscar (Nakajima Ki-43) stealthily following from a port-side blind spot, behind the large oval fin and rudder. That enemy pilot, I thought, knew his business. The Japanese foe also exhibited immense bravado in subjecting himself to the same anti-aircraft fire that targeted our bomber.

My throat mic, for communicating with crewmates, was plugged into a black Bakelite switchbox dangling by a leather strap positioned around my neck. To talk, I had to locate the switchbox hanging down in front of me and then hit a press-to-talk switch. Frantically, I searched for this dangling box in order to report the Oscar, and what must have been Willy's scream from the rear turret, but I gave up in disgust after a moment or two and focused, instead, upon warding off the menacing fighter.

Meanwhile, the emboldened Oscar pilot, growing more confident, stuck his nose a little forward and fired away at the Liberator. Suddenly, our port inner engine gushed a huge sheet of flame, which, as I witnessed, melted the de-icing boot on the port fin.

I fired a burst from my 50-calibre Browning at the fighter. Briefly, a wisp of flame appeared from under the Oscar's cowling. In response, and to avoid the backward-streaming flames from the bomber's damaged engine, the Oscar pilot dipped his starboard wing with the intention of getting underneath the Liberator.

Remembering my mid-November target practice on sharks when returning from an op, I fired my gun into the empty space between the Lib's port elevator and the fuselage, where I expected the fighter to re-emerge. Back in November, the empty space was behind the target, a shark, and the forward movement of the Liberator walked the bullets right into the target. Now, I hoped, it would be the Japanese aviator's piloting, not John's, which brought together target and bullets.

As if on cue, the fighter flew right into the stream of .5-inch bullets. I saw the canopy shatter. Suddenly, the fighter slid off to pass under the Liberator's belly and disappeared astern.

I believed I had shot down the fighter and cured the pilot's headache, perhaps permanently, with my 50-calibre prescription. I later learned that aircrew aboard two other Liberators, shortly after my gunnery display, noted a dark red fire thought possibly to be an aircraft crash site.

With the immediate danger of further attack from that lone Oscar likely arrested, I found my press-to-talk switchbox and reported the fighter attack and port inner engine fire to John. By then, John was well aware of a night fighter and the flaming engine outside of his cockpit window. Immediately, he threw the aircraft into a steep and prolonged corkscrewing dive that eventually succeeded in losing the searchlights and, of even more pressing concern, extinguishing the fire. The air temperature warmed during the rapid descent; we were down to 800 feet when John levelled off.

Going aft, I found Willy slumped against the side of the turret. Opening the doors at the rear of the turret, I half-hoped Willy had only been knocked out, but when I moved his head it was painfully obvious that he was dead. Blood was everywhere.

Willy was far too big for me to move, and his feet were caught under the guns so I called on the intercom for John's assistance. With Flt Lt West taking the controls temporarily, John joined me aft. Between us, we extricated Willy from the turret and reverently laid him on the fuselage floor.

Crying quietly, we stood looking down at Willy, our loyal, sometimes exasperating, but always beloved crewmate dating back to 1653 Conversion Unit at Burn in the summer of 1942. 'A grand lad was he,' was all that I could utter before breaking down in sobs.

John well knew that Willy had volunteered for three extra ops and had also lobbied for reassignment back to the Gauntlett crew to help protect his admired skipper in the homestretch of their tours together. Guilt-ridden, John blamed himself for Willy's death.

Touching me on the arm, John motioned that I accompany him forward. I nodded, took a moment to bid Willy goodbye, and followed John. When entering the bomb bay, we were shocked to discover petrol pouring in from a punctured tank in the port wing. In the rush to reach Willy in the rear of the aircraft, John had failed to notice the leak. John and I now realised the fire hazard from both the spilling liquid and the fumes; one spark would spell disaster. I did not care to die in the flash of a massive explosion as had my mate Ben back in October, only a few miles from where we were then flying.

Another shock presented itself in the forward end of the bay: the overpowering odour of hydraulic fluid indicating further combat damage that might impact our capability to land.

Back on the flight deck, John once again took control of the Liberator, now limping along on three engines. 'Get a QDM to Dhubalia. We're lost,' he commanded.

'Think I ought to get out an SOS?' I asked, tapping John on the sleeve. Hesitating for only a second, John nodded his head. In plain language, I transmitted our course, height, and airspeed as well as an approximate position determined by Harry. Then, soon after my broadcast, I received an acknowledgement from Group in Calcutta; at least someone had heard me.

John called me forward again to say that we had barely enough petrol to reach our own lines and ask me to get a QDM for the RAF landing strip at Chittagong, on the east side of the Bay of Bengal and 230 miles short of our base at Dhubalia. Calling Chittagong, I raised a response, but one that was barely audible. I passed the necessary course heading to Harry to plot and to John to fly so I sat back. I knew that if the Japanese were attentive, they would plot these transmissions and have a night fighter waiting somewhere on our course to Chittagong, but I kept those thoughts to myself.

Harry advised, 'Get me a QDM for Chittagong every fifteen minutes.'

Agreeing, I continued to give Harry and John courses to steer at regular intervals. The Chittagong ground station was so much on the ball that if I did not call up at the stated time, they would call me.

Although the petrol loss had been acute, the self-sealing tanks had operated as designed, and there was firm hope that we would make it to Chittagong. As we neared the station, the signals became stronger. Finally, I asked for and received permission to land. The hydraulic fluid level seemed adequate for braking, if the hydraulic system was coddled, so Flt Lt West lowered the flaps manually and Sgt McKay worked the hand crank to drop and lock the undercarriage. John touched down easily enough at 1.30 a.m., after seven hours and fifty-eight minutes in flight, only to realise that the severity of damage had rendered the brakes useless. We braced for a crash and waited. The bomber ran off the runway, through a paddy field, and eventually came to a halt in a cloud of dust against a brick embankment, with no resulting injuries.

We all exited the aircraft smartly in case of fire, but thankfully, no flames erupted. EV843, however, was a write-off, too damaged to be repaired on site, especially as Chittagong was a forward airfield far from a proper Liberator station. On the long haul back from Rangoon to Chittagong, we had stripped Willy of his rupee belt, parachute harness, and revolver, placing them in his parachute bag. I had also divested myself of my money belt and revolver to be more comfortable.

The CO of the unit at Chittagong told us to leave our gear in the aircraft until the following morning and that he would put a guard on it. On receiving this assurance, we went wearily to debriefing and then to bed to bring the night's ordeal to a close. It had been a rough one.

We were told that Willy's funeral would be at 10 a.m. the next morning, but although we waited, no vehicle came by to pick us up for the funeral. Later, we learned that Willy had been buried at 4.30 a.m. Apparently, there was such a high water table at Chittagong that the burial party dug a hole, put the casket within, and covered it up straightaway before the hole could fill with water. Learning that our mate had been buried so indecently, without any of us having even been invited, added to our bitterness.

Eventually, we went out to see our pranged bomber. The first thing that hit us was the noise. Millions of flies were feasting on the blood in the rear turret. We then checked on our gear, only to find that someone had stolen Willy's revolver and also mine. Surprisingly, our money belts were untouched. 'Thieving bastards!' I muttered in disgust.

We did not stay inside the Liberator for long; the memories were too vivid and the flies disgusting. We climbed out for our first good look at the aircraft that had brought us home against the odds. It was poised with its tail sticking up into the air, and there were many holes, particularly in the wings.

I grabbed Harry by the arm and pointed to a large hole behind the port outer engine. 'Look at that, Harry,' I marvelled. 'Do you realise what it means?'

Harry shrugged. 'Flak, I guess. So what?'

I shook my head impatiently. 'Flak, alright, but when that shell penetrated the wing and a petrol cell, it allowed the petrol to flow through the wing for some time until the self-sealing membranes of the leaking tanks closed it off. Don't you get it? Petrol was flowing past the inner engine, which was on fire!'

Harry viewed the hole with renewed interest. 'Bloody hell!' he gasped, 'It only wanted one rivet to weep and, boom, we wouldn't be here now!' He looked at the hole steadily for some time. 'Jesus!' he swore; there was a mountain of meaning in the word.

I then admitted to Harry that I had prayed over the target. Seeing Harry's surprise, I added hastily that it had been half a curse and half a prayer; I had said, 'Jesus Christ, get us out of this. Just let me live to be thirty!'

Solemnly, Harry looked at me. 'Reckon He heard you then, Enoch.'

On the slightly crumpled nose of the aircraft, my painted wench now looked as if she was sitting on the dirt road adjacent to the brick embankment, not just lying back with her hands behind her head. I had intended on painting the words 'Erotic Edna' beneath the reclining woman but now realised it would never get done. As a write-off, *Erotic Edna* would never fly again.

Two other 159 Squadron Liberators came back from the Kemmendine railway station raid with wounded aboard, following night fighter attacks from astern in the vicinity of Rangoon. One, EV870, with the rear gunner and a beam gunner injured by enemy fire, crashed in a spectacular heap at Alipore, a Calcutta aerodrome, when landing gear collapsed. Remarkably, although the Liberator was a write-off, additional injuries amounted to nothing more than shock. The other Liberator, BZ960, was able to return to Dhubalia with battle damage and a wounded rear gunner.

All three Liberators set upon by fighters that night were victims of aggressive attacks from astern. The rear turret position carried the most ammunition for a good reason, but the 1–2 April op also demonstrated the vulnerability of the rear gunner.

Late in the day, on 2 April, a Liberator landed at Chittagong to fly our crew back to Dhubalia. EV864, piloted by 159 Squadron's WO Murphy, took off from Chittagong at 5.30 p.m. for the eighty-minute flight home.

At Dhubalia, the CO, Hoppy Hopkins, greeted John, Harry, and me with the words, 'OK. You've finished your tours. Well done.' We three combat-tested airmen, so close to finishing the full thirty-three-op tours we had every intention of completing, looked blankly at one another.

Finally, Harry spoke quietly. 'Pity Willy couldn't be with us to hear you say that, sir.' With a sigh, Wg Cdr Hopkins nodded in agreement.

Doc Kelly, the medical officer, also stood awaiting our return from Chittagong.

The Gauntlett crew survivors accompanied him to the Station Sick Quarters, where he handed us a ration of rum. We finished off the bottles by the evening and slept deeply that night.

My logbook entry for the harrowing thirty-second op, not meant to be a diary, succinctly summarised a bleak experience:

> 32—Operations—Rangoon. D. C. O. [Duty Carried Out] Caught & held in searchlights. Hit by flak & night fighters. Fired back at fighter. Own Damage—Rear Gunner killed. No 2 engine U/S [unserviceable, or needing maintenance]. Hydraulics hit. Petrol tanks hit. Transmitted S. O. S. Crashed at Chittagong—no brakes. 8.00 [flight duration].

159 Squadron Relocates Back to Digri

Not every decision made with 159 Squadron in mind was ideal. The hasty decision to relocate 159 Squadron's home base from Digri to Dhubalia in early March was acknowledged as unsatisfactory by the bigwigs in the highest levels of the RAF command structure in India. Despite the numerous problems at under-prepared Dhubalia, it was one issue above all others that forced a relocation back to Digri after little more than a month: the Dhubalia runway was unable to take the weight of Liberators in its present condition. Another move was essential.

On 6 April, an advance party of twenty-six airmen proceeded by rail from Dhubalia to Digri with a limited amount of equipment. A provisional air party joined them on the 11th. Two days later, the first road party set out from Dhubalia for Digri, and again, as in the previous month, great difficulty was experienced in getting transport across the river at Krishnagar. At last, the party arrived at Digri late in the day on the 14th. Then, on the 15th, the main air party flew to Digri and the main rail party also departed Dhubalia.

By the 17th, the move back to Digri was completed, and the squadron was deemed ready again for operations.

20

RAF Service after the 1–2 April 1944 Operation

My RAF Service after 2 April

I glanced around the 159 Squadron Sergeants' Mess at Digri while sitting there one evening in April 1944. I hardly knew anyone. Looking at some young airmen at a nearby table, I wondered if they would know intense comradeship such as I had experienced on 159 Squadron or the heartbreak of losing friends killed on active service with the squadron. It seemed strange that my crewmates and I, who had been so intimate and close, should be split up with so little concern as if we were packages to be sent here and there at the whim of the powers-that-be.

For a time, I helped in 159 Squadron's Intelligence Section, but I felt oddly out of sync and watched, sometimes with a pang of envy, as the aircraft took off to bomb some distant target. I knew that the war still had a long way to go before it was finished and that I would have to do another tour in six months' time, but for the moment, I was safe.

After my orders came through to instruct on wireless matters at 231 Group Navigation School in Calcutta, I left Digri without so much as a backward glance. I soon began referring to my time on 159 Squadron, for which I would later be awarded a DFM, as 'ancient history'.

I had been charged with the loss of my firearm when it was stolen back at Chittagong, and—something that especially infuriated me—so was Willy. The charges took months to be adjudicated. One sunny morning at my next posting in Calcutta, I was paraded before some top brass. Although sympathetic, they insisted that RAF law be upheld. The ruling was that I would lose six months' seniority, and I must pay an exorbitant sum for the missing revolver.

As Willy, deceased, had been 'in no fit state to guard his sidearm', the cost of his missing revolver—his sidearm—would merely be deducted from his credits. I hit the roof. Was it not enough that Willy had given his life? Who were these cheese-paring bastards who charged a dead man for a piddling little revolver, and who would now force his family to settle the financial burden months after his death? The CO let me carry on for quite some time and then, with a nod to the disciplinary warrant officer, brought the hearing to a close.

At lunch, almost weeping with rage, I was taken to one side by the stores sergeant. 'You have to sign the 664b,' he told me. Speechless only for a second, I rounded on the man with a damning vitriol. The stores sergeant, expecting my reaction, grinned broadly and raised his hand. 'Hold it!' he said, 'I was at the hearing, and I'm as disgusted as you. Here.' He held out the offending sheets—one for my stolen revolver and one for Willy's. Puzzled, I took them and looked at the man. 'There are two guns the Air Force is not going to get paid for,' offered the stores sergeant. With a wink he was gone, leaving me with the sheets showing the offending articles and, on each page, a blank space for a signature. I could not help but grin as I tore the sheets into pieces. Sometimes, I mused, the little people do win in the RAF after all.

I was bored stiff at RAF 231 Group Navigation School trying to instil wireless gen into the heads of conceited Mosquito navigators, mostly commissioned officers. I was saved by a telephone call from Sqn Ldr J. M. Hillier, with whom I had flown on ops four times. On 159 Squadron, he had been Flight Commander on 'B' Flight before being elevated to Officer-in-Charge of 231 Group Air-Sea Rescue.Desperate to replace undertrained Americans, Sqn Ldr Hillier invited me to fly with the United States Army Air Force as a wireless operator on air-sea rescue Catalina flying boats.

I jumped at the chance. Ops thirty-three through fifty-eight of my second tour were flown between November 1944 and April 1945 with an American skipper and a mixed-nationality Catalina crew on a USAAF detachment on 231 Group Air-Sea Rescue Squadron and then on the USAAF 7th Emergency Rescue Squadron. The majority of these ops were tedious patrols and unsuccessful searches for downed or missing aircraft, or dinghies in the Bay of Bengal and Indian Ocean, but I was especially proud of my forty-fifth op flown on 24 February 1945.

My logbook sums it up: '45 OPS. Search for B-29 crew. Sighted same aboard launch. Landed alongside & picked up eight survivors from B-29. Two injured. Damaged port float.'

In addition, some trips were of a more cloak and dagger variety and were distinctly hairy.

In late April 1945, I transferred to RAF 292 Squadron, an air-sea rescue unit primarily flying Liberators out of India. The unit disbanded in June 1945, its duties being taken over by Nos. 1347, 1348, and 1349 Air-Sea Rescue Flights operating independently. I continued with the Liberators of 1349 Air-Sea Rescue Flight.

The seventy-second and final official op of my RAF career was a nine-hour Liberator sortie with 1349 Air-Sea Rescue Flight flown in daylight on 5 September 1945. From my logbook: '72. Operations—Search Sundarbans area. Sighted two parachutes & fire in mangrove swamp area. Guided launch to area.'

With the cessation of hostilities against the Japanese, the frequency of my flights dropped to just a few hours per month. I only flew two more sorties that were comparable to wartime ops, though they were no longer credited as ops. The second of these, an unsuccessful six-hour-and-twenty-five-minute search for two naval rafts on 23 February 1946, was my final flight of any kind in the RAF. From my perspective, I guess I had more than my share of good luck in the RAF.

Arnie, John, Harry, and Fred after 1–2 April 1944

In late April 1944, into May, Harry and Fred joined me for a second restful leave in Naini Tal, the same hill station where we had shared our leave the previous year, then also joined by our crewmates Willy, Arnie, and C. J. Nicholls. This time Harry, Fred, and I were accompanied by Ernie Richards, who had flown nine ops with us as an air gunner and had finished his 159 Squadron tour of ops earlier than the rest of us.

Arnie remained on 159 Squadron a little longer than John, Harry, Fred, or I. Following the ordeal of the Gauntlett crew—his former crewmates—on 1–2 April, Arnie flew seven more sorties with 159 Squadron and finished his first tour of ops on the night of 1–2 May.

On 26 July 1945, nearly fifteen months later, he was killed with thirteen others in the aerial collision of two Liberators of the Air Fighting Training Unit stationed at RAF Amarda Road aerodrome in India. I had remained closely in touch with Arnie until the end. On the night before his death, I had eerily experienced a ghostly visitation from him. We were 300 miles apart at the time and I guarantee that I was as sober as could be.

I never saw John, Harry, or Fred depart 159 Squadron for their new assignments in the spring of 1944 as I was in hospital with psoriasis; when I returned from hospital to the squadron at Digri, they were already gone. Having completed a tour, each was posted to a so-called rest assignment befitting his experience and trade.

John flew frequently as a Liberator instructor pilot on 1673 Heavy Conversion Unit at Kolar, India, providing training to airmen new to the four-engine behemoth. This inherently dangerous flying, so different from ops, was hardly a true rest period, but John loved to fly, and his hard-won expertise was put to valuable and practical use here.

Then, in January 1945, he was back on ops, again with 159 Squadron, as Flight Commander on 'B' Flight, and holding the rank of squadron leader. For a stretch in January 1945, he was acting CO of the Squadron. In April 1945, he moved to 99 Squadron to finish his second tour of Liberator flying.

Fred later flew a second tour as an air gunner on a newly formed Liberator unit based in India, 358 Squadron, which focused upon dangerous Special Duties ops, dropping supplies and agents behind Japanese lines. His skipper was another ex-159 Squadron pilot, Ken Jones. Their crew included Ernie Richards, our erstwhile crewmate on 159 Squadron (ten ops with Fred and nine ops with me), and with whom Fred, Harry, C. J. Nicholls, and I had spent a leave in Naini Tal in late April and early May 1944.

Harry's flying duties concluded with 159 Squadron and the difficult 1–2 April 1944 op. Eventually, he made a safe return by ship to his beloved Canada.

21

1971

Recuperating and Reminiscing on Stronsay

I sat on a lonely beach with my wife, Marie, on the island of Stronsay in the Orkneys. It was a beautiful morning in 1971. The sand was almost white, the sky was a clean, cold blue such as one sees in the northern latitudes, and the sea sparkled in the sunshine. It was a day to gladden the heart, but Marie and I were sad.

We were on holiday as a result of an offer by a benevolent policeman where we lived in Horsforth, just outside of Leeds. A native Orcadian, the policeman invited us to Stronsay after we lost our son Miles in a tragically fatal accident just ten days short of his fifteenth birthday. Staying with relatives of the policeman, we were touched by the extreme kindness afforded to us.

The solitude of Stronsay acted like a balm to our feelings. We were fascinated by the bird life and the seals, which amused us greatly. Watching a common tern, I was intrigued by the bird's superb flying qualities. It hovered on the breeze only about twelve feet above the water with its neck extended downwards as it searched the water below. Suddenly, the bird swooped, dipped its pointed beak below the surface and rose into the air with a small fish.

Seeing Marie observing the bird, I nudged her and nodded towards the rapidly departing tern. 'That's life, lassie. Here today, gone tomorrow.'

She nodded glumly, and I subsided into silence, mindful that I had said the wrong thing.

We had been sitting for some time before I became aware of the approaching sound of a heavy piston-engined aircraft. Glancing skyward, I excitedly poked Marie in the ribs. 'Bugger me, it's a Liberator!' I exclaimed. At this, Marie displayed some interest, as she had often heard me speak of Liberators.

The aircraft was coming directly towards us. I was puzzled. Sure enough, it had four engines and twin fin and rudder units, but the shoulder wing seemed to be mounted lower than I remembered.

As the aircraft drew closer, I realised my mistake. It was an Avro Shackleton, obsolescent but still used for maritime reconnaissance. As it flew steadily over us, I thought of the crew. Were they anything like my wartime pals? I doubted it and gave a slight chuckle. If I were to meet the Shackleton crew, I surmised, they would regard me as some kind of dinosaur.

With their aircraft stuffed full of electronic gadgetry, they lived in a differently defined grim age than that which I had faced during my war of many years earlier. They had to be on alert at all times, watching for the unthinkable on their modern cathode ray tubes.

Memories of my long-deceased crewmates on 159 Squadron came flooding back to me. There was Ben Blue, who would stay in the skies forever, and dear old Willy Kirby. I hoped there was an abundance of ciggies to keep Willy supplied with dog-ends wherever he was. There was also Arnie Bridgman, killed in a needless mid-air training collision in 1945, only three weeks before the whole stupid game played itself out. How had his widow managed to cope with grief?

I was moderately successful in my post-war signwriting business and with my hobby shop, *Models and Militaria*, but I had suffered many nightmares in the years since my 159 Squadron tour ended with the harrowing last trip to Rangoon on the night of 1–2 April 1944. My second tour in the Far East, aboard Catalina flying boats and Liberators, added further scarring. Marie, bless her, endured my undefined traumas and always stood by me, and I regarded her with affection as she joined me in watching the Shackleton disappear beyond the horizon.

While musing over wartime memories, I wondered about all the young men who had died in the Far East. The British Empire was long gone, given away with almost indecent haste by the politicians after the war. I would not have minded if the world had become a better place as a result, but as I saw things, it had not. Instead, it had stood on the brink of incineration at times, and stupid clots at the top were still playing silly games.

I had persevered during harsh times before, but what was most challenging now was unrelated to world politics. Instead, it was a deeply personal wound that Marie and I, as parents, had to endure and conquer. Our Orkneys sojourn offered hope for the future.

As I pondered these thoughts, I tossed and caught what others might have wrongly assumed was a coin. Instead, it was a reminder of the past that I always carried with me—a tiny enamel lapel badge upon which was depicted the figure of a tiny mouse. It was my Teddy Tail League membership badge from late 1942. Smiling gently while remembering my old crewmates, also Teddy Tail Leaguers, I put it in my pocket for safekeeping and held out my hand to Marie.

'Come on, love, let's be off.'

Turning our backs on the sea, we returned to the village, and to our hosts.

Epilogue

'Here Today, Gone Tomorrow'

Lamentably, Bill's 1971 comment to his wife applies to most, maybe all, of those cited in his memoir. While a small number may still be alive today, many of those who were not lost during the war are known to have died since the war's end in 1945.

William Arthur Kirkness DFM—Enoch to his wartime RAF mates—passed away in 1994. His Liberator skipper on 1349 Air-Sea Rescue Flight in late 1945 and early 1946, Ken Tame, attended his funeral. In 1998, Ken, now also deceased, commented on his crewmate's passing: 'Alas, and sadly, my old friend died on 30 October 1994, and an RAF Standard was paraded at his funeral.'

Marie passed away on 18 October 2012.

Enoch's parents, Gwendoline and Arthur, who had been so hospitable to Enoch's crewmates on leave, passed away in 1951 and 1972, respectively.

His sister Sheila succumbed to cancer in her fifties.

Minnie Bracewell—Gran, his maternal grandmother—died at age sixty-eight in 1947. At her public house, The Queens Arms, she had proudly welcomed Enoch home from the war in 1946 with the bottle of whiskey put aside in 1942 for a future celebration.

John Gauntlett DFC died on 27 September 1994, a month before Enoch. A single, divorced man for many years, John had no children.

Having survived the war, Harry Hartshorn returned to the family shoe last business in Canada. In 1986, he was killed by a bus while crossing a Kingston, Ontario street. He was survived by his widow, Gloria, their two sons, and their daughter.

No. 197830 PO Lewis Arnold 'Arnie' Bridgman and the thirteen others with whom he died on 26 July 1945 lie in Collective Grave 9.A.1-14 in Madras War Cemetery, located in Chennai, India. Arnie's grave marker is inscribed with the couplet 'Treasured memories/silently kept'. Arnie's widow, Marjorie, remarried in 1947 and gave birth to a son and daughter. Widowed a second time, Marjorie passed away in 2005, survived by her two grown children.

No. 1314663 FS Cyril 'Willy' Kirby lies buried in Grave 6.E.4 of Chittagong War Cemetery in Bangladesh.

No. 656440 WO William Gibson 'Ben' Blue and the seven others with whom he died on 9 October 1943 lie in Collective Grave 4.J.1-8 in Rangoon War Cemetery in Myanmar.

Arnie, Willy, and Ben's graves are magnificently maintained by the Commonwealth War Graves Commission.

Fred Rozee, residing west of London in Stanford le Hope, Essex, passed away in 1985 in Hackney, London—one year before his old crewmate Harry's death 3,600 miles across the Atlantic Ocean.

The Selby pub where the Gauntlett crew first socialised together in 1942, The Friendship, was torn down following two arson fires in 2012 and replaced by modern housing. The establishment where Bill's gran treated the Gauntlett crew to a memorable evening's entertainment in 1942 still operates in the centre of Selby. In 2017, its name changed from The Londesborough Arms to The George Inn.The Queens Arms, Bill's gran's historic pub, continues to be a popular and friendly haunt in Horsforth.

Enoch and Marie's daughter, Susan Olsson, resides in Australia, but she still retains her Yorkshire accent.

APPENDIX I

The Wartime Operational Flights of Bill 'Enoch' Kirkness

Flight durations for each op and cumulative flying times are listed in hours and minutes. The durations of the flights for Enoch's first tour of ops with 159 Squadron are as recorded in his logbook. Some totals differ by a minute or more from what was recorded in the 159 Squadron Operations Record Book. The ORB durations, where different from Enoch's, are shown in parentheses.

The data for op no. 65 is noteworthy as there is a logbook error; although listed as having the serial number EV296, no such Liberator serial number existed.

The two 1946 flights marked with double asterisks were not credited as ops; they would have been deemed ops during the war. Enoch's last credited op was 5 September 1945, three days after Japan signed the Instrument of Surrender.

11	15–16 Nov	Pegu railway station, Burma	Lib III BZ900 'C'	Flt Lt Gauntlett	8.55 (9.00)	94.30
12	27–28 Nov	Rangoon, Botataung Wharves and railway depot, Burma	Lib III BZ906 'A'	Sgt Ellis	8.50 (8.44)	103.20
13	23–24 Dec	Bangkok, Bansuk marshalling yards, Siam	Lib III BZ906 'A'	Sgt Ellis	10.50 (10.52), plus 2.15 from base to ALG	116.25, including the 2.15 from base to ALG
14	30–31 Dec	Rangoon, Mahlwagon marshalling yards, Burma	Lib III BZ855 'B'	WO Jones	10.10 (10.09)	126.35

1944

Op No.	Date	Target or nature of flight	Aircraft type/ serial	Pilot	Duration	Cumulative time on ops
15	10–11 Jan	Moulmein minelaying, Burma	Lib III BZ840 'E'	Fg Off. Brailsford	11.50 (11.52)	138.25
16	16–17 Jan	Rangoon central railway station, Burma	Lib III BZ900 'C'	FS Hedley	9.45	148.10
17	22–23 Jan	Meiktila railway station, Burma	Lib VI BZ962 'D'	Flt Lt Gauntlett	7.30 (7.22)	155.40
18	31 Jan–1 Feb	Mingaladon aerodrome, Burma	Lib VI EV843 'E'	Flt Lt Gauntlett	9.30 (9.27)	165.10
19	4–5 Feb	Heho aerodrome, Burma	Lib VI EV843 'E'	Flt Lt Gauntlett	9.00 (8.56)	174.10
20	10–11 Feb	Bangkok, Makasan railway workshops, Siam	Lib VI EV843 'E'	Flt Lt Gauntlett	11.25, plus 2.00 from base to ALG	187.35, including the 2.00 from base to ALG

1943

Op No.	Date	Target or nature of flight	Aircraft type/ serial	Pilot	Duration	Cumulative time on ops
1445 Flight (ferry flight, UK to India):						
1	29 March	UK–Gibraltar leg of transit flight to India	Lib II AL597	Fg Off. Gauntlett	7.25	7.25
2	31 Mar–1 Apr	Gibraltar–Middle East leg of transit flight to India	Lib II AL597	Fg Off. Gauntlett	10.50	18.15
RAF 159 Squadron:						
3	13–14 May	Heho aerodrome, Burma	Lib II AL597 'R'	Fg Off. Evans	8.20	26.35
4	22–23 May	Rangoon, Burma (not located—poor weather); coast road near Sandoway, Burma, bombed	Lib II AL597 'R'	Fg Off. Evans	10.10	36.45
5	12–13 June	Mandalay marshalling yards, Burma	Lib II AL597 'R'	Fg Off. Evans	9.00	45.45
6	12–13 Oct	Pyinmana railway station, Burma	Lib III BZ840 'E'	Flt Lt Evans	7.30 (7.28)	53.15
7	21–22 Oct	Heho aerodrome, Burma (not located—clouds); Thedaw landing ground, Burma, bombed	Lib III BZ906 'A'	Flt Lt Gauntlett	8.35 (8.36)	61.50
8	24–25 Oct	Rangoon central railway station, Burma	Lib III BZ855 'B'	Flt Lt Gauntlett	9.05 (8.55)	70.55
9	5 Nov	Akyab, Burma	Lib III BZ906 'A'	Flt Lt Gauntlett	5.35 (5.32)	76.30
10	11–12 Nov	Insein (Rangoon) locomotive sheds, Burma	Lib III BZ900 'C'	Flt Lt Gauntlett	9.05 (9.02)	85.35

30	20–21 Mar	Prome railway station, Burma	Lib VI EV843 'E'	Flt Lt Gauntlett	7.00 (6.54)	277.40
31	29–30 Mar	Rangoon, Victoria Lake storage dumps, Burma	Lib VI EV843 'E'	Flt Lt Gauntlett	9.00 (8.59)	286.40
32	1–2 Apr	Rangoon, Kemmendine railway station, Burma	Lib VI EV843 'E'	Flt Lt Gauntlett	8.00 (7.58)	294.40
USAAF Detachment to RAF 231 Group Air-Sea Rescue:						
33	6 Nov	Search	Catalina 902	Lt Worthington	5.10	299.50
34	11 Nov	Search	Catalina 902	Lt Worthington	12.10	312.00
35	27 Nov	Patrol	Catalina 901	Lt Worthington	10.45	322.45
36	29 Nov	Search	Catalina 902	Lt Graham	9.50	332.35
37	29–30 Nov	Search	Catalina 901	Lt Worthington	19.45	352.20
38	3 Dec	Search	Catalina 901	Lt Worthington	16.00	368.20
39	9–10 Dec	Search	Catalina 901	Lt Worthington	14.35	382.55

1945

Op No.	Date	Target or nature of flight	Aircraft type/ serial	Pilot	Duration	Cumulative time on ops
40	25–26 Jan	Search	Catalina 901	Lt Graham	21.00	403.55
41	1 Feb	Patrol	Catalina 902	Lt Graham	11.30	415.25
42	7 Feb	Patrol	Catalina 901	Lt Worthington	8.30	423.55
43	19 Feb	Patrol	Catalina 902	Lt Graham	12.55	436.50
44	24 Feb	Patrol	Catalina 901	Lt Spelman	9.10	446.00
45	24–25 Feb	Search	Catalina 902	Lt Graham	9.00	455.00
46	26–27 Feb	Search	Catalina 901	Lt Graham	18.00	473.00
47	2 Mar	Patrol	Catalina 901	Lt Bleier	13.00	486.00

21	15–16 Feb	Bangkok terminus railway station, Siam (Aiming Point not identified—dense ground haze); Moulmein railway jetty, Burma, bombed	Lib III BZ924 'F'	Flt Lt Gauntlett	13.25 (13.23)	201.00
22	18–19 Feb	Mandalay marshalling yards, Burma	Lib VI EV843 'E'	Flt Lt Gauntlett	7.30 (7.21)	208.30
23	21–22 Feb	Sagaing shore railway station, Burma	Lib VI EV843 'E'	Flt Lt Gauntlett	8.55 (8.54)	217.25
24	23–24 Feb	Moulmein barracks, Burma (Aiming Point not identified); Moulmein railway station and south railway jetty bombed	Lib VI EV843 'E'	Flt Lt Gauntlett	10.50 (10.47)	228.15
25	29 Feb–1 Mar	Rangoon, Mahlwagon marshalling yards, Burma	Lib VI EV843 'E'	Flt Lt Gauntlett	8.55 (8.43)	237.10
26	3–4 Mar	Mingaladon aerodrome, Burma (Aiming Point not identified—dense ground haze); Zayatkwin aerodrome, Burma, bombed	Lib VI EV843 'E'	Flt Lt Gauntlett	9.30 (9.23)	246.40
27	10–11 Mar	Kamaing-Mogaung Road, Mogaung village storage dump, and probable troop concentrations, Burma	Lib VI EV843 'E'	Flt Lt Gauntlett	7.30 (7.31)	254.10
28	14–15 Mar	Rangoon, Victoria Lake storage dumps, Burma	Lib VI EV843 'E'	Flt Lt Gauntlett	8.55	263.05
29	17 Mar (take-off was at 00.01 on 17 Mar)	Ywataung south landing ground, Burma	Lib VI EV843 'E'	Flt Lt Gauntlett	7.35 (7.34)	270.40

65	30 June	Search	Lib 'M' EV296	Flt Lt Pocock	6.10	651.35
66	10 July	Patrol	Lib VI KH269	Fg Off. Kitt	11.30	663.05
67	14 July	Patrol	Lib VI KH269	Fg Off. Kitt	10.10	673.15
68	27 July	Patrol	Lib VI KH319	Flt Lt Pocock	11.50	685.05
69	30 July	Search	Warwick BV479	Fg Off. Andrew	6.30	691.35
70	4 Aug	Search	Lib VI KH269	WO Whitehead	9.30	701.05
71	12 Aug	Search	Lib VI KH319	Fg Off. Kitt	9.15	710.20
RAF 1349 Air-Sea Rescue Flight:						
72	5 Sept	Search	Lib VI EW244	Fg Off. Andrew	9.00	719.20

1946

Op No.	Date	Target or nature of flight	Aircraft type/ serial	Pilot	Duration	Cumulative time on ops
**	17 Jan	Patrol	Lib VI KH194	WO Tame	6.30	725.50
**	23 Feb	Search	Lib VI EV818	WO Tame	6.25	732.15

USAAF 7th Emergency Rescue Squadron:						
48	12 Mar	Patrol	Catalina 901	Lt Bleier	12.45	498.45
49	17 Mar	Patrol	Catalina 974	Lt Bleier	12.40	511.25
50	20 Mar	Search	Catalina 986	Lt Bisland	12.35	524.00
51	26 Mar	Search	Catalina 986	Lt Fraser	8.00	532.00
52	28–29 Mar	Patrol	Catalina 961	Maj. Prim	13.15	545.15
53	31 Mar	Patrol	Catalina 901	Lt Spelman	5.00	550.15
54	2–3 Apr	Search	Catalina 986	Capt. Walker	8.20	558.35
55	7 Apr	Patrol	Catalina 961	Lt Col. Prim	10.30	569.05
56	14 Apr	Search	Catalina 982	Lt Hubbs	4.15	573.20
57	15 Apr	Search	Catalina 982	Lt Hubbs	11.15	584.35
58	16 Apr	Search	Catalina 901	Capt. Bleier	5.45	590.20
RAF 292 Squadron:						
59	20 Apr	Search	Lib VI EW273	Plt Off. Dunn	8.50	599.10
60	24 Apr	Search	Lib VI EW273	Plt Off. Dunn	14.00	613.10
61	2 May	Search	Lib VI EW240	Plt Off. Dunn	12.15	625.25
62	14 May	Patrol	Lib VI KH319	Fg Off. Kitt	7.00	632.25
63	22 May	Patrol	Lib VI KH319	Fg Off. Kitt	7.20	639.45
64	26 May	Patrol	Lib VI KH269	Fg Off. Kitt	5.40	645.25

APPENDIX II

Distinguished Flying Medal Citation for Bill 'Enoch' Kirkness

Announced in the *London Gazette* 22 August 1944

Distinguished Flying Medal
Flight Sergeant William Arthur KIRKNESS, 1114254
No. 159 Squadron

This airman has been on active operations in this theatre of war for over a year and has at all times set an excellent example to other Wireless Operators. In April 1944, he displayed extreme coolness and courage when his aircraft was severely damaged by a night fighter attack. The rear gunner was killed in the first attack and the attacking fighter was shot down by the accurate return fire from Flight Sergeant Kirkness's gun. On the return flight, it was largely due to his very skilful use of his wireless equipment under adverse circumstances that the aircraft was safely flown to base. Throughout his operational tour this airman has at all times shown a fine fighting spirit and great enthusiasm.

APPENDIX III

Hamilton Spectator Newspaper Story, Ontario, Canada: 2 September 1944

The details refer to the 1–2 April 1944 ordeal of 159 Squadron's EV843 'E', skippered by John Gauntlett. Enoch was credited with shooting down the Oscar night fighter which killed Willy Kirby, the rear gunner, and nearly destroyed EV843. Not all of the newspaper's facts are correct; comments and corrections are shown in brackets.

His rear gunner dead and his Liberator bomber badly mauled by flak and fighters over Rangoon, Flt Lt Johnny Gauntlett, a Canadian in the RAF, ploughed his aircraft into a brick embankment and thus ended his first operational tour on the Burma front.

Three other Canadians flew with Flt Lt Gauntlett, who attended Connaught public school in Regina and whose mother now resides in Orilla, Ont., as he dived at 330 mph over the Burmese capital from 12,000 to 800 feet to shake the Jap attacker.

Second pilot was Flt Lt Johnny West, Vancouver. Fg Off. Dave Bruce, Kenora, Ont., was navigator and WO1 H.T. Hartshorne [Harry Hartshorn], Preston, Ont., was air bomber.

Johnny Gauntlett, the squadron's heavyweight, was in England studying history at Bristol University and joined the British Army two days after war was declared. He transferred to the RAF in March, 1941, to win his wings. After operating on Ferry Command in the Middle East he came to India on Liberators. He's marking time now but expects to fly his second tour in the Far East.

Now captain of his own aircraft, *Goofy*, Flt Lt West, whose wife resides at 47 Barclay Avenue, Hamilton, Ont., told the story of Flt Lt Gauntlett's hair-raising tour. Flt Lt West instructed at Dunnville, Ont., and Calgary and was assistant supervisory officer at High River, Alta., before going overseas.

'Just as we were on the run-in they caught us in searchlights and a Navy Zero [a Japanese Army Air Force Oscar] night fighter came at us twice,' he said. 'On his first attack the Jap killed our tail gunner, shot away our hydraulics and our inner port motor. Our gas tanks were hit and petrol poured into the bomb bays.

'Once they had us coned we went into a dive at 12,000 feet and all the way down to 800 feet the Zero followed us [not per Bill Kirkness's account] and the ground defences kept banging away.'

One of their gunners [Bill Kirkness] got in a long burst at the Zero and they later saw an enemy fighter ablaze on the ground below.

Limping to their own coast, the crew made an emergency landing. With no brakes, the kite swung off the runway into a brick embankment. Surviving members of the crew were not injured but the aircraft was 'written off.'

'We didn't smack into the embankment on purpose,' said West, 'but next day we found we were in luck because we were heading for a water reservoir.'

APPENDIX IV

Letter from Bill 'Enoch' Kirkness to His Parents: 20 April 1944

One explanation is shown in brackets.

Mr & Mrs A. Kirkness
215B Low Lane
Horsforth
Leeds
Yorkshire
England

1114254 FS Kirkness
159 Sqn RAF India
20/4/44

Dear Mum & Dad,
Sorry I have not written to you lately, but many things have been happening which prevented me from writing—& I'm afraid you will have to be content with that excuse as I can not say what! Tomorrow morning I am going on leave with Harry & Fred to Naini Tal. Unfortunately, poor old Willy caught it through the head & was killed instantly, but again, no details except that Johnny's skill saved the rest of us. We miss Willy a lot, but I guess he had to go. You do not need to worry about me now for a long long time. The leave should give clues.

We have been awarded the '39–43 Star. It's rather a nice ribbon. I received the Defiant kit [a model aircraft kit]—& 400 Senior Service cigarettes. Many thanks. Glad Dad received his shoes. Sorry this is abrupt. Will write long letter from Naini. I'll spend my birthday up there—what a thought—Beer, Beer & more Beer. My regards to Mrs Freer now. Will send you something Mum.
All My Love, Bill. XXXXX
P.S. Receiving your mail OK.

APPENDIX V

1945
Hometown Newspaper Story

The identity of the newspaper and the precise date of publication are unknown. If not a Leeds newspaper, it could very well be the *Wharfedale & Airedale Observer*, covering Horsforth. Corrections to errors in the report are shown in brackets.

Horsforth DFM in Rescue Crew

Believed to be the first rescue of its kind on the Burma air front, a landing was made on Tuesday, January 23 [the correct date was Sunday, 25 February 1945], by an American/British [and Dominion] team in an amphibious Catalina on the Bay of Bengal to pick up the crew of a drifting bomber. The wireless operator of the Catalina was W/op W. A. Kirkness, aged 23, of Horsforth, who recently won the DFM with an RAF Liberator squadron in India. The captain of the plane was an American, and the crew included an Australian and a Canadian. For three [five] months, these USAAF, RAF and Dominion flyers have been 'crewed' together on life saving patrols off the India and Burmese coasts.

Sighting the bomber crew in two dinghies by the light of flares, the pilot, with a tropical moon flickering on the water, put the amphibian down a hundred yards away and taxied over.

Taking off again with a full load of survivors on board, they landed on a Bengal airfield, and within a few minutes the rescued men were being treated in hospital.

Warrant Officer Kirkness received the DFM in August. He is the only son of Mr. and Mrs. Arthur Kirkness, 'Oxbridge,' Low Lane, Horsforth. He attended Aireborough Grammar School, and as a schoolboy served in the old 52nd (Leeds) Squadron, Air Cadets, and was a member of the Leeds Model Aero Club. He has been in the RAF since he was 18, received his training in this country, and afterwards served in Egypt, Malta and India. He was in Malta for six months during the blitz period. [He was only in Malta from 12 May to 19 May 1942.]